*The Subject of Coexistence*

# BORDERLINES

A BOOK SERIES CONCERNED WITH REVISIONING GLOBAL POLITICS

David Campbell and Michael J. Shapiro, Series Editors

Volume 28  Louiza Odysseos, *The Subject of Coexistence: Otherness in International Relations*

Volume 27  Denise Ferreira da Silva, *Toward a Global Idea of Race*

Volume 26  Matthew Sparke, *In the Space of Theory: Postfoundational Geographies of the Nation-State*

Volume 25  Roland Bleiker, *Divided Korea: Toward a Culture of Reconciliation*

Volume 24  Marieke de Goede, *Virtue, Fortune, and Faith: A Genealogy of Finance*

Volume 23  Himadeep Muppidi, *The Politics of the Global*

Volume 22  William A. Callahan, *Contingent States: Greater China and Transnational Relations*

Volume 21  Allaine Cerwonka, *Native to the Nation: Disciplining Landscapes and Bodies in Australia*

Volume 20  Simon Dalby, *Environmental Security*

Volume 19  Cristina Rojas, *Civilization and Violence: Regimes of Representation in Nineteenth-Century Colombia*

Volume 18  Mathias Albert, David Jacobson, and Yosef Lapid, editors, *Identities, Borders, Orders: Rethinking International Relations Theory*

Volume 17  Jenny Edkins, *Whose Hunger? Concepts of Famine, Practices of Aid*

Volume 16  Jennifer Hyndman, *Managing Displacement: Refugees and the Politics of Humanitarianism*

*For more books in this series, see page vi.*

# The Subject of Coexistence: Otherness in International Relations

LOUIZA ODYSSEOS

BORDERLINES, VOLUME 28

University of Minnesota Press

Minneapolis

London

Earlier versions of material published in this book have appeared as the following: "Dangerous Ontologies: The Ethos of Survival and Ethical Theorizing in International Relations," *Review of International Studies* 28, no. 2 (2002): 403–18; "Radical Phenomenology, Ontology, and International Political Theory," *Alternatives* 27, no. 3 (July/September 2002): 373–405; and "On the Way to Global Ethics? Cosmopolitanism, 'Ethical' Selfhood, and Otherness," *European Journal of Political Theory* 2, no. 2 (2003): 183–207; reprinted by permission of Sage Publications, Ltd.

Published by the University of Minnesota Press
111 Third Avenue South, Suite 290
Minneapolis, MN 55401-2520
http://www.upress.umn.edu

Library of Congress Cataloging-in-Publication Data

Odysseos, Louiza.
   The subject of coexistence : otherness in international relations / Louiza Odysseos.
      p. cm. -- (Borderlines ; vol. 28)
   Includes bibliographical references and index.
   ISBN 978-0-8166-4854-2 (hc : alk. paper) -- ISBN 978-0-8166-4855-9 (pb : alk. paper)
   1. International relations--Philosophy.   2. International relations--Methodology.   I. Title.
   JZ1305.O39 2007
   327.101--dc22

                                        2007001080

Printed in the United States of America on acid-free paper

The University of Minnesota is an equal-opportunity educator and employer.

*To Aris*

# BORDERLINES

Volume 15  Sankaran Krishna, *Postcolonial Insecurities: India, Sri Lanka, and the Question of Nationhood*

Volume 14  Jutta Weldes, Mark Laffey, Hugh Gusterson, and Raymond Duvall, editors, *Cultures of Insecurity: States, Communities, and the Production of Danger*

Volume 13  François Debrix, *Re-Envisioning Peacekeeping: The United Nations and the Mobilization of Ideology*

Volume 12  Jutta Weldes, *Constructing National Interests: The United States and the Cuban Missile Crisis*

Volume 11  Nevzat Soguk, *States and Strangers: Refugees and Displacements of Statecraft*

Volume 10  Kathy E. Ferguson and Phyllis Turnbull, *Oh, Say, Can You See? The Semiotics of the Military in Hawai'i*

Volume 9  Iver B. Neumann, *Uses of the Other: "The East" in European Identity Formation*

Volume 8  Keith Krause and Michael C. Williams, editors, *Critical Security Studies: Concepts and Cases*

Volume 7  Costas M. Constantinou, *On the Way to Diplomacy*

Volume 6  Gearóid Ó Tuathail (Gerard Toal), *Critical Geopolitics: The Politics of Writing Global Space*

Volume 5  Roxanne Lynn Doty, *Imperial Encounters: The Politics of Representation in North–South Relations*

Volume 4  Thom Kuehls, *Beyond Sovereign Territory: The Space of Ecopolitics*

Volume 3  Siba N'Zatioula Grovogui, *Sovereigns, Quasi Sovereigns, and Africans: Race and Self-Determination in International Law*

Volume 2  Michael J. Shapiro and Hayward R. Alker, editors, *Challenging Boundaries: Global Flows, Territorial Identities*

Volume 1  William E. Connolly, *The Ethos of Pluralization*

# Contents

Acknowledgments     ix

Introduction: Subjectivity, Coexistence,
and the Question of Heteronomy     xi

1. Manifestations of Composition     1

2. Toward a "Hermeneutics of Facticity"     29

3. An Optics of Coexistence: Dasein's Radical
   Embeddedness in Its World     57

4. Becoming-Proper: Authenticity
   and Inauthenticity Revisited     95

5. Recovering the "Ethical" Self:
   Global Ethics in Question     119

6. Coexistence, Community, and Critical Belonging     153

Conclusion     177

Notes     187

Index     241

# Acknowledgments

A work is always a debt. This book began as a doctoral thesis in international relations at the London School of Economics and Political Science (LSE), where a great number of people, staff and fellow students, provided intellectual stimulus as well as professional and emotional support. Michael Bank's Concepts and Methods in International Relations seminar opened up a path for thinking differently about international politics. His personal encouragement and willingness to support this kind of philosophical curiosity was instrumental (although we had plenty of debate as to the meaning of this particular word) in getting this project started. A different kind of stimulus was offered at the offices of *Millennium: Journal of International Studies*. This was truly where the journey of this book started, as colleagues such as Hideaki Shinoda, Hakan Seckinelgin, Paris Yeros, Michi Ebata, Ralph Emmers, and Nelli Kambouri all "called for thinking." Hakan Seckinelgin especially deserves the warmest of thanks for his encouragement and advice, as well as for always pointing to the need for even deeper questioning.

At the LSE's numerous research workshops, especially "Postmodernism in International Relations" and "International Political Theory," a great many interlocutors provided welcome critique and advice: I thank especially Erica Benner, Chris Brown, Margot Light, Nicola Short, Peter Weinberger, Helen Kambouri, Pavlos Hatzopoulos, Cathleen Fitzpatrick, and Fabio Petito. At the

School of Oriental and African Studies the intellectual environment made the question of otherness a concrete and worldly matter, and I would like to thank my colleagues Stephen Hopgood, Sudipta Kaviraj, and Mark Laffey for their encouragement. Moreover, I would like to thank Fred Dallmayr, Tarak Barkawi, Patrick Thadeus Jackson, Kimberly Hutchings, Richard Shapcott, Nicholas Rengger, and David Owen, who discussed parts of the book at conferences and other settings and helped improve the work and make me aware of its limits. Most important, however, heartfelt gratitude goes to Mark Hoffman, who as my doctoral supervisor always made time in his busy schedule for advice, support, and critical engagement toward my ideas.

Last but not least, I would like to thank Stefan Elbe, whose combination of critique and companionship made this book both possible and an experience to remember. To my parents, Marios and Maro Odysseos, I owe everything. But for their unfaltering support, this book would never have existed. Finally, Aris arrived as the book was being finalized and made our world a happier one. Therefore, it is only fitting that it be dedicated to him.

Brighton, December 2006

# Introduction: Subjectivity, Coexistence, and the Question of Heteronomy

## THE ISSUE OF COEXISTENCE AND INTERNATIONAL RELATIONS

Coexistence could be said to be paramount for international politics. Exploring what coexistence might mean and what it might entail, however, has not been directly addressed by the discipline of international relations (IR). That is not to say that IR scholars have not turned their attention to specific and diverse issues of cohabitation or living in common, but rather to suggest that what is considered to *be* coexistence has yet to receive proper questioning. "Coexistence," in other words, is not presently regarded as a question for world politics; it is, instead, a term whose meaning is considered to be self-evident. Endowed with the literal meaning of copresence, its study is bounded within a set of assumptions and parameters that serve to revoke its status as a *question,* restricting reflection on coexistence as an aporia of international politics.

The seeming self-evidence of "coexistence," however, is rendered unstable by world events, which often unsettle and disrupt the everyday activities of world-political actors, what one might call, in its collective form, "international praxis." States, governments, international organizations, and other nongovernmental bodies alike are (whether they are aware of it or not) continuously preoccupied by specific concerns that arise from the fundamental question of coexistence. As will be shown in greater detail, international praxis is thus constantly required to address coexistence as a *question*.[1] Such preoccupation centers on issues *within* state borders, such as civil war, secession disputes, resource conflicts, civic debate within multi-ethnic or other diverse communities about issues of cultural diversity, and so on. Additionally, it is an issue at the level of international interaction for intergovernmental bodies that become increasingly concerned with the regional or global repercussions of states' internal disputes, such as refugee protection, asylum provision, and economic migration. Especially since 1989, such interaction has frequently resulted in military interventions in the form of assisting in the cessation of hostilities and violence. These activities are usually undertaken in the name of certain values often considered to be humanitarian, whose protection is regarded as imperative to the current human rights regime. Interventionist measures, moreover, are intended to promulgate these values in the aftermath of conflict in the wider cause of international peace and order, although their critics often consider these a disguise for power politics. Indeed, recent preoccupation with the vertiginous changes brought about by economic and cultural processes of globalization has made "coexistence" all the more pertinent to policy makers and politicians. New measures and policies are now regarded to be necessary to facilitate multicultural coexistence, population movements, and increased economic and cultural interaction.

It can be claimed, therefore, that while coexistence has hitherto not been deemed particularly question-worthy for international thought, it is nonetheless constantly surfacing as a problem for international praxis. In this regard, international thought has clearly failed to keep pace with international praxis in its consideration of the meaning of "coexistence." In the context of this book, co existence is therefore taken to be a concept whose aporetic nature is obscured in international thought, and yet constantly preoccupies international praxis, but is usually dealt with under other, more specific, guises. This book illustrates how, in the absence of direct questioning about coexistence, its more general meaning can only be discerned from an examination of the ontological premises of international relations. Among these premises the modern subject stands out in its ontological centrality[2]—IR theory being embedded in the larger context of modern philosophical and social inquiry.[3]

Within this larger theoretical context, the modern subject is generally understood as a completed self, already fully constituted when it enters into relations with others, relations that are considered ontologically secondary to the subject itself. Its main attributes are self-sufficiency, nonrelationality, and autonomy; these become instrumental in determining coexistence as the presence of multiple units, in other words, as a composition of otherwise nonrelational subjects. The book contends that, based on this ground of modern subjectivity, coexistence can only be articulated through what might be called the "logic of composition." When being-with-others is understood solely as a composition of previously unrelated entities, the constitutive role of otherness in coexistence, and for selfhood itself, is obscured. In particular, the other's participation in the constitution of the self, what might be called the "heteronomous constitution of selfhood," remains concealed. The other is grasped, instead, as a similar nonrelational subject, its otherness reduced to what is knowable about the self.[4] Unless this heteronomous constitution of selfhood is allowed to show itself,[5] coexistence appears only as the mere composition of units or entities, as is often assumed in IR, instead of being the prior and constitutive condition of their being.

Before providing a fuller articulation of the juncture of subjectivity, coexistence, and heteronomy,[6] however, it is important to review the historical trajectory of IR discourses about coexistence in order to bring to the fore the reduction of coexistence to the copresence of entities. As will be shown in the next two sections, this reduction runs through both cold war *and* post–cold war debates of world politics. Despite the common assumption that these two eras of world politics represent radically different historical configurations, there is in fact an inherent unanimity in their prevalent determinations of coexistence as copresence or composition. This continuity suggests that received thinking about coexistence in international relations implicitly relies on deeper assumptions about subjectivity that need to be excavated and questioned more thoroughly—which this book sets out to do.

## THE COLD WAR, COEXISTENCE, AND IDEOLOGICAL COMPETITION

In the post-1945 world, various forces practically and conceptually affected the meaning and study of coexistence. In the years following the end of World War II, societal and political concerns revolved primarily around the imminent nuclear confrontation between the two superpowers. The very presence of nuclear arms meant that conflict resounded with the possibility of worldwide destruction. Thus, the conflictual workings of the state system, without any higher authority to guarantee peace, called for concerned academics, politicians, and international activists alike to bring about "a conception of coexistence which matches the needs of the nuclear age."[7] "[T]he emergence of the thermonuclear truce of the cold war"[8] meant that thinking about the notion of coexistence revolved exclusively around the nexus of survival.

Among politicians in the so-called first and second worlds, the copresence of divergent political systems became the centerpiece of a strategy aimed toward the accommodation of the ideological differences of the superpowers. It was widely regarded that such coexistence of contradictory, yet totalizing, ideological positions was required for the very survival both of their incompatible political systems and of the human species as a whole, considering the nuclear context within which the struggle among their competing ideologies took place. Related to the potentially cataclysmic repercussions of nuclear conflict, coexistence also became the sole means of survival when one reflected on the various paths to development and modernity available to postcolonial, developing countries that were inevitably caught up in the international politics of the cold war.

Moreover, coexistence was established as a central concern for peace movements that attempted to diffuse the nuclear tension by calling for an end to the superpowers' ideological struggle. Within the antinuclear activist movement it was felt that the entanglement brought about by the nuclear age rested with the politicians' inability to extract themselves from an old age of strife. "Pride, arrogance, fear of loss of face, and ideological intolerance have obscured their power of judgement,"[9] insisted one of its most vocal members, British philosopher Bertrand Russell. In his extensive writings against nuclear armaments, Russell clarified further the association between survival and coexistence. "Coexistence," he wrote in the early 1960s, "must be accepted genuinely and not superficially as a necessary condition of human survival."[10] That coexistence was the hoped-for antidote to the possibility of nuclear annihilation served to affirm and highlight the assumed opposition of coexistence and conflict. This sanctioned the assumption that coexistence is the condition that *surpasses* conflict; however, this has also led IR to neglect its consideration as the *primary* condition in which entities find themselves and to regard it as a state that must be actively, and secondarily, brought about.

Despite the calls for a notion of coexistence to accommodate the particularities of the nuclear age, it was a primarily conflictual configuration of the concept that prevailed in the international political world. In the 1950s Nikita Khrushchev revived the Leninist term "peaceful coexistence" both to signal that nuclear confrontation was not only undesirable and unnecessary and also to suggest that "peaceful coexistence" was a requirement for the progression of socialism.[11] While for many political commentators in the West military and political coexistence with the USSR was considered inconceivable, coexistence of the diverging systems was a *fact* of international political life. As Y. Frantsev noted, "Socialism and capitalism exist on the same planet and their coexistence is historically inevitable."[12] Ironically, V. I. Lenin had argued, it was "general economic world relations, which compel them [capitalists] to establish intercourse with us."[13]

Khrushchev's revival of the term "peaceful coexistence" reasserted the political necessity of promoting the copresence of conflicting ideologies and political systems in order to avoid war with capitalist states. He agreed in this regard with Lenin's earlier argument that, at the interstate level, coexistence between capitalist states and communist countries was possible and the struggle against capitalism could be carried out on the level of ideas. "Peaceful coexistence" in the post-1945 world entailed, therefore, the desire to avoid interstate warfare in the name of ideological opposition, but revived the pledge to maintain and encourage confrontation in the realm of ideology in order to bring about the collapse of the capitalist system.[14] As Khrushchev himself proposed in an article in *Foreign Affairs*, peaceful coexistence intended "to keep the positions of the ideological struggle, without resorting to arms in order to prove that one is right."[15] It could be argued, then, that in the 1960s, "peaceful coexistence between countries regardless of their social system" came to form "the bedrock of international affairs."[16]

Despite some political opposition, the West prudently embraced the chance to challenge the Soviet articulation of the concept of peaceful coexistence in order to reshape it for its own ends. The

Commission to Study the Organization of Peace, a member of the American Association for the United Nations, defined "peaceful coexistence" as "primarily a state of affairs in which the so-called sovereign states seek to protect and promote their conflicting national interests by means other than war, or organized and systematic intimidation based upon the threat of war."[17] In its report on this issue the commission reiterated that peaceful coexistence should be considered as a compromise because this concept lay "between war in the literal sense and peace in the ideal sense."[18] As a compromise necessitated by the nuclear context, "peaceful coexistence" accepted that ideological struggle was the means of confrontation and a mechanism of "diffusion" of the nuclear situation. With its rearticulation of peaceful coexistence, the association sought to counter the Soviet hegemony over the term and to reiterate it in ways that accorded a much greater role to international law in the workings of international politics, in recognition of the fact that, in a time of nuclear proliferation, "national security is unobtainable by military force alone."[19]

Peaceful coexistence, therefore, mitigated nuclear *war* by allowing ideological *competition* among the superpowers, a contention that resulted in many a proxy war fought with conventional weapons in the periphery, as well as in the often violent intervention into the political systems of developing and postcolonial countries.[20] Opponents of peaceful coexistence in other countries, as well as several social movements, resisted its initial acceptance by emphasizing that Khrushchev's proposal for "peaceful coexistence" included the notion of ideological struggle as the site of contestation of the capitalist world system and, as a result, "coexistence" became a paradoxical term: "Bitter ideological struggle is central to their idea of coexistence," denounced Christopher Paget Mayhew, a British politician in the 1960s.[21] When peaceful coexistence is the condition where state interaction allows for a sustained *ideological* struggle, then one can be said to be "waging peaceful coexistence," no matter how counterintuitive or oxymoronic this may seem.[22] This resistance to the ideologically contentious configuration of coexistence once again highlights the assumption that coexistence was regarded as a state that transcends conflict and enables survival.

Furthermore, many in the West noted the danger that such an ideological competition still entailed: the acceptance, and even encouragement, of ideological propaganda on both sides of the world-political spectrum, argued opponents of peaceful coexistence, could lead to the reduction of ideological variety and complexity arising from the multifarious social systems in the international political world. Intense ideological struggle as the means of engagement between the two superpowers discouraged worldwide multivocality and reduced the possibility of multiple interpretations of the world system. More important, it captured the terms of international discourse and limited the alternatives available to political thought at a time when they were most needed. Such a reduction of variety to two monolithic ideologies was tantamount to the creation of ideological myths that were "a prime cause of international tension and a major barrier to disarmament and peace."[23]

Among those who attempted to think outside the parameters of peaceful coexistence, a different type of concern as to the future of peace arose precisely from the presence of too many voices. In 1957, Sir Kenneth Grubb equated coexistence with the existing international system of sovereign states and their political interactions. Understood in this way, coexistence meant taking "for granted an unlimited compatibility of national aspirations"[24] whose acknowledgment did not, however, provide the requisite conditions or guidelines for the prevention of nuclear conflict. The fact of coexistence alone, in other words, did not suggest how one may coexist. Taken literally, *coexistence is nothing more than copresence.* As Grubb noted, "Presumably coexistence simply means side by side: it does not require that we live together in any meaningful way; it merely records that we live in the same limited space, the inhabited world,"[25] astutely observing the spatial determination of coexistence, where it is understood as copresence or the composition of units. In this way, international thought and praxis about coexistence in the post-1945 era reduced the term to a primary concern with the organization of a multitude of units, and the sustenance of the international state system and its principle of state-centricity, whose survival was far from assured in the nuclear context. Grubb called for a more meaningful and instructive definition of what kinds of interaction coexistence might entail, and highlighted the need to move beyond "mere coexistence . . . into a closer partnership or community" among states and peoples.[26] Coexistence, understood as the cohabitation of *sovereign* states, harbored "a terrible lie," suggested Grubb. This was, of course, the norm of state sovereignty, which accorded the state absolute control within its territorial boundaries. Such sovereign cohabitation "almost seems to sanctify evil and condone the effects of tyranny,"[27] he noted, advancing an opposition to the kinds of actions that were subsumed under the heading of coexistence, such as war, violent incitement to struggle, proxy wars in the periphery, and, finally, sustained ideological propaganda.

During the cold war era an understanding of peaceful coexistence evolved to accommodate the nuclear threat. While there was a general acceptance of the progress that the concept of peaceful coexistence brought to cold war political life, theoretically it sustained the conceptual opposition between coexistence and conflict and led to the ossification of the meaning of coexistence as the tentative and dangerous copresence of ideologically incompatible units. Coexistence, then, came to connote an ephemeral state, as it contained within it the acceptance that conflict was inevitable, albeit momentarily restricting it to the realm of ideology. The mitigation of nuclear war in this way entailed the toleration of intense ideological struggle and transposed actual conflict to the periphery, where proxy wars were fought throughout the post–World War II years. This brief exposition suggests that international relations literature and institutional or political practice were largely preoccupied and sought to address the continued danger brought about by the production and deployment of nuclear arms on the one hand, and the perceived ideological incompatibility of capitalism and really existing communism on the other.

## COEXISTENCE IN CONTEMPORARY INTERNATIONAL RELATIONS

Since the collapse of communism, the parameters of thought that had guided international coexistence between opposing ideological camps during the post-1945 era have undergone major changes. Contrary to the political preoccupation with the possibility of nuclear annihilation during the cold war, since 1989 concerns with potentially precipitous ideological competition have largely dissipated, leaving concerns about issues of coexistence to evolve along three main trajectories.

In the context of the first path, a certain unease and source of concern was visible, arising from the perception that the West [was left] without markers to identify potential threats to its way of life or reasons to be prepared. With the collapse of communist regimes in Eastern Europe, followed by the dissolution of the Soviet Union itself, the global ideological confrontation that had served so well to identify friend and foe vanished.[28]

Cold war thinking about ideological struggle, as a result, transformed its content by discursively shifting away from superpower conflict toward "civilizational tension or struggle." The most widely known example of this strand of thinking is Samuel Huntington's "clash of civilizations,"[29] although his theorization of the post-1989 international political scene has come under severe criticism, not only from critical theorists but also from more mainstream authors.[30] Embedded within an alarmist ontology of decline, IR thinking about civilizations sought to replace the formulaic role of cold war ideological and military oppositions with mapped cultural differences.[31] As Marc Lynch argues in this vein, "Huntington's 'clash of civilisations' initially defined the terms of debate within a realist conceptual universe which simply replaced 'states' with 'civilisations.'"[32] As such, it remains wedded to an understanding of civilization, not as diverse and polymorphic, but as unitary.[33]

The second trajectory reveals that the discipline of international relations has been increasingly called on to theorize coexistence, not among sovereign states where its traditional expertise lies, but rather of substate groups and individuals. The emerging concern with the coexistence of people as an issue that requires attention in IR is evident when one considers the rise in civil wars, ethnic conflicts, and other such internal matters that have preoccupied the international community in the post-1989 world.[34] Similarly, there is an increased scholarly focus toward individual or group conflict at a more localized level, usually in the form of specific case studies. The concerns of conflict resolution scholarship evolve around peacemaking and, in terms of peace maintenance and postconflict reconstruction, include peacekeeping and peacebuilding. This strand of thinking about coexistence inevitably responds to the considerations of the international community about localized conflicts, either couched in humanitarian language or considered with regard to their international repercussions, or both.

As Eva Bertram argues, a certain extension of the scope of multi-lateral (usually United Nations) peace operations can be noted since 1990, when there occurred a move from the prevention of hostilities to the active building of "the political conditions for a sustainable peace,"[35] a task that amounts to "remak[ing] a state's political institutions, security forces, and economic arrangements," in short, nation-building.[36] Such on-the-ground widening in the scope of operations within international praxis, as has occurred since 1989, has thus far not been accompanied by a deepening of scholarly focus or punctuated with reflection about the more general, yet foundational, terms that bound that scope. Deepening of that sense would serve to better clarify *what* it is that these operations are trying to achieve, namely, coexistence, and would, moreover, enable the consideration of this concept beyond specific issues of technical management of transitions and cessation of hostilities.

It must be noted that the confrontational politics of the cold war, compounded as it was by its location in a nuclear context, afforded the tragic opportunity of reflecting on the meaning of coexistence as such despite the fixing of dichotomies between coexistence and conflict that that location had imposed on thinking. The post-1989 focus on peacemaking, peacekeeping, and peacebuilding has thus far restricted itself largely to the technical issues of conflict prevention or management within the generalized context of the "upkeeping" of the world system. Despite its difference from the civilizational path of post–cold war thinking, it, too, has the tendency to consider coexistence in the post–cold war context as copresence in a new political geography. It can be argued, therefore, that "a new political geography of the world" has begun to dominate political understanding, where new kinds of wars are associated with "violence-prone areas," which necessarily require the mobilization of world-political resources for the management of international peace and security.[37]

These reflective restrictions and self-imposed limitations of scholarly scope and debate, however, are understood by the discipline of international relations not as limitations but, on the contrary, as prudent responses to what is now perceived to be the mere maintenance of the international system.[38] This level of comfort only makes sense if located within the "end of history" so optimistically heralded by Francis Fukuyama,[39] which leaves but one historical alternative: liberalism. Roland Paris has argued that the guiding paradigm of post-1989 peace operations is liberal internationalism with its premises of free-market-oriented economy and liberal democratic polity, which he collectively unites in the phrase "market democracy."[40] Fukuyama's proposition about the end of history, and the prevalence of liberalism more generally, illustrates the acceptance of the modern subject at the center of the political ontology of IR, despite widely held pessimism in philosophical and social scientific circles about the assumptions of modern subjectivity.[41] Furthermore, the widespread orientation toward technicity occludes the status of coexistence as a question; it presents research as multiple and varied, whereas, upon closer examination, such apparent multiplicity takes place within the bounds of a greater unanimity about the *subject* of coexistence. Moreover, there are no attempts to think about the meaning of coexistence and its conditions of possibility, nor are there any discernible attempts to explore the possibility of grasping coexistence as anything other than composition or copresence of already constituted units.

The third and final contemporary strand of thinking about coexistence comprises international attempts to encourage the "extension of moral inclusion in world politics."[42] It is suggested that in international society, just as within the structures of national societies, inclusion "depends crucially on finding ways of bringing disadvantaged groups, women or men into the political process."[43] This mandate of greater inclusion has arisen more recently from the destabilizing effects brought about by the globalization of world politics and the intensification of social relations across a number of spheres of interaction. There are two broad discourses aiming at greater moral inclusion. The first and more influential discourse wishes to achieve "higher levels of universality" by extending the international human rights regime.[44] Cosmopolitan thinkers such as Ulrich Beck and Jürgen Habermas read "globalization" as a movement away from the Westphalian "international society of states" that underpinned human rights (in the sense that human rights were instruments of positive law, grounded in state constitutional arrangements, and safeguarded as such) and toward a "world society of individuals" in which human rights are prior to and serve to legitimate states. In other words, this is a movement away from international law (where states are prior) toward cosmopolitan law (where rights-bearing subjects are prior), which expands, these authors suggest, ethical regardedness toward the other and aims to provide protection through legal entitlements applicable internationally.[45]

The second discourse is related to the first in that it suggests that something akin to a post-Westphalian era is now approaching, which, in turn, might signal a more inclusive approach to the state and community.[46] This discourse provides an analysis of the impact of processes of globalization on territorially sovereign nation-states, as well as their evaluation of the possibilities arising from novel political arrangements for the future of community, such as the European Union. Constituting the community with the inclusion of the other in mind is the bedrock of this new approach to international relations, as seen in Andrew Linklater's recent work. Linklater's monograph *The Transformation of Political Community* sets out to move beyond the statist Westphalian "blind alley"[47] in order to make the notion of community less exclusionary. For Linklater, the drive for greater inclusion works both by reconstructing "the modern state and the international state system to permit the development of higher levels of universality" and by "transforming exclusionary political communities so that higher levels of respect for cultural difference can evolve."[48] This transition toward a post-Westphalian international environment entails the reworking of states and communities where "universalistic loyalties have to be reconciled with strong emotional ties to specific communities."[49] Linklater calls for a cultivation of a universality that encompasses sensitivity and respect toward otherness, despite the traditional opposition between the two. In this regard Linklater joins Beck and Habermas as "proponents of a liberalism hospitable to particularities" and similarly exhibits a concern with otherness that aims to bestow upon it "equality in the sense of legal egalitarianism."[50]

Both manifestations of this third trajectory—the extension of human rights and the transformation of community—question current modes of exclusion of the other, a task that appears to cohere with this book's interest in why and how coexistence understood as copresence occludes the role of otherness. Their inquiry into otherness, however, is limited both as to how community might be *expanded,* as if greater inclusivity in terms of numbers alone might be the decisive issue, or how others might be included and protected through the bestowal of human rights instruments. These attempts, moreover, do not engage with the even more fundamental and prior issue—central to this book—as to how one could allow existence to show itself as other-determined, that is, as being heteronomous and coexistential from the start. As Werner Hamacher writes in response to the debate on inclusion, thinking about politics and coexistence must seek to go beyond addition, beyond mere counting.[51] This requires not only an other-sensitive universality, as Linklater seems to suggest, but also the calling into question of the edifice or institution of the modern subject on which such liberal cosmopolitan accounts rest.[52] As Diana Coole argues, "where the prevailing liberalism is grounded in a philosophy of the subject," as the majority of these perspectives are, "the radical challenge is to rethink the political" and coexistence in a more fundamental way, a challenge that

> must entail something more fundamental than placing rational individuals within a communicative situation: what is needed is an ontology of this interworld, in order to grasp the way rational forms are engendered within the thick, adverse space between subjects. The analysis of politics no longer begins with the juridico-theoretical model (as Foucault will call it), with the state at its zenith and juridical subjects beneath, but with struggles for coexistence.[53]

The reliance of the majority of these literatures on predominant variants of the modern subject thus suggests that such attempts for greater inclusion are limited in their ability to rethink coexistence, unwittingly reducing its consideration to composition. This reduction is what I will refer to throughout as "the logic of composition"[54]—a logic that will receive a fuller articulation later, where it will also be shown how its reliance on prevalent assumptions about the modern subject renders it inadequate for thinking about coexistence in international relations.

## INTERNATIONAL ONTOLOGICAL COMMITMENTS AND THE LOGIC OF COMPOSITION

Reflecting on the status of coexistence in international relations brings into view a paradoxical situation. While the issue of coexistence ought to be paramount for world-political understanding, its meaning is taken as self-evident; in other words, coexistence is not addressed as a question. Since coexistence is not regarded as an aporia, there is no scholarly debate about what it is, how difficult it might be to define and grasp, or, moreover, what other related theoretical issues about ethics and community, for example, it might both reveal and conceal. According to the prominent stories that IR tells about an anarchical society or system of sovereign nation-states and, more recently, stories about individuals or substate groups, the term "coexistence" is implicitly understood as a condition of entities coming together to cohabit a particular geographical, social, and political space, as well as requiring the explicit act of staying together. The definition of coexistence as a *state* of staying together, therefore, presumes that it is a secondary condition: it is a state of being that must be yielded from some prior purposive action. In this sense, coexistence is "postontological" for IR, a term denoting a condition not investigated at the level of the existential structures of these entities, but rather one that rests on *other* ontological assumptions.

What are those assumptions, and can they be traced to a single basis or guiding principle? Despite the substantially differentiated contexts within which attempts to think about coexistence have arisen, it can be argued that, in modernity, their grounding has been centered on the individual subject, the historical development of which is examined in greater detail in chapter 1. IR theory presents the state *as subject* in much the same way as social theory takes the self or individual as subject, in the sense of a unitary observable and purposive agent.[55] Where IR turns to issues of individuals, as in recent preoccupations with human rights, expanding the community, or postconflict transitions, it joins other related social sciences in its grounding on the modern subject.[56]

Stephen K. White usefully describes this modern subject as an "assertive, disengaged self who generates distance from its background (tradition, embodiment) and foreground (external nature, other subjects) in the name of accelerating mastery of them. This teflon [that is, nonstick] subject has the leading role in the modern stage."[57] David Carr, similarly, notes that the modern subject has invoked mastery over others and self-control "centered in such notions as the cogito, the 'I think,' consciousness, self-consciousness, self-transparency, self-determination."[58] Chapter 1 will outline these characteristics of modern subjectivity in much greater detail, but suffice it to say at present that the two main features of modern subjectivity are its nonrelationality and self-control, features that are often discussed as the values of autonomy and sovereignty. Nonrelationality, in this context, does not suggest that the modern subject does not engage in relations with others, which of course it does, but rather that these relations are not considered *constitutive* of the subject; they tend to be viewed as nonconstitutive for selfhood.

In the past, discussions of the modern subject were customarily conducted not in such critical terms, but rather more neutrally and without explicit exploration as to how its main features affect the subject's relationality toward others. In fact, until recently the modern subject remained largely underthematized in the social sciences, a historical outcome that ought to be taken as "at least a measure of modernity's self-confidence."[59] Perhaps it is a rising insecurity about the modern subject, a dissipation of the once prevalent modernist confidence about its foundational capacities, that has led to recent attempts to evaluate assumptions about human existence, to gain access to the kind of entity "which we ourselves are,"[60] part of a type of inquiry called "ontology." Scholars in philosophy, along with social and political theorists, have recently expended considerable energy criticizing the hold that modern subjectivity has over inquiry in the modern era and have called for different thinking about "ourselves, and being in general."[61] Such unconventional and challenging thinking is essential because ontology grounds political narratives about political order (and coexistence).[62] This can be seen explicitly in international relations where coexistence is determined, on the basis of the self-sufficient and nonrelational subject, as mere copresence. While there has been a reluctance to engage in ontological examination, due in part to the largely epistemological focus of the third debate, ontology remains essential for reevaluating what "the international world is made of"[63] and for determining "what actors there are, how they relate to one another, and what methods are appropriate for the type of research we want to do."[64]

This book endorses the call for an examination of the ontological premises of IR, but understands this to require a more fundamental reconsideration of the subjectivist ground of international relations as a modern social science.[65] It argues that this traditional ground of modern subjectivity has severely constrained the ability of the discipline to think through the question of coexistence in two key respects. First, it becomes apparent that on the basis of this modern subjectivity coexistence can only be thought of and articulated through a "logic of composition."[66] This logic ultimately leads to a phenomenologically unsatisfactory reduction of coexistence to mere copresence. Second, the resulting mutual reinforcement of the subject and practices of composition further ends up obscuring the constitutive role of otherness in the formation of subjectivity, leading to what one might call at this stage a disconcerting effacement of heteronomy. These two limitations are explored in the next two sections.

### The Modern Subject and the Logic of Composition

When inquiry is grounded in modern subjectivity, theoretical articulations of coexistence become limited to composition. Put differently, the ground of modern subjectivity ultimately restricts the possibility of understanding coexistence as anything but a collection of already constituted or preformed individuals. It is therefore also the implicit commitment to the modern subject that continues to determine, indeed *limit,* what being-together or coexistence might mean for international political thought, and this necessitates closer examination. Nancy, for example, observes how the construction of the modern subject, the individual, is widely heralded as "Europe's incontrovertible merit of having shown the world the sole path to emancipation from tyranny, and the norm by which to measure all our collective or communitarian undertakings."[67] Yet, he asks, how can this construct be considered a triumph, an achievement of European thought, when it is at the center of the dissolution of coexistence, more generally, and of community, more specifically? "By its nature—as the name indicates, it is the atom, the indivisible—the individual reveals that it is the abstract result of a decomposition. It is another, and symmetrical, figure of immanence: the absolutely detached for-itself, taken as origin and as certainty."[68] Within the metaphysics of the detached and atomistic modern subject, coexistence can only be grasped *as* composition of already formed subjects.[69] Put differently, subscribing to the "logic of composition" means that the predicate "together . . . is in fact only a qualification extrinsic to subjects, not belonging to the *appearing* of each as such, designating a pure and indifferent juxta-position; or, on the other hand, it adds a particular quality, endowed with a literal sense, which must realise itself for all subjects 'together' and as an 'ensemble.'"[70] The understanding of coexistence as extrinsic to the subject illustrates the power of the ontological commitment to determine coexistence as little more than a situation of subjects being simultaneously present, its reduction to copresence.

Based on modern subjectivity, with its key features of self-sufficiency and mastery prescribing a relation of mere copresence, the logic of composition suggests that units or entities are nonrelational in their constitution until "composed." This determination of coexistence, however, does not arise from the phenomena, the facticity of entities; rather, it is based on an interpretative preconception, what Martin Heidegger calls "a fore-having,"[71] brought to considerations of coexistence and affecting its articulation: this presupposition is the nonrelational subject, whose ontological attributes render coexistence as a secondary and fragile condition, as an act of composing previously unrelated and preformed subjects. The decisive effect of the logic of composition is thus the restriction of relationality to mere copresence of preconstituted entities.

One might object, asking whether the logic of composition can be reduced to its reliance on the human subject in international relations. What about the system of states that provides the parameters for the discipline of world politics? Surely, one might argue, the system of states defies this logic by concentrating on the state as the type of unit involved in coexistence. However, the logic of composition involves the understanding of collectivity according to the principle of the subject. It not only assumes that collectivities are made up of multiple individual subjects but also that *as* collectivities they behave as subjects, which works by a reduction of the "we" to an "I." In other words, just as individuals within the state are thought to coexist on the basis of preformed subjectivities, so too does much of international relations theory assume the state to embody a unitary, nonrelational subjectivity.

This logic of composition is not merely an aberration of the philosophy of some thinkers, of liberalism, and so on, easily exorcized or denounced. Rather, it becomes the sole means of grasping togetherness once the metaphysics of the subject has become prominent. On the basis of assumptions about modern subjectivity, coexistence becomes a technical problem instead of an irreducible aporia. The tension between "self" and "society," the "I" and the "we," arises only with the arrival of the modern subject as the ground of inquiry:

> Only because insofar as man actually and essentially has become
> subject is it necessary for him, as a consequence, to confront the
> explicit question: Is it as an "I" confined to its own preferences and
> freed into its own arbitrary choosing or as the "we" of society; is it
> as an individual or as a community; is it as a personality within the
> community or as a mere group member in the corporate body; is it
> as a state and nation and as a people or as the common humanity of
> modern man, that man will and ought to be the subject that in his
> modern essence he *already* is?[72]

In other words, the question of self and collectivity cannot be asked
from any other position; it is a comprehensible concern only from
the perspective of subjectivism.

Since the question of being-in-common becomes settled through
the logic of composition, the question of the status of coexistence
is never properly raised: "An inconsequential atomism, individualism tends to forget that the atom is also a world."[73] The atom, the
indivisible unit that the modern human subject is assumed to be, *is*
a world, that is, it is enclosed within itself in its certainty and mastery. Its relations are relations of grasping, of presenting that which
is (beings) to itself as its object. Thus, thinking about coexistence
falls within a larger "metaphysics of the subject," understood as
part of, or equal to, "the metaphysics of the absolute for-itself—be
it in the form of the individual or the total state—which means also
the metaphysics of the *absolute* in general, of being-ab-solute, as
perfectly detached, distinct, and closed: being without relation."[74]
"Being without relation" does not mean that there are no actual
relations of the subject to that which is (world and other beings).
Rather, it suggests that the subject, having established itself as complete and absolute, can only strive to preside over its relations; it is
unencumbered; it is solitary; it is unaffected in its self-constitution
by the objects of its representation and reflection.

Within this metaphysics of subjectivity the question of coexistence
can only be asked as that of composition, of a technical arrangement
of units, its success always fragile, its descent to conflict never surprising, always expected. Expectation of incompatibility and surprise at
any achievement of coexistence betrays that the logic of composition
determines it as an afterthought, as a secondary condition. This also
helps to clarify why in IR coexistence is primarily considered as the

tentative state that might always slip back into conflict: it is because the "with" is seen as that which must be constructed from the starting point of subjectivism that it becomes a precarious achievement. There is, in other words, a subterranean theoretical linkage between coexistence and conflict that is sustained even by the people who wish to imbue coexistence with a different meaning and those who wish to emphasize that coexistence is a matter crucial to human survival. Coexistence appears as a technical issue of how to arrange units in a certain manner to bring about this condition of togetherness crucial to "survival."

I argue, therefore, that if coexistence is to be theorized otherwise in IR, the disciplinary reliance on the premises of modern subjectivity must first be questioned. The current juncture of uncertainty attributed to globalization, to the retreat of the state, to emergence of concerns ungraspable within IR's traditional parameters, might present an opportunity for sustained ontological examination to "unwork modern subjectivity"[75] by, first, problematizing the ontological commitment to the subject and, second, suggesting a recovery of selfhood that, first and foremost, coexists. But why should problematization of the reliance on the modern subject be considered so vital a task for IR? I suggest that the uncritical acceptance of the modern conception of subjectivity severely limits IR's ability to thoroughly address the question of coexistence and that this leads to more than theoretical neglect: the logic of composition, more importantly, fails to recognize the *priority* of coexistence and the fundamental role that otherness plays in the constitution of selfhood, a role that one might call "heteronomy." As the next section illustrates, the logic of composition remains blind to the self's heteronomous constitution; it effaces heteronomy because its assumptions about the modern subject make it impossible to recognize that the self, as Heidegger argued, is always already thrown into a world of otherness.

### The Effacement of Heteronomy

Understanding human existence under the sign of modern subjectivity not only leads to a reduction of coexistence to copresence, it also obscures the constitutive role of the other in the formation of the self. Modern subjectivity produces a set of assumptions about the entity "we all are, in each case" and assumptions about the other, based on "a mindset of valuation, disposal, management, and objectification in our care for our lives, a mindset whose overpowering force hems us in throughout our everyday world, confuses freedom with the condition of possibility for certain types of subjectivity, and gives priority to correctness and measurement in matters of truth."[76] It is through the production of certain assumptions about ourselves, Charles Scott argues, that "we make ourselves present to each other by reference to values that commonly identify us and have proven trustworthy for our survival and well-being."[77] Yet the values that are customarily considered as trustworthy guides for life are located within "a history of thought and practice in which engagement in the disclosure of beings is thoroughly overlooked and excluded from thought."[78] The ontology of modern subjectivity does not allow entities and beings to show themselves as they are; by assuming *that* they exist, this ontology neglects to ask about their "facticity," that is, how they are in the world with others. In this way, "[t]he disclosiveness of beings is thus distorted into their presence and their quality of will regarding other beings."[79] Therefore, to be is to be present, and to coexist is to be copresent. When self-sufficient subjectivity is the ground on which the question of "with" is thought, coexistence becomes an act of bringing together subjects and managing their copresence.

The attempt to shed light on heteronomy is thus of the utmost importance to the critical enterprise within social science because it refuses the effacement by modern subjectivity *of its own constitution by otherness;* moreover, it allows otherness and selfhood to be disclosed outside of a subjectivist grasping. Rethinking the relationship between selfhood and otherness, Thomas Trezise suggests, does not merely seek to "reverse an oppositional dissymmetry while leaving the opposition and its terms intact"; rather, the consideration of heteronomy "seeks to articulate a relation other than that of opposition itself, a relation of differential intrication in which the involvement of terms with each other constitutes their only identity or quidity."[80] The first step toward the grasping of heteronomy and the enabling of coexistence beyond composition must begin with a challenge to the assumptions of nonrelationality and self-sufficiency, usually bound up in the notion of autonomy. Autonomy has to do with freedom and "absolute autoactivity, a spontaneity and a power of man to determine himself on his own."[81] But why, asks Paul Standish, "should we have anything to say against autonomy, why feel any reservations about this sort of ideal," intricately related as this is "in a fundamental way with many aspects of our freedom and with the related notion of our individuality."[82] Yet, what I seek to challenge is precisely the fallout from this kind of autonomy as an attribute. As Ute Guzzoni notes, autonomy has, in many a configuration of the modern subject, been related to mastery over otherness: "The subject is posited as *autonomously determining* in relation to an object which is determined by it; its autonomy is revealed in a relation of domination over everything which is not itself."[83] Raising the question of heteronomy, however, shows that the mandate of otherness refers not only to really-existing others, it also shows an equal interest in the suppression of the otherness or strangeness of human existence, which autonomy similarly effaces.

Prior to further exploration of the ontological basis of coexistence, "heteronomy" as a term should defy a fixed definition, because any definition, which might be given presently, has to come from within a subjectivist ground. Yet, awareness of the futility of accessing heteronomy within the language of the subject does not obviate the need for something like a working definition of the term. The term "heteronomy" ought to be taken at this stage as nothing but a *formal indication,* in the sense that it indicates a potential meaning without strict determination, leaving open the definition of heteronomy to be illuminated through the discussion (see chapter 2). Thus, the term "heteronomy" should be considered as a placeholder (Heidegger would say "formal indicator")[84] for a phenomenon still obscured by subjectivist thinking, still to be properly discussed.

The usage of "heteronomy," therefore, warns of a phenomenal awareness of something like heteronomy, but its determination (which may very well require a reformulation in the assumptions of formally indicated "heteronomy") will be gradual. In some sense, "heteronomy" means "constitutive otherness," but also entails within it another meaning, that of being-other-directed.[85] Furthermore, and this is the meaning that challenges the predominant feature of nonrelational subjectivity, "heteronomy" could be seen to indicate being-radically-in-relation. Yet another possible sense of the term arises when one asks what it is that compels thinking toward the questioning of modern subjectivity. How is an aporia created in something as complete and self-actualizing as the constellation of modern subjectivity? As Foucault noted, the achievement of subjectivity is a continuous process, a "ceaseless task" within which is contained the possibility of the failure of totalization and closure.[86] To think of this failure is to think of the space in which ~~subjectivity~~ (putting this term under erasure) can be rethought. "The subject is thus indeed already, between the lines (and thanks to a retrospective reading), what *threatens*. . . . But why is the subject threatening? And what is it, in the subject, that threatens?"[87] What is it "which, in the subject, deserts (has always already deserted) the subject *itself*" and leads to "the dissolution, the defeat of the subject or *as* the subject: the (de)construction of the subject or the 'loss' of the subject—if indeed one can think the loss of what one has never had, a kind of 'originary' and 'constitutive' loss (of 'self')"?[88] It will be argued that not only something in the subject threatens its own construction, but that in its making itself secure it fails to adequately efface its own heteronomous constitution. Heteronomy, then, is the remainder that subjectivity could not erase.

Finally, heteronomy also denies the premise of individuality understood as self-constitution, but highlights instead the fact of *singularity* because "behind the theme of the individual, but beyond it, lurks the question of singularity."[89] As Nancy argues, "[S]ingularity never has the nature of individuality. Singularity never takes place at the level of atoms, those identifiable, if not identical identities"; rather, singularity has to do with the inclination or disposition to otherness.[90] It will be argued in the course of the book that it is only when selfhood is grasped beyond the subject that coexistence itself will be thought beyond addition or composition and the phenomenological inadequacy of the self-understanding of self *as* subject will be revealed, making possible a different disclosure of the self as a coexistentially heteronomous being. In either case, it means there are three concerns about otherness motivating the discussions of the book. The first is how the logic of composition reduces the phenomena of coexistence to copresence of already constituted subjects; the second is how the other's role in the constitution of the self, its heteronomy, is concealed by this logic and how this might be reversed; and the third relates to how the self's otherness, how it is other to itself, is obscured when it is grasped as subject.

## THE STRUCTURE OF THE BOOK

The introduction and the first chapter are illustrative of manifestations of composition in the grounding tradition of international political thought.[91] They provide a brief historical trajectory of the modern subject and examine the interplay of subjectivity, otherness, and coexistence in Thomas Hobbes's account of the social contract arising in the state of nature, which is one of the most lasting and powerful manifestations of the logic of composition, especially for international relations. The discussion of Hobbes's contractarianism remains a brief illustration of the logic of composition, however, because the book seeks to investigate the possibility of another ontological account that allows the articulations of coexistence as a *question* and gestures toward a possibility of theorizing it otherwise than composition. The conditions of possibility for an alternative framing of coexistence lie in the initiation of a process of "unworking modern subjectivity," which is the focus of chapters 2 through 4. For this purpose, an ontological examination of the being normally conceived as subject is called for in order to let its heteronomous facticity, *how* it is, be seen. This process, however, must have as its starting point the search for a method through which to access and express the facticity of entities. This is found in the early thought of German philosopher Martin Heidegger and his rearticulation of interpretative phenomenology, which is examined in chapter 2.

The turn to Heidegger for the purpose of unworking modern subjectivity is familiar to readers of philosophy and political theory. However, the claim that this unworking is undertaken in order to prevent the effacement of heteronomy by the logic of composition may be rather more surprising. The primary reason for this is that Continental philosophy and to some extent international relations have become suspicious of Heidegger's thought, following Emmanuel Levinas's critique that his thought is emblematic of the broader Western tradition's blindness to the other.[92] Furthermore, Levinas's concern was that phenomenology, the tradition within which he himself worked, is a philosophy of power and violence; his work has, therefore, engendered a certain cautiousness toward, and one might say a certain neglect of, Heidegger's thought *when it comes to the thought of otherness.* Chapter 2 thus describes the phenomenological method alongside Levinas's objections—objections that are invaluable because they have sensitized us to the question of the other within Heidegger's thought. The turn to Heidegger, therefore, is advocated precisely in light of Levinas's critique. Put differently, Levinas's challenge that phenomenology and ontology are philosophies of violence leads us to *return* to Heidegger to show precisely that within the ontological and hermeneutic turn that Heidegger gives to phenomenology in *Being and Time* there can be found an account of the self (in Heidegger's term "Dasein") as an other-constituted and coexistential being, a being determined through and through by otherness.

Chapter 3, then, undertakes the phenomenological examination of *Dasein*[93] largely contained within Heidegger's seminal work *Being and Time*. Responding to Levinas, the chapter argues that an "optics of coexistence" can be found within Heidegger's phenomenology of everyday existence, comprising a host of elements that unwork the presuppositions of the subjectivist ontology of IR and illustrate the primary role of otherness. Through these elements, coexistence is shown phenomenally to be the primary fact of Dasein's existence. Theoretically, such an account of primary sociality renders unstable the terms of subjectivist discourse through which coexistence is conceptualized. Such an optics puts forward a *heterology* or a discourse where the other is primary, but also an *other* discourse, one that attempts to defy the dominance of subjectivity and that shows that selfhood is coexistentially heteronomous.[94] Heidegger's "optics of coexistence" and his "calls for the overcoming of subjectivity as the constitutive feature of man"[95] engage in a process of "unworking of subjectivity," which lets heteronomy show itself. Following this discussion, chapter 4 continues this task by discussing how the self becomes aware of its own heteronomy through a process of becoming-proper for the kind of being that it is. The discussion, moreover, examines various prominent concerns about Heidegger's account of the self in order to better illuminate the contribution made by such a coexistential reading of Heidegger's analysis to a thought of coexistence beyond copresence.

The task of the book does not stop here, however. It must be noted that the account given by Heidegger in *Being and Time* amounts to an *existential* heteronomy, which calls into question the determination of coexistence as composition. The unworking that chapter 3 undertakes does not seek to replace the subject with an-

other account of ontological certainty. On the contrary, it problema-
tizes subjectivist assumptions and aims at creating the possibility for
thinking of coexistence beyond composition, a task taken in parallel in chapters 5 and 6. Chapter 5 examines recent cosmopolitan attempts to protect others and conceive of coexistence by extending the
international human rights regime. It illustrates how the optics of
coexistence aids in the recovery of an ethical self that understands
itself as an opening to otherness and that, paradoxically, calls the
reliance on legal instruments and ethical construction into question.
Universal ethical construction based on rights is challenged through
the cultivation of silence and hearing that allow the voice of the
other, which Dasein carries within it, to be heard. This brings the
discussion back to Levinas's incitement to recover from the analysis of Dasein a selfhood that understands itself as an opening to
otherness.

Chapter 6 brings this recovery of the ethical self to bear on the political realm by examining how community and coexistence might be
conceptualized beyond the logic of composition. Yet, any discussion
of political coexistence deriving from the thought of Heidegger also
faces an additional difficulty: is not the thought of Heidegger marred
by his own political involvement with the National Socialists in the
1930s? I discuss the impact of the debate on Heidegger's politics on
the attempt to reconceptualize coexistence and point to Heidegger's
problematic discussion of community as containing critical possibilities within it. Using the recent work of Peg Birmingham, I explore
the constitution of community as occurring through a process of
critical mimesis and leading to a mode of identification that might
be called critical belonging, which hopes to avoid both the reduction of coexistence to copresence according to the logic of composition and also the determination of it according to an essence, which
would be equally blind to otherness.

Finally, the conclusion brings together the trajectories of the
book, highlighting the contributions of this *heterologous* reading of
Heidegger in light of the questions of coexistence and otherness for
international relations.

# Manifestations of Composition

*We think restlessly within familiar frameworks to avoid thought about how our thinking is framed.*
WILLIAM E. CONNOLLY, *POLITICAL THEORY AND MODERNITY*

How does coexistence come to be articulated through the logic of composition, as a condition of joining distinct, previously unrelated units? The equating of coexistence and composition, it is argued here, becomes possible when political thinking is based on modern subjectivity. It is necessary, therefore, to examine in greater detail the historical emergence of "the subject," in order to better illustrate the ontological commitment of international relations to modern subjectivity and how this determines coexistence according to the logic of composition. On the ground of modern subjectivity, as described briefly in the introduction, a number of accounts of political coexistence (and more specifically, of communal constitution) have arisen in the modern age[1] that take different perspectives on government and the creation of political order. Martin Wight's reflections on the traditions of international political thought suggest, in this regard, a number of political philosophic accounts on which the theoretical perspectives of international relations are grounded. Wight distinguished between realist, rationalist, and revolutionist legacies, loosely associated with Thomas Hobbes, John Locke, and Immanuel Kant respectively.[2] Despite their diversity, these traditions determine coexistence on the basis of composition to a greater or lesser extent.

Although it is beyond the scope of this project to exemplify in detail how the logic of composition operates in all the traditions and the breadth of thinkers included in Wight's typology, this chapter seeks to illustrate how the assumptions of subjectivity affect the understanding of coexistence in what may well be the most prevalent traditional discourse prominent in IR. Examples of this effect are certain aspects of the political philosophy of seventeenth-century English philosopher Thomas Hobbes, as received within the disciplinary boundaries of IR. Hobbes is chosen for a variety of reasons. First, Hobbes reconfigures the emerging attributes of early modern subjectivity for the purposes of his political theory by specifically formulating reason and mastery into a self-interested subject concerned with survival and self-preservation. The Hobbesian infusion of danger into the ontological basis of the modern subject inserts the notion of self-preservation as part of the mastery of the subject. Hobbes's account is an example of how different modern philosophies rearticulate the main features of modern subjectivity. Although such rearticulations can vary widely, there exists a basic concern about the subject that is distinctive of modern philosophy. As Dieter Sturma and Karl Ameriks argue, modern philosophy "has combined perspectives that construct and criticize the standpoint of subjectivity . . . but without thereby giving up the notion of the self."[3]

Second, Hobbes's account of the creation of a civil and orderly commonwealth out of a state of nature through the mechanism of the social contract has been one of the more lasting and powerful manifestations of the logic of composition, a composition that, in his case, is permeated by danger. Third, Hobbes's political philosophy clearly illustrates the interconnectedness of subjectivity, composition, and otherness. Hobbes's *Leviathan* contains an extensive *heterology*, a logos of/about the other, which sustains his political theoretical construction. Specifically, his reconfiguration of modern subjectivity leads to a specific understanding of the other-as-enemy, where the other is encountered through an éthos of survival as an enemy that must be survived.[4] The result of the interplay between subjectivity and composition is a political theory of coexistence, which exhibits all the characteristics of the logic of composition as outlined in the introduction, namely, tentativeness, tendency to failure, and nonconstitutive, controlled relationality.

There is a final reason for choosing Hobbes's account with which to illustrate the logic of composition, and it involves its reception in international relations. Even when acknowledged as an origin to be surpassed or being currently transformed, the Hobbesian parameters still hold sway over the disciplinary imagination. Even recent important contributions to the theoretical understanding of communities such as that of Andrew Linklater or the delineation of systemic environs by Alexander Wendt all begin from this account.[5] In this sense, what is important here is how IR understands the Hobbesian account rather than its authenticity.

## THE MODERN SUBJECT IN HISTORICAL CONTEXT

"The modern subject has been at the centre of social and political inquiry even if by negation," write Simon Critchley and Peter Dews in their influential volume on subjectivity.[6] The modern subject has been holding court over the philosophical endeavors of the modern era, and in this century it has become the focus of numerous divergent philosophies with often contradictory aims and ends. To talk about the modern subject is not to claim that a unifying conception of it holds for all of modern philosophy. Rather, its importance suggests that modern philosophy might be seen as "a set of variations on a theme" of the subject,[7] which originated in Continental philosophy, and where it received extensive attention but also substantive critique.[8]

Jane Flax suggests that since the seventeenth century two related but distinct views about the subject dominated philosophic debate:

> One is the Cartesian idea of the self as an ahistoric, solid indwelling entity that grounds the possibility of rational thought. In turn the self is accessible and transparent to such thought. The defining characteristic of this self is to engage in abstract rational thought, including thought about its own thought. . . . The second idea is the Humean-empirical one. This self and its knowledge are derived from sense experience.[9]

From its philosophical origins, the modern subject has become the cornerstone, the underlying premise, of much theoretical inquiry and has provided the unit of analysis for the majority of the social sciences. In order to elucidate the problematic of coexistence as one that obeys a certain logic of composition, it is necessary to provide an account of that which is operative in this logic and, moreover, of that which makes this logic possible. This is to ask the question "what is meant by *subject*?" The answer that this chapter offers can only sketch, in summary form, a historical trajectory of the institution of the subject, while bearing in mind that any narration of its story in such a setting can never be fully inclusive of the resistances and critiques rendered against "the subject" nor of the forms of its many reassertions.[10]

### Subject as *Hypokeimenon*

"Subject," at first glance, appears to translate the term *hypokeimenon*, which in Greek philosophy meant that which lies under, that which predicates something else. This apparent relation or identity between "subject" and *hypokeimenon* requires careful consideration because the concept of the subject has undergone a reformulation in the modern era that prohibits such an immediate equivalence. In Greek philosophy *hypokeimenon* was generally understood together with the term "substance" *(ousia)* because "[s]ubstance is the underlying, persisting foundation which supports everything else."[11] For something to *be*, therefore, it had "[to be] a substance or to be a property or predicate of a substance. Substance exists in the primary sense, everything else exists 'in' substance and thus has a merely secondary and dependent way of existing."[12] In Aristotle's *Physics* and *Metaphysics, hypokeimenon* refers to "that of which all other entities are predicated but which is itself not predicated of anything else," that which does not require further foundation.[13] For the Greeks, then, subject indicated a predicate that acted as a foundation that "persists through change, the sub-stratum, and which has a function analogous to matter *(hule)*. It is matter which persists through the changes that form *(morphe)* imposes on it."[14] These brief references to a premodern meaning of "subject" as *hypokeimenon* make clear that the term "names that-which-lies-before, which, as ground, gathers everything onto itself."[15]

What is missing from this description of what "subject" meant in a premodern context for ancient Greek philosophy is any relation or equation of *hypokeimenon* to man or human being. As Martin Heidegger argued, "This metaphysical meaning of the concept of subject has first of all no special relationship to man and none at all to the I."[16] Opposing a subjectivist rereading of Greek philosophy,[17] Heidegger emphasized the sea change that came about in modernity, particularly with the principle *ego cogito, ergo sum* put forward as the essential feature of subjectivity by French philosopher René Descartes in the seventeenth century.[18] Heidegger understood "all metaphysics" to be "characterized by 'subjectity,' but in modern philosophy this is transformed into 'subjectivity.'"[19] Whereas *subjectum* or *hypokeimenon* had meant the underlying, unchanging predicate that itself required no further foundation but denoted no relation to man or the "I," with the advent of modern metaphysics man asserts himself as this final ground.

## Man as Subjectum

The inception of subjectivity is closely related to the increasing concern with the ego or the individual in the seventeenth century. As Paul Barry Clarke notes, "This is no mere accident"; such an interest in the individual as subject is "a clear consequence of the breakdown of the medieval order"[20] and is evident in several thinkers of that time. The creation of a relationship between man, seen as the ultimate predicate *(hypokeimenon)*, and constancy, in the sense of continuous presence and certainty, must be grasped within the context of seventeenth-century metaphysics and the space created by the loss of certainty associated with premodern cosmology. The collapse of divine ultimate foundations, however, required the formulation of a new ground. Man as final foundation

> had not only to be itself one that was certain, but since every standard of measure from any other sphere was forbidden, it had at the same time to be of such a kind that through it the essence of the freedom claimed would be posited as self-certainty.[21]

Thus, the disavowal of medieval metaphysics seeks a modernist grounding that, in effect, works as "man's making himself secure as *subiectum*."[22] As Ernesto Laclau and Chantal Mouffe explain,

> [T]he seventeenth century [brought about] the collapse of the view of the cosmos as a meaningful order within which man occupied a precise and determined place—and the replacement of this view by a self-defining conception of the subject, as an entity maintaining relations of exteriority with the rest of the universe.[23]

Heidegger sought to provide a sustained critique of early modern metaphysics and, particularly, of the infiltration of all science by subjectivity since the seventeenth century; for him, the philosophy of Descartes, specifically, played a grounding role in the establishment of man as subject.[24] Cartesian thought enabled the philosophical development of modern subjectivity as the primary ground by emphatically placing the subject as the final foundation of rigorous science. As Robert C. Solomon and Kathleen M. Higgins note in their overview of the history of philosophy, "Descartes was the philosopher who most dramatically insisted on the simultaneous turn to subjectivity and the use of logic . . . to argue his way to objectivity."[25] David Carr goes as far to suggest that, in fact,

> beneath the surface of a language that metaphysically valorizes the "objective" over the "subjective" . . . lies an ontology that [is] precisely the reverse. For in spite of all orientation towards the objective, in modern philosophy and especially science, it is the subject . . . which exists in the primary sense, while the objective is reduced to something secondary.[26]

The modern articulation of reflection as constitutive for subjectivity, in the form of the Cartesian cogito, played a grounding role for subsequent philosophizing and theorizing. Heidegger regarded that

> at the beginning of modern philosophy stands Descartes' statement *Ego cogito, ergo sum*, "I think, therefore I am." All consciousness of things and of beings as a whole is referred back to the self-consciousness of the human subject as the unshakable ground of all certainty.[27]

The liberation of man from the medieval schematic of salvation required the creation of a different, human-based, and self-sufficient kind of certainty.[28] Descartes enabled this by grounding *"the metaphysical ground of man's liberation in the new freedom of self-assured self-legislation"*[29] and provided in this way a "foundation for the freeing of man to freedom as the self-determination that is certain of itself."[30]

The distinguishing feature of metaphysics in the modern age, therefore, "is that the metaphysical foundation is no longer claimed to reside in a form, substance, or deity outside of the human intellect but is rather found in the human being understood as subject."[31] The assignment of man as subject came about, Heidegger argued, because Cartesian inquiry relied on the existing idea of substance with which to grasp the essence of man. Descartes disregarded an analysis of man that would adequately account for his embeddedness *within* the world, relying instead on the idea of substance to describe the world and inner-worldly entities.[32] Descartes equated the Being of the world with substantiality, while defining the human being by its *distinction* to substance, as the entity defined by its reflective capacity, the "I think."

What about the human subject? Descartes' *ego cogito* is distinguished from the *res corporea*, which is understood as *res extensa*, namely, as "extended substance."[33] Examining solely the *ego cogito* and defining it in distinction to substance led Descartes to forgo serious investigation of the latter part of his now famous maxim: of the *sum*, the "I am." By focusing on the *cogito*, Descartes created an opposition between the reflective "I think," which makes me certain that I am this entity, and the facticity and embodiment of the "I am." This oversight resulted in the equivalence of the "I am" with that against which the "I think" is distinguished, namely, "extended substance." According to Heidegger, then, Descartes understood human being "in the very same way as he takes the Being of the *res extensa*—namely, as substance," though to equate the "I am" with the *res extensa* and substantiality in general was not phenomenally adequate.[34]

In sum, what distinguished the modern age from the prior medieval era and from Greek philosophy is that in modernity "man, independently and by his own effort, contrives to become certain and sure of his human being in the midst of beings as a whole."[35] Michel Foucault concurs years later not only that certainty is self-instituted but that "the modern *cogito* . . . is not so much the discovery of an evident truth as a ceaseless task constantly to be undertaken afresh."[36] This echoes Friedrich Nietzsche's insight that "[t]he subject is multiplicity that built an imaginary unity for itself."[37] The process of securing man as the ground of certainty is, in other words, continuous and reiterative and has to be asserted through the subject's relations with others within its world.

Instituting man as foundation was far from effortless and involved two related steps. The first is the pivotal role of thinking-as-representing, and the second is the representing-as-securing, which, taken together, render man as ground. "The freeing of the subject to freedom" liberated man from the medieval schema in which he had been incorporated. Man as subject, however, inversely "assume[d] a definitive relationship of domination with regard to the world in which it represent[ed] itself as living."[38] The relation of man-as-subject to existing entities was a relation of mastery: the subject relates to the world, and entities within the world, as object. Dalia Judovitz suggests, "The subject signifies a new way of being human, one that has to do with the rationalization of human capabilities through their delimitation and economization in order to master the world through representation."[39]

### The Representing Subject

The "ceaseless task" of subjectivity is intricately connected to representation not only of entities as objects but also of the subject to itself *as* the subject of re-presentation, the subject that presents itself to itself *as* subject.[40] Having already noted that to exist for a subject is "to be an object or representation for it," it has been argued that the relationship of human being to the world, to other entities and other human beings within the world, becomes one of subject and object.[41] Richard Polt suggests, "Subjectivism pictures the human situation in terms of the subject, object, and a representational connection between the two."[42]

This reduces relationality to representation. "What can appear is determined in advance as what can be represented to a subject, a subject whose self-representation is the ground of all that it represents to itself," argues Bernard Flynn.[43] But what does that mean for otherness? In the first instance, it reduces the spectrum of relationality to self and other, grasped as subject and its object of representation, leaving no space for an understanding of the self as permeated by alterity, constituted through and through by otherness. Far from further elucidating the self's constitution, the subject of representation "is supposed to be in complete command of its own consciousness, perfectly self-present or at least potentially so."[44] The very character of this subject is representation. Otherness, as the object, "is supposed to be a thing that occurs as present within a neutral space," becoming something knowable and intelligible because "by representing it, that is, by following some procedure that will yield the correct picture or account of the object" it is determined as an object distinct and nonrelated to the subject that presents it to itself.[45] Representation, thus, "make[s] the object available for manipulation,"[46] whereas "[t]he *human* subject—as self, ego, or conscious, thinking thing—becomes the ultimate foundation upon which entities are rendered intelligible, that in virtue of which entities are understandable in their Being."[47] The representing subject reduces relationships with otherness and with the world to a process of representation and knowledge, although this knowledge is not of entities as they are but rather a conflation of otherness to sameness. Subjectivity "takes over all being by objectifying it and reducing it to calculable representations, framing it within a world-picture which is a product of subjective (human) activity."[48] Through this will and activity "in the philosophical era extending from Descartes to Hegel, subjectivity ultimately negates its own negation, sublates the other as or into itself."[49]

As well as revealing the relations of domination woven by the concept of the subject, the relationship between subjectivity, intelligibility, and representation is of great ontological significance for the very institution of subjectivity itself. Through the grasping and determination of otherness as *object* the subject secures itself: in representing the "object" "the subject is supposed to be capable of representing itself with the object."[50] Thinking-as-representing, therefore, does not affect only otherness. The invocation of the dichotomy of subject and object recalls "the very *interval* constitutive of the modern metaphysics of subjectivity, in which a subject entirely present to itself confronts an object present or op-posed to that subject."[51] The emphasis placed on representation and intelligibility, in other words, puts into focus the *ego cogito:* man as subject becomes himself reduced to his reflective capacity and his mind. Richard Williams and Edwin Gantt suggest, "The intellectual spirit of modernism is captured and preserved in its finest creation, the individual mind as subject, *standing over against the world* conceived as object."[52] Carr further argues, "primary being or subjectivity . . . is conceived as the activity, striving or will"[53] reified as a mind distinct from its embodiment and in control over it. With mind in the ascent, the material world and otherness become purveyed and thought of as nonconstitutive, the result of which is the consideration of world and people as "resources."[54] The opposition of subject/object, most prevalently taken as the pursuit of knowledge of the world and inner-worldly entities in the name of manipulating them or putting them to use, is best exemplified in the domain of scientific inquiry where science is transformed into human science.

### Science as Human Science

The transformation of science into human science is of great importance in the historical emergence of modern subjectivity. Foucault argued,

> The simple fact that man, whether in isolation or as a group, and for the first time since human beings have existed and have lived together in societies, should have become the object of science—that cannot be considered or treated as a phenomenon of opinion: it is an event in the order of knowledge.[55]

Political knowledge is, naturally, of special interest to us, and its epistemic transformation from the classical age to modernity illustrates three evident changes. First, "the claim of scientifically grounded social philosophy aims at establishing once and for all the conditions for the correct order of the state and society as such. Its assertions are to be valid independently of place, time, and circumstances, and are to permit an enduring foundation for communal life, regardless of the historical situation."[56] Second, the transition from knowledge into praxis is now considered a merely technical problem. General conditions for social and political order are considered knowable, resulting in narrowing the task of politics to "the correctly calculated generation of rules, relationships, and institutions."[57] The third change, most importantly, involves the subject of politics, whose behavior now becomes "the material for science," itself transformed into the deduction and "construction of conditions under which human beings, just like objects within nature, will necessarily behave in a calculable manner."[58]

The assertion of man as subject and its characteristic self-certainty "leads to a conception of knowledge as information gathering and processing, which can then be exploited to serve the interests of the subject."[59] Thus, all science becomes, in some sense, anthropology: in other words, science is now understood from man's perspective. "Anthropology," in this instance, "designates that philosophical interpretation of man which explains and evaluates what is, in its entirety, from the standpoint of man and in relation to man."[60] As Foucault concurred years later, "the anthropological configuration of modern philosophy" suggests that "the pre-critical analysis of what man is in his essence becomes the analytic of everything that can, in general, be presented to man's experience."[61] It is not, however, just that this scientific configuration evinces technicity and calculability: the transformation of science into human science or anthropology entails overtly political determinations because "the modern enterprise is thus also inextricably tied to a kind of 'metaphysical politics' . . . striv[ing] for a complete universal self-authorization."[62] In other words, the subject's positing of itself as the object of science and the reduction of science to what is representable to the subject as part of its experience involve the desire toward self-knowledge and the ability to make total claims about the world. In this way, "we come to know the world 'outside' by looking 'inside.'"[63] This paradoxical "arrogance of knowledge coupled with the seeming humility of critical self-examination," however, means that a largely situated perspective can make global claims about the objectivity of its knowledge amassed subjectively.[64] Thus, the rise of the subject is not merely synonymous with the "apotheosis of reason, and the successful pursuit of knowledge"; rather, the story of science as the institutionalization of thinking-as-representing and representing-as-securing is "also a story of power and politics."[65] Nevertheless, Heidegger argues that

> man assumes a special role in metaphysics inasmuch as he seeks, develops, grounds, defends, and passes on metaphysical knowledge— and distorts it. But that still does not give us the right to consider him the measure of all things as well, to characterize him as the center of all beings, and establish him as master of all things.[66]

### The Subject of International Politics

While philosophy has been preoccupied with notions of subjectivity for the better part of this century and has initiated a process of self-critique since the very advent of the Enlightenment,[67] it appears that in the more applied fields of the human and social sciences the modern subject has taken hold and is still generally accepted as the basis of social and political inquiry. C. Fred Alford has observed that in political theory and political science, as well as social science more generally, theorizations of the "self" always involve trade-offs. Often authors will "weaken, split, and shatter the integrity of the self, in order to render it more tractable, or more ideal."[68] The purpose of these manipulations of the self is, of course, to write social or political theory that fulfills certain functions and allows certain normative concerns to be realized theoretically. The self, thus, is considered to be little more than "a dependent variable in this or that social theory."[69] If Alford is correct in his view, this might also explain why ontology is not a major concern in social and political theory, although in some respects this may be changing.[70] Alford contends, not without irony, that for most social scientists "more subtle and complex models [of the self] may be interesting, but they are not necessary to do real social science."[71] It is interesting to ask as to the extent to which his comment, ironic as it may be, would not also be appropriate for IR as a social science, and significantly for IR as a social science not really concerned with people at all, although again exceptions can be found.[72] Furthermore, "subtle and complex models" of the self might be what is required for a reconsideration of coexistence as an issue of primary importance for international politics.

It might be contentious to suggest that the ontological assumptions on which IR grounds coexistence are centered on the individual subject, given the presumed divergence between the three traditions or paradigms and also the discipline's focus on "states." However, IR as a social science lies within the modernist tradition and shares its fundamental metaphysical positions about the subject as sovereign and self-sufficient. Wight classified IR theories into three schools made up of realists, rationalists, and revolutionists because these perspectives take their assumptions from philosophical movements or schools that bear those names, although, as he rightly notes, these took hold in IR with some "debasement."[73]

Can one really claim, however, that these modern philosophies, as well as the theoretical traditions they have engendered in IR, rest on a common understanding of subjectivity? Is this really the claim put forward here? Not at all: the claim here suggests not identity among philosophies of the modern era about their consideration of subjectivity, but an inherent centrality within them of the notion of the subject. The suggestion is that, with modernity, philosophy and also social science become grounded in the human being as subject, although there are a number of differentiated features of that subject proposed by various thinkers and schools of thought. Cartesian philosophy effected a change in the terms of discourse so that in the post-Cartesian era philosophical and social thought takes its problematic from the *cogito*.

Much like the modern philosophical endeavor in which it is located, the discipline of IR avails a view of the ontological centrality of the modern subject. Despite the renowned and sharp differences regarding the characteristics they attribute to subjectivity, and the theoretical result of these differences, modern subjectivity is what allows the realist, rationalist, and revolutionist[74] traditions to articulate their political thought. Far from agreeing on the particulars, these paradigms put the attributes of modern subjectivity to work in radically differentiated political theories, which are united by their grounding on modern subjectivity even if their reformulations of it are varied. For example, as will be shown extensively, the realist tradition based on Hobbes uses the features of modern subjectivity, such as mastery and capacity for reason, to arrive at the subject's self-induced vulnerability that provides the context of an ontology of danger and as a result a political theory of the social contract with an absolute sovereign. By contrast, the rationalist school based on Locke reinterprets many of the same features of the modern subject as proprietary consciousness in order to arrive at a conception of society as "a body composed . . . of independently moving individuals" who voluntarily consent to constitute themselves as a "body."[75]

Generally speaking, the ontological centrality of the modern subject for IR is evident in three ways. First, IR as the study of the interactions of states seen through their statesmen and diplomats engages with the modern subject in its utmost interpretation, namely, the secular, self-interested subject of modern politics.[76] Second, the collective entities of IR undergo a process of anthropomorphization so that nonhuman or pluralistic actors, the most prevalent being the state, assume a number of the characteristics attributed to human being as subject, such as purposive behavior, self-sufficiency, and rationality. This is not only an occurrence in IR but is the case with social theory in general, which takes its object of inquiry, society or community, as the "absolutization of subjectivity."[77]

Third, the resurgence of critical theorizing in IR has returned disciplinary attention to, and has largely brought about an acceptance of, the study of individuals.[78] This had been customarily neglected by political realists, who took their unit of analysis to be the sovereign state (as subject), especially following the pervasive turn to structuralism in the late 1970s.[79] Of course, liberal international theory assumes "individual human beings as the primary international actors" and states as pluralistic actors whose interests and functions are determined by bargaining, elections, and contestations among groups of individuals.[80] Until the early 1990s, realism was harshly distinct from its opposing paradigm, liberal internationalism, but a most interesting development since the 1990s is what Ole Waever and others have called the "neo-neo synthesis," between neorealist and neoliberal approaches to IR after the discipline's "third debate." In this synthetic move, methodology and key assumptions of the two perspectives appear to have converged, particularly regarding anarchy and rationality.[81] The neo-neo synthesis offers a unique opportunity for ontological examination because it reveals for the first time the unanimity between these two alternative worldviews on international politics, which both accord a pivotal position to the subject while making different assumptions about its nature.

As an important illustration of the neo-neo synthesis, Alexander Wendt's constructivist international theory, whose most influential statement is *Social Theory of International Politics,* takes as its premise the state as a "purposive actor" and argues that in its social interactions, the state is equivalent to a subject or a self. Despite his commitment to a "synthetic view" on structure/agency questions, Wendt suggests that "states *really are* agents," that is, they are endowed with reason and a form of rationality conducive to purposive action.[82] He invests the units of analysis in IR with subjectivity, directly related to the action-directed and rational subject of modernity. Relations with other such subjects are at least partly determined, he suggests, from the type of self these units are (and partly structurally). Wendtian social theory, then, seeks to reinforce the view that "states are also purposive actors with a sense of Self—'states are people too'—and that this affects the nature of the international system."[83] Wendt's account depends on an understanding of the state as the subject of intentionality and agency exhibiting several key attributes of modern subjectivity, because his concern is rightly to counter the hegemony of a neorealist structuralist account, which reduces the workings of the international system to the effects of structure. This strategic commitment to the proper consideration of state agency, however, encloses his account of the state to subjectivism and, as a result, risks compromising his in-depth ontological examination and, particularly, his efforts to provide a synthetic view of unit between holism and individualism.[84] Wendtian constructivism, therefore, must be understood in part as a call to place selfhood or subjectivity as the bedrock of international politics.[85] It is not unusual, Williams and Gantt argue, for critical analyses to display such "perverse" faith to sovereign subjectivity. The denunciation of Cartesian subjectivity on the basis of empirical or psychological evidence does not usually amount to a fundamental questioning of the self. Rather, even empirically-minded skeptics "retain the individual self as *locus,* or bearer, of all a person is or knows. This privatizes knowledge and makes the individual the principal focus of the (perhaps misnamed) 'social' sciences."[86]

Having examined the historical emergence and disciplinary manifestations of the modern subject, I now turn to consider how it is that modern subjectivity is central to a determination of coexistence according to the logic of composition. For this purpose the remainder of this chapter examines the prominent configuration of the subject by Thomas Hobbes, whose shaping of specific features of modern subjectivity results in a particular manifestation of coexistence within the political theory of the *Leviathan.* I argue that the Hobbesian configuration of subjectivity still forms the starting point for much of international political thought, even in efforts to negate it, and that this entails its own effacement of heteronomy.

## THOMAS HOBBES, SUBJECTIVITY, AND THE SOCIAL CONTRACT

Jürgen Habermas has argued that modern social philosophy largely arose out of the pragmatic political concern with the maintenance of human life. The primary concern of modern philosophers "is how human beings could technically master the threatening evils of nature."[87] For modern philosophers, like Hobbes, "[t]he pragmatic forms of heightening the agreeableness and strength of life retain their reference to the positive, to the mere maintenance of life."[88] I examine how Hobbes's concern with the maintenance of life leads him to reformulate the features of modern subjectivity in a unique way and how this affects IR's understanding of coexistence.

### Configuring Subjectivity: Danger and Reason

The Hobbesian configuration of the subject must be contextualized as the locus of a social philosophy responding to the revolutionary climate and chaotic political and social situation of England in the 1650s, wherein Hobbes's seminal philosophical text, *Leviathan,* was conceived. Heavily influenced by this context, Hobbes provided an imaginary description of social existence prior to the creation of, or in the absence of, the state as an anarchical "state of nature" wherein people are enmeshed in a "war of all against all" and in which all persons were enemies to others. The Hobbesian account of what is widely known as anarchy elucidates self/other constructs as self/enemy, whence the other is always already encountered through what might be called an éthos of survival.[89]

> Whatsoever therefore is consequent to a time of Warre, where every man is Enemy to every man; the same is consequent to the time, wherein men live without other security than what their own strength, and their own invention shall furnish them withall.[90]

The presocial world, in other words, is understood as dangerous. Danger is inevitable due to two related principles put forward by Hobbes, a materialist understanding of man's nature and the lack of a natural harmony of interests, which necessitate the presence and efficacy of a sovereign authority to maintain peace and order. However, the locus of danger is Hobbes's conception of the other-as-enemy: pervasive enmity makes the notion of anarchy dangerous and establishes survival as the predominant preoccupation of the subject in the state of nature.

The causes of war, strife, and lawlessness are to be found in every man's nature. Hobbes writes in this respect "that in the nature of man, we find three principall causes of quarrell. First, Competition; Secondly, Diffidence; Thirdly, Glory." It is important to elaborate that Hobbes does not identify the state of nature in actual fighting and enmity. Rather, he explains that "the nature of War, consisteth not in actuall fighting; but in the known disposition thereto, during all the time there is no assurance to the contrary."[91] The universal disposition to quarrel arises from the equality among men:

> Nature hath made men so equall, in the faculties of body, and mind; as that though there bee found one man sometimes manifestly stronger in body, or quicker of mind then *[sic]* another; yet when all

is reckoned together, the difference between man, and man, is not so considerable, as that one man can claim to himselfe any benefit, to which another may not pretend, as well as he.[92]

Equality, in this regard, leads to a universal desire for material possessions or glory "which neverthelesse they cannot both enjoy"; for this being impossible, men who desire the same thing "become enemies; and in the way to their End . . . endeavour to destroy, or subdue one an other."[93] Yet, in addition to the drive for material goods, the Hobbesian subject comes to desire power in itself. John McCumber argues that the materialist desire for specific objects, which distinguishes the Hobbesian subject, is supplemented "with the general desire for power."[94] When Hobbes suggests that there is in mankind "a generall inclination . . . a perpetuall, and restlesse desire for Power after power, that ceaseth onely in Death,"[95] he thereby transforms power from being "the universal means to satisfying desires into a universal object of desire on its own account."[96] It is this transformation that delivers us to the state of nature and to an understanding of the enemy as the *other* person in competition for power, as well as for material goods.

Moreover, man's ability to transcend his "inclination to quarrel" becomes possible by another feature of Hobbesian subjectivity, namely, Hobbes's distinction between danger and sin. When man is described as *evil,* this refers to "dangerous" and should be understood not as theological evil but as "the innocent evil of the beasts."[97] Prior to the laying down of his rights by agreeing to the covenant, man is at liberty to do as he pleases. Given the absence of sovereign authority in the state of nature, there are no limits to his rights and liberties. He is dangerous because of his quest for power, yet this endless quest for power is largely the result of lacking security to ensure his own survival. The evil of man is not theological but rather is grounded in materialist competition, itself pursued due to the lack of other means to security. Hobbes does not have a notion of sin, other than one tied to the disobedience to the covenant and the laws stated by the covenant.[98] He denies a theological conception of evil while, at the same time, he attributes danger to man's dispositions. Similarly, the other-as-enemy is not evil but dangerous. This distinction between danger and evil is crucial as it explains, William E. Connolly argues, how the Hobbesian self has the reason to recognize the need for society but does not have the nature for it and must be educated and controlled.[99]

The conditions in the state of nature lead man to seek self-preservation or survival, and in order to ensure it he may lay down all his rights but the right to his own life. The only inalienable right, which may not be given up to the Leviathan, is the right to life: "man cannot lay down the right of resisting them, that assault him by force, to take away his life; because he cannot be understood to ayme thereby, at any Good to himself."[100] Survival is, in this way, connected to man's natural right, which exists in the state of nature and becomes the etiology for the creation of the Leviathan. Since man has an inalienable right to life, it is his responsibility to himself to ensure that he does survive: to transcend the state of nature fulfills one's responsibility to oneself, that is, the responsibility to survive. Thus, transcendence of the state of nature becomes the foremost responsibility of the self and, as such, should not be seen merely as a pragmatic response to danger. Leo Strauss explains that Hobbes's "contention that the State originates only in mutual fear and can only so originate had thus moral, not merely technical, significance."[101] Survival serves as the constellation of the attributes of mastery and control, and the modernist concern with the maintenance of human life over and against the world and entities within the world.

Survival and mastery of self and others are both intimately woven into Hobbesian subjectivity. This becomes apparent when, as Connolly suggests, the state of nature is seen as a construct expressing Hobbes's political preoccupations:

> When Hobbes discusses the state of nature he is talking to people already in civil society. He is not trying to convince them to move from a stateless condition to a state, from a condition in which the passions are wild to one in which they are domesticated. Rather he is persuading imperfectly domesticated subjects that they, in their present state, should consent to remain there and should commit themselves more fully to the habits and principles that ensure the stability of their condition, even though that condition does and must carry many "inconveniences."[102]

Thus, Connolly argues, the purpose of the state of nature is to simulate "what it would be like to live amongst others in a condition where civil power has been removed."[103] In this respect, for Hobbes, the description of the state of nature has an instrumental and disciplinary intent: "the state of nature is shock therapy. It helps subjects to get their priorities straight by teaching them what life would be like without sovereignty. It domesticates by eliciting the vicarious fear of violent death in those who have not had to confront it directly."[104]

Hobbesian subjectivity is thus shaped by the confrontation with the possibility of violent death. Fear of death becomes the means by which the subject, although having no limits to his natural right, cultivates a disposition toward its own survival. In this manner, with the possibility of death, the right to pure self-determination is relinquished, giving way to sovereign government: "when one confronts the fear of early and violent death, one becomes willing to regulate oneself and to accept external regulations that will secure life against its dangers. The fear of death pulls the self together."[105] As John Dunn suggests, for Hobbes, "human political authority is a rational response to the overwhelming motivation of human fearfulness. It rests practically upon a systematization of the passion of fear."[106]

Hobbes's configuration of subjectivity is, therefore, well served by the accentuation of man's immature and quarrelsome sociability and his disposition to strife. According to Connolly's analysis, this "is a useful passion, useful to an ordering of the self and to peace and quiet in the social order."[107] The quarrelsome disposition of man is at once a cause for concern for man's own life and, at the same time, the means that leads man to choose an orderly society, that is, to ensure that his survival is safeguarded by a state. Transcendence of the danger that man posed to one's self and to others was possible because, as was noted above, the Hobbesian self is a curious entity.

> The Hobbesian individual is, first, not a given but a formation out of material that is only partly susceptible to this form [social life] and, second, not merely an end in itself but more significantly a means to the end of a stable society. The Hobbesian individual is thus in part a product of the civil society which is to regulate it, and the Hobbesian problem is how to form it so that it will be able and willing to abide by the natural laws and contracts appropriate to civil society.[108]

To shape such a subject is to bring to bear another feature of modern subjectivity on the artifice that is the Hobbesian self: reason.

Transcendence of the state of nature is only possible due to man's "flash of reason," by which Hobbes meant man's ability to "recognize as the real enemy not the rival, but 'that terrible enemy of nature, death.'"[109] Eager to advocate against the collapse of civil order, Hobbes theorized the transcendence of the state of nature toward orderly coexistence through man's calculation of his interest to avoid violent death and his ability to agree to a covenant. Hence, man self-interestedly chooses to transcend the dangerous state of nature by abandoning the multiplicity of wills present among the people at large and relegating responsibility for survival to the Leviathan as the only means of temporally and spatially transcending anarchy. The Hobbesian solution to the dangerous ontology of "the state of nature" created a fragile peace within a "commonwealth." Maintenance of this peace required the vigilance of a state apparatus, the Leviathan. This man-made covenant, by which order is brought about, is a product of man's rationality and self-knowledge and, as such, resisted any continuity with the medieval age where covenants were contracted between the people and a godly, or princely, sovereign. In Hobbes, the social contract is brought into being solely through man's action and, therefore, is radically individualist in its conception. It can be seen, therefore, that this configuration of subjectivity, through the attributes of danger but not sin, reason but also nonrelationality and omnipresent enmity, conceptually enables transcendence of the state of nature through the subject's decision to agree to a radical transformation of the *structural* conditions. Connolly writes, "The self-interested self is an artifice, an artifice celebrated by Hobbes as the one most conducive to a well-ordered society."[110] At the same time, retaining the nonrelational subject after transcendence allows Hobbes to frame coexistence as a tentative and fragile copresence, and to justify the constant and unceasing need for sovereign civil authority.

### Heterology in the State of Nature

The Hobbesian account, it was argued above, frames the relation to the other as one of self/enemy and regards enmity as omnipresent ("all against all") by definition. Such a framing occurs largely because coexistence in the state of nature is potentially a war of all against all since it is grounded on a subjectivity whose modernist aspects are configured through a systematization of innate fear, danger, and desire for mastery over others. It is important to note that the dangerous ontology of the state of nature, where proximity to others is theorized as a "warre of all against all," determines sociality through an overriding imperative: survival. The "essence of man," according to Hobbes, is utilized to connect danger and subjectivity, and as a result it reduces proximity to a relation of enmity. When the mode of relating to those residing in proximity to the self is examined at length, survival is revealed to be the predominant relational schema of the Hobbesian account. Survival, then, can be seen as a *particular* kind of relationality whose focus is the protection of the self and the surviving of the other. The relation to the other becomes a relation of danger, one to be transcended according to the subjective and ethical imperative of self-preservation. Strauss noted in this regard, "Self-preservation and the striving after peace for the sake of self-preservation are 'necessary,' because man fears death with inescapable necessity."[111]

The extensive and pessimistic heterology of *Leviathan* reduces otherness to the same (self) since the other is determined as, and represented to, the subject according to the attributes of the very same Hobbesian selfhood. In this way, encountering the other as a competitor for material goods and power against the background of structural insecurity, as well as an enemy against whom one has the responsibility to preserve oneself, assimilates the other's terrifying otherness to the self's knowable nature. The other is tamed and his enmity transformed to that same enmity that the Hobbesian subject identifies in itself. The subject represents and thus reduces the other to those attributes that are at once accentuated and lamented in itself so that they can form the building blocks of the edifice of the Leviathan. The other's very alterity is expunged and subordinated to the well-structured construct that is designed to achieve a workable political philosophy. Through the "éthos of survival" a peculiar process of "othering" occurs, enclosing the other within a schema of sameness. Yet this process also indicates the mastery and control exerted over the self's own otherness. Both of these moves are made possible by Hobbes's manipulation of subjectivity as the centerpiece of his political thinking. The self-interested and rational subject holds mastery over the other, as well as itself, by politically determining the fate of otherness for the purpose of the "pragmatic maintenance of life."

### Composing Social Life through the Contract

The social contract has undoubtedly provided political thought with a powerful and lasting mechanism that inseparably links state, co-existence with others, and subjectivity. The imaginary of the state of nature or, more generally, the notion of anarchy has become a staple of political theorizing and analysis. Stuart Umphrey argues, in this regard, that "[Hobbes's] teaching . . . remains to be overcome in fact. Our way of regarding things political is still predominantly Hobbesian."[112] Mary Dietz, a prominent Hobbes scholar, concurs when she writes that "[Hobbes's] political theory . . . is at least partly constitutive of the ways in which we continue to understand and describe our own political practices."[113] Furthermore, the lasting imaginary of the Hobbesian description of the world as presocially dangerous has even greater significance in international relations where it has provided the ground for the perspective of political realism, and this importance has long been recognized within the discipline.[114]

Brian C. Schmidt writes:

> From an early point in the history of academic international relations, scholars embraced the view that the topics of central concern to the field—topics that included the study of the factors leading to war and peace, international law, international organization, colonial administration, and the means of achieving world order reform—were grounded in an ontology of anarchy. The idea that international relations was characterized both by the presence and absence of sovereignty has provided the intellectual paradigm within which the academic discourse of international relations has taken place.[115]

Once order is brought about by the covenant and safeguarded by the Leviathan, danger is relegated to the *outside* of state boundaries in the form of others-as-enemies. As Leo Strauss once noted in this regard, "the state of nature continues at least in the relationship between the nations."[116] James Der Derian concurs, noting that "Hobbes's solution for civil war displaces the disposition for a 'warre of every man against every man' to the international arena."[117] A parallel can be discerned where the state behaves in the international (the outside) in the same fashion as man behaved in the state of nature. The state acts to promote its own survival and mastery over the system, creating what Der Derian calls "an ethico-political imperative embedded in the nature of things."[118]

The link between anarchy and danger in the international sphere relates to the absence of principles that have brought about order inside the Leviathan. *Arche,* meaning both principle and order, enables us to look at anarchy as that condition that lacks the principled order brought about by a sovereign power. Thus, danger imposes on us an *anarchic,* or unprincipled, environment reminiscent of the state of nature, where the other-as-enemy is defined as a like-entity, that is, as another Leviathan among many. The international, understood as the outside of the Leviathan, remains in the state of nature and offers no security.[119] Beate Jahn has claimed, moreover, that understanding of "the international" as a state of nature "is the defining claim of IR, its very *raison d'être.*"[120]

With regard to the coexistence of individuals, the linkage of subjectivity and danger is resolved through the creation of a commonwealth by an agreed-on contract in which men give up the multiplicity of their wills because they have a responsibility to survive. The covenant, however, does little to dispel or deconstruct the Hobbesian subject. On the contrary, the need for the contract and the resulting commonwealth establish the subject as unsociable, that is, as having no capacity to be with others without the regulation of rules and principles. Hobbes's institution of an ontology of danger through the elaboration of the social environment of an anarchical state of nature, in which the other is encountered as an enemy, serves to emphasize the features of the logic of composition, that is, the notion that coexistence is a postontological and fragile copresence of presocial individuals.

Highlighting the nonrelational attributes of the subject, even after the transcendence of the state of nature, sustains the anarchical assumption that coexistence is fragile and as such it will still require watchful authority and general vigilance against its tendency to collapse, since the condition of staying-together, following the act of joining-together, is, in some ways, unnatural to the Hobbesian subject determined in large part by the assumption of nonrelationality. The already constituted subjects that compose coexistence must have autonomy and rationality in order to choose the contract but also to retain that right which underlies the whole edifice: the right to self-preservation. Furthermore, the mechanical construction of coexistence or sociability amounts to "a physics of sociation."[121] The contract, in other words, composes nonrelationality into the controlled arrangement of the Leviathan. It, additionally, imbues sociality with the need for domination and control by merely modifying the structural conditions of the state of nature, but leaving unchanged and unchangeable the ground on which the political solution is based, the Hobbesian subject.

Therefore, prior to the social contractarian solution to the problem of dangerous anarchy, coexistence is regarded as the copresence of preconstituted subjects bearing the features of the modern subject, such as mastery, nonrelationality, and reason. As Georges Van den Abbeele argues, "the notion of social contract assumes the *prior* constitution of self-determining subjects who 'freely' aggregate to form a community"; not only does the notion of contract occlude the *whence* of its subjects' constitution (usually through the delegation of it to human nature), but it also "forgets the differences between subjects."[122] The notion of the contract, moreover, serves to reinforce the particular type of nonrelational, belligerent subjectivity, the existence of which necessitates the creation of a civil commonwealth through the contract. Subsequent to the contractarian solution, coexistence is reduced to a fragile composition sustainable solely by the contractarian mechanism (which has achieved the composition) and by the exercise of absolute power by the sovereign. Coexistence is not the primary state of being for the Hobbesian subject but must be politically achieved. The contract, therefore, is constitutive of the sociality (coexistence) of the already formed, completed selves of the Hobbesian schema. It is this type of subjectivity that maintains the belief that social and political arrangements among subjects like itself are fragile and require vigilance against their tendency to fail. In other words, the Hobbesian subject justifies strong political arrangements because its posited nonrelational nature means that coexistence is seen as tending toward a certain disorder and fragility. This generalized fragility is among the features, as was noted in the introduction, of the logic of composition according to which coexistence is articulated. Hobbesian political philosophy, in conclusion, illustrates how the reconfiguration of subjectivity determines coexistence through the logic of composition and highlights the interconnection between subjectivity, otherness, and coexistence. The social contract, taken here as an example of compositional logic, becomes a necessity for a thought that is grounded in the subject because of the nonrelational nature attributed to this subjectivity, as was shown extensively earlier.

## "UNWORKING" THE MODERN SUBJECT: POSSIBILITIES FOR COEXISTENCE

This chapter began with an overview of the emergence and establishment of the modern subject as *the* subject of social and political thought, a broad field of inquiry that includes international relations. Hobbes's particular configuration of the features of modern subjectivity for the purpose of constructing his political philosophy has had a lasting impact on theories of international relations, especially on the dominant school of political realism but also, more generally, on IR perspectives that invoke an ontology of danger and anarchy. As the earlier discussion illustrated, the ontological centrality of the modern subject in Hobbes's manifestation of social contractarianism constructs a specific schema of survival, formed by the interplay of subjectivity, self-interested rationality, and danger within an overall *heterology,* logos about the other, of enmity. This relational schema, or "éthos of survival," has been extremely influential and is still at play within international relations despite the emergence of recent attempts toward ethical theorizing and inclusion of the other.[123] The effect of the ethos of survival is the determination of coexistence as a tentative and continuously fragile composition of preconstituted subjects. This is what has been called herein the "logic of composition," which leads, as was argued in the introduction and illustrated in the specific case of Hobbes, to the reduction of coexistence to mechanistic copresence and the resulting effacement of heteronomy. The other is grasped according to this schema as an enemy who is endowed with the very attributes of the modern subject, characteristics that circularly permit the neglect of coexistence as a question-worthy issue and disregard the role of otherness in the very constitution of the self.

In order to be able to articulate an understanding of coexistence beyond composition and to avoid the effacement of the constitutive function of otherness in the articulation of selfhood, two conditions must be met. First, a substantive account of the self is required that does not start from the presuppositions and assumptions of the modern subject, since it is those nonrelational attributes of modern subjectivity, such as autonomy, nonrelationality, and mastery, that reduce coexistence to the composition of already constituted units. What is needed is an account of selfhood that takes into view the multiple ways in which others are part of the world, indeed, the ways in which others meaningfully *create* the world that the self considers to be hers. This substantive account must call into question the nonrelationality of the modern subject and its presumed inability to relate to others in nonmasterful ways.

Yet how does one provide such a substantive account of selfhood, an account that is first and foremost attuned to the other but also aware of its constitution by otherness, its heteronomy? One could, as Alford noted above, "twig" modern subjectivity to insert more relational characteristics or to erase elements that are not conducive to a more inclusive understanding of coexistence. This, however, is a highly problematic suggestion, given that it is a contingent construction based on the subjective needs or desires of one or another social theorist (in this case, myself). It would be much more useful to avoid the construction of a subject to merely suit a social or political theory of coexistence that I might consider desirable and to seek instead to capture or to map what some have called the facticity of life, that is, how selves are manifested in their location in the world with others. In other words, it is more pertinent to become attentive to the phenomena of selfhood and its relations to others and otherness within its world. This may also help to avoid the ossification of theoretical assumptions about the "subject," such as nonrelationality and self-interested rationality in political theorizing, and renew the questioning of what the self might be in the historical constellation of late modernity. In order to be able to undertake such questioning, however, a *method* is needed that offers a different mode of access to the facticity of entities, a method other than the theoretical (re)construction or "twigging" of the modern subject. This is the second condition that enables a discussion of coexistence, the delineation of a method for ontological questioning, which in fact must precede and enable the discussion of a substantive account of heteronomous selfhood.

The remainder of this book sets out to fulfill these two interconnected tasks, the requirement of a method and the need for a richer substantive account, through the philosophy of German philosopher Martin Heidegger and, in particular, his phenomenology of average everydayness, which contains what chapter 3 calls "an optics of coexistence." To readers of Continental philosophy, turning to Heidegger to unwork the modern subject is by now a familiar move; to such readers and also to those familiar with the critical perspectives of international relations, however, the claim that one can retrieve out of Heidegger's existential analysis an account of heteronomy, of a self that is other-constituted and amenable to noncompositional understandings of coexistence, is not quite so straightforward. In part, this is the result of the long-standing critique of phenomenology and ontology by the French philosopher Emmanuel Levinas, whose concerns are addressed in depth in chapters 2 and 4. Suffice it to say at this stage that our turn to Heidegger is not a dismissal of Levinas's concerns with phenomenology in general, and with Heidegger in particular. On the contrary, Levinas's critique inspires this turn to Heidegger, which becomes a *return*—a return for the purposes of precisely highlighting in Heidegger's analysis of human existence, of retrieving from his thought, those elements that attest to the self's heteronomy. Such a critique, then, bears fruit in the sense that Levinas makes necessary a rereading of Heidegger's text that is *heterologous,* that attends to the other in Heidegger's thought.

Specifically, the next chapter turns to Heidegger's search for a method with which to access and express the facticity of the being too easily designated as "subject" in a modern configuration. The next chapter shows, however, that the method and the substantive account are indeed related aspects of his thought. Heidegger's path toward a radicalized phenomenology is instructive of the methodological issues at hand in challenging modern subjectivity and forms the first step in a process that might be called "unworking subjectivity." Following that, the third chapter subsequently delves more deeply into the substantive account revealed through the phenomenological questioning of the self; this account attests to the primacy of coexistence in the very understanding of the self and thus enables a proper consideration of coexistence, away from mere composition and toward the consideration of an ethical attitude that is open to otherness and that can inform an account of political coexistence and community constitution not bound to the logic of composition.

# 2

## Toward a "Hermeneutics of Facticity"

The subject of modern politics is the subject of certainty and mastery. As was shown in relation to Hobbesian subjectivity, this subject is assumed to voluntarily enter into arrangements of regulated sociability, such as the mechanism of the social contract. Yet, on the basis of this kind of subject, coexistence is reduced to mere copresence, to the fragile composition of already constituted selves. Therefore, coexistence can only be rethought beyond this logic of composition if the subjectivist understanding of human existence is challenged; only then, moreover, will it be possible to illuminate the constitutive role of the other.

How might this occur? Should theorists of international relations attempt to (re)construct, or to "twig" modern subjectivity in the words of C. Fred Alford, in order to insert more relational characteristics or in order to erase elements that are not conducive to an understanding of coexistence that reveals the role of otherness?[1] Should they resort, in other words, to a theoretical construction that is a variation of the modern subject to suit their needs and preferences for conceptualizing coexistence? I argue that this path would merely provide an arbitrary basis for coexistence, which would be as much a construction as Hobbes's dangerous subject that facilitates the contractarian artifice. In order to avoid thinking coexistence on the basis of such a highly contingent construction, the present chapter examines the development of a method that attempts to be more attentive to the "facticity of selves." This means considering the following questions: First, how are selves manifested in their location in the world with others? And, second, how does one *investigate* such manifestations of the phenomena of selfhood and coexistence? Stated differently, it is not only important to provide a substantive account of the self beyond the assumptions that various social sciences have long held about modern subjectivity; it is equally important to explore a *method* with which to access the facticity of human existence that can then lead to an understanding of coexistence beyond copresence. In this search for a method, I turn to the German philosopher Martin Heidegger, whose attempts to avoid the presuppositions that philosophy held about modern subjectivity led him to question and radicalize Edmund Husserl's phenomenological method. Indeed, Heidegger wanted to challenge the reliance of the ontological tradition of philosophy on the subject, asking,

> How does man come to play the role of the one and only *subject* proper? Why is the human subject transposed into the "I," so that subjectivity here becomes coterminous with I-ness? Is subjectivity defined through I-ness, or the reverse, I-ness through subjectivity?[2]

Heidegger challenged the use of the modern subject, which had grounded post-Cartesian philosophy, on the basis of prior presuppositions and sought a method with which to gain access to the facticity of existence, to existence *as* it shows itself. For this reason, the brief examination of Heidegger's project that follows helps situate the discussions of the following chapter, where it is suggested that in the analysis provided in Heidegger's *Being and Time* one can discern an "optics of coexistence," that is, an account of the self as always already social, as wholly indebted to the other for its self-understanding and for the meanings and orientations that it has of, and within, the world that it inhabits. Contrary to the masterful and self-sufficient subject posited as the ground of the social sciences and international political thought, Heidegger's existential analytic contains within it an account of existence as both heteronomous and coexistential. Such a coexistential understanding of the self as a "being in the world with others" is not a theoretical construction, competing with that of Hobbes or other political and social theorists. Heidegger wished to find a method that would allow him to move beyond the theoretical construction of the modern subject in order to access lived experience. Therefore, the following discussion is centered on Heidegger's larger project, the pursuit of which led him to question the appropriateness of theoretical construction for ontology and, eventually, to rearticulate the phenomenological method for gaining access to lived experience, exposing its coexistential and heteronomous aspects, and laying open the undeniable role of otherness for the constitution and existence of the self. Outlining the development of Heidegger's project provides the background in which his challenge to modern subjectivity can be meaningfully understood, as well as acting as a reminder that his discussion of the other-determined character of human existence *arises* within a project that seeks to restate the question of Being as the question of philosophy. Following this discussion of Heidegger's project, I examine radical phenomenology more closely as precisely the attempt to get at the facticity of human existence, concluding with Emmanuel Levinas's critique of Heidegger's phenomenology, reading it not as a dismissal but, on the contrary, as providing the impetus and the inspiration for the retrieval, out of Heidegger's "hermeneutics of facticity," of an "optics of coexistence"—a host of elements highlighting the heteronomous constitution of human existence—in the next chapter.

## HEIDEGGER'S PROJECT

Heidegger's project revolved around restating "the question of Being" as the question of philosophy.[3] In order to refocus philosophical inquiry toward the question of Being, Heidegger suggested that the question asked by traditional ontology, namely, "what is the being of entities?"[4] had to be preceded by a question about the meaning of Being, in other words, questioning the "conditions for the possibility of having any understanding whatsoever."[5] Contrary to the assumptions of mainstream Heideggerian scholarship, Heidegger's own concern was with "what gives or produces being as an effect,"[6] what "lets things be what they are, what 'determines entities as entities' in their various ways of being."[7] As early as 1922, when Heidegger wrote the essay "Phenomenological Interpretations with Respect to Aristotle,"[8] his program was twofold: first, to inquire into the meaning of Being, what he called fundamental ontology, inseparably accompanied by the second part, namely, the destruction of ontology, where "destruction" does not imply the rejection of the ontological tradition but rather a critical stance toward it and a reappropriation of its positive aspects (*Being and Time,* ¶6).[9] It is helpful, therefore, to first outline Heidegger's early engagement with the ontological tradition prior to examining his radicalization of phenomenology beyond subjectivity and toward the facticity of existence.

## Heidegger and the Ontological Tradition

The genesis of ontology in ancient Greece can be seen as a development facilitated in part by the peculiarities of the Greek language, where the existence of distinct terms for "beings" *(ta onta),* "to be" *(einai),* and "the nature of beings" as expressed in the abstract noun "being" *(ousia)* led to the question

> whether there is a unified meaning of *being* that accrues to all beings (in contradistinction to "what is not") or whether *being* has irreducibly many different meanings that fall into different categories, depending on the kind of entity that is under investigation.[10]

Could there be, in other words, a "unitary concept that demarcates the realm of being as such"?[11] The Greeks, John van Buren argues, variously "experienced being as a stable *noeton topon,* an intelligible place (*Republic* 508c),[12] an open area of truth in the sense of unconcealment *(aletheia),* light *(phos)* or radiant appearing *(phainesthai),* and emergence *(physis).*"[13] Despite the apparent variety, however, Being was understood "to be the *aition* of beings (the cause of beings in the pre-modern generic sense of what is responsible for something)" so that in Greek thinking the question of ontology became formulated around a unitary concept, resulting in an understanding of "being *(Sein)* or beingness *(Seiendheit)* of beings in the sense of a causal ground for beings."[14] As a unitary concept, "Being as ground was also taken to be itself a being, the most beingly being *(to on ontos),* that is, the highest and most honored being in the hierarchical-teleological order of the cosmos."[15] Because the "Greeks ultimately saw in being the divine *(to theion),*" they "stood in an ocular relation" of seeing, gazing, and wonderment to being.[16] However, despite the phenomenological possibilities of the Greeks' *seeing relation*—"letting appear *(phainesthai),* making manifest *(deloun)* and unconcealing *(aletheuein)*"—this was mediated through *logos* "in the inclusive sense of theory, thought, and assertion."[17]

Their understanding of being as ground or as substance, there-fore, restricted the possible answers that the Greeks were capable of providing to their ontological inquiries within a limited space. The fundamental metaphysical positions that established themselves in Greek thinking appeared as "competing answers: for example, being (Parmernides), *logos* (Heraclitus), idea (Plato), category, being-in-work (Aristotle)"; this competition, however, took place within a "deeper unanimity [which remained] concealed in the very un-questioned question about being as ground" that discouraged any attempt to articulate the question of Being differently or direct it toward a different path.[18]

While Plato posed the question of Being in *The Sophist*, calling it a *gigantomachia peri tis ousias*, it was Aristotle's doctrine on the manifold meanings of Being that prevailed in the history of Western metaphysics.[19] Frede argues that "Aristotle distinguished as many meanings of 'being' as there are categories of entities." He divided Being into "a primary category of *substance*, designating natural 'things' that exist in their own right," while regarding other beings as "*attributes of substances* either inhering in them or standing in some other relation to them (quality, quantity, relation, place, time, action, affection, possession, position)."[20] Thus, for Aristotle, Being had manifold meanings, with physical entities being accorded the *dominant* meaning of substance and the rest becoming reduced to qualitative attributes of it. Yet, it is important to note that "Aristotle regarded the categories as distinctions contained in the nature of things; they are *read off* nature and are not schemas read into or imposed on nature by us."[21] With Aristotle's doctrine of the cate-gories, "[s]ubstances are the only entities that can exist in their own right"[22] because they remain "continuously present throughout all change"[23] "while all other entities are attributes that need substances as the substrate for their existence."[24] For ontology, this implies that "'to be' then means either to be a substance or to be (one of the nine other kinds of) attributes of a substance" allowing for "no unified sense of 'being' that could be predicated in all categories" because, as Frede explains, "the being of a substance and any of the attributes are *irreducibly different*."[25] Heidegger believed that the acceptance of Aristotle's doctrine of the manifold meanings divided into *cate-gories* brought about the neglect of the "question about the meaning of Being" (*Being and Time*, 21). He was concerned, moreover, that the question of the meaning of being, of a "unitary concept that demarcates the realm of being as such," had ceased to be a *question*[26] for ontology (31).

Heidegger's goal with respect to the ontological tradition, therefore, was to problematize "the idea that reality must be thought of in terms of the idea of substance at all." Heidegger considered the reliance on substance or ground as the enduring principle of reality as a "metaphysics of presence" because substance is what "remains continuously present throughout all change." It is this reliance on *substance* that has facilitated dichotomous ways of philosophizing, such as "either there is mind or everything is just matter; either our ideas do represent objects or nothing exists outside the mind." These, Heidegger claimed, "are derivative, regional ways of being for things," which are "remote from concrete lived existence."[27] This problem of theorizing about reality was central to both his doctoral thesis as well as his qualifying dissertation *(Habilitationsschrift)* and led him toward Husserlian phenomenology. Specifically, both works challenged the acceptance of Aristotle's theory of categories within the ontological tradition and attempted to overcome the difficulties with the "substance ontology" that permeated it. The thesis, titled "The Doctrine of Judgement in Psychologism" (1913), provided a critique of psychologism associated with Franz Brentano and the early Edmund Husserl, and it illustrated "that the key to *meaning* cannot lie in the empirical observation of the actual psychological processes that constitute our thoughts."[28] Rather, Heidegger suggested that it was more important to explore "how *meaning* as a whole is embedded in the *actual life* of the person who entertains a thought"[29] to investigate the location of meaning into the "facticity" of life, an interest that moved him toward a sustained engagement with Husserl's phenomenology.

In the *Habilitationsschrift,* published as *Die Kategorien- und Bedeutungslehre des Duns Scotus* (The theory of categories and meaning of Duns Scotus), Heidegger refined further the question of Being. He expressed an interest in Duns Scotus because the latter considered the Aristotelian system of categories to be "only one of several such systems, a subclass that fits one special part or specific realm of being but does not exhaust reality as such."[30] Duns Scotus's concerns largely arose from the need to expand the ontological categories for theological reasons. Scotus did not merely seek to expand or diversify the categories of the Aristotelian tradition, nor did he only "assign different realms of reality to the different subject matters of different disciplines"; in fact, the scholastic philosopher "saw the need for a new conception of *reality* as such":[31]

> If different disciplines import different (senses of the) categories, then the categories of reality cannot simply be *read off* nature, as they were for Aristotle, but they are obviously also read *into* nature by us, or rather into reality as a whole.[32]

Thus, for Heidegger, "[t]he 'question of being' becomes then the question of the givenness of the object to the subject."[33] Heidegger showed that in Scotus the conditions and means by which the subject takes hold of, or interprets, its objects, which Scotus had called the "conditions of *subjectivity*," attain paramount importance: "all objects depend on the meaning that is bestowed on them by the subject, and . . . they are always part of a wider network of referential totality."[34] Scotus considered that it would be philosophy's purpose to understand "in what sense there is a *structure of meaning* that stands in relation to or conditions what one might call the *structure of reality*," and, therefore, explored how language, particularly its grammatical structure, imposes a discernible *form* on our thinking.[35] Heidegger's examination of Scotus urged him to challenge Aristotelian metaphysical realism and to question the consequences of reflection and theorizing on reality: "the categories of 'all that is' become the categories of our *understanding of being*: the categories become the 'elements and means of the interpretation of the meaning of what is experienced.'"[36] The idea that categories of "what is" are categories of the *interpreter's understanding* of being, crucially led Heidegger to conclude that reality was framed by the subject's understanding, and this led to his attempt to find a way to access a pretheoretical attitude toward the world and reality.[37] Thus, he set out to access a sense of beings outside theorizing and reflection by studying "the way [entities] show up in the flux of our everyday, pre-reflective activities."[38]

Heidegger's engagement with Duns Scotus also led him to argue that the objectifying outlook of the subject toward the object originated not so much in the natural sciences (as Husserlian phenomenology and neo-Kantianism, the two prominent philosophical movements of the early twentieth century, had claimed) but "from the theoretical attitude itself."[39] Scotus's insights provided the impetus for Heidegger's search for a method for ontology that could avoid imposing categories onto everyday experience in the way that modes of theoretical thinking did. Theoretical thinking, Heidegger concluded, served to "un-live" human experience and objectify existence.[40] Importantly, however, it is not necessarily the case that Heidegger was against *theory;* rather, Heidegger aimed to interrogate anew what it is to be a human being, and for this purpose he needed a new approach toward prereflective activity, "a phenomenology of 'mindless' everyday coping skills as the basis of all intelligibility."[41] In this vein, Heidegger subsequently "made it his task to show that there is a meaningful concept of the being of all beings, a conception that underlies all our understanding of reality."[42] This task found expression in a

> holistic conception of human existence as "Dasein," that is, as being-in-a-world, or of "care" as the meaning of our existence, which comprises and unifies in its understanding all the different conceptions of what there is, let alone of temporality as the transcendental horizon of the overall meaning of being as such.[43]

This is perhaps an opportune juncture at which to focus more specifically on Heidegger's search for a method for ontology, which he found through a critical engagement with phenomenology.

### RADICAL PHENOMENOLOGY AS THE METHOD OF ONTOLOGY

Although providing a generally valid definition of phenomenology is a difficult task, there are certain means and tasks of inquiry generally accepted within this diverse field.[44] According to John Sallis, phenomenology

> is, in the first instance, the methodological demand, that one attend constantly and faithfully to the things themselves. It is the demand that philosophical thought proceed by attending to things as they themselves show themselves rather than in terms of presupposed opinions, theories, or concepts.[45]

Phenomenology attends to "the perceptual object as it shows itself," while acknowledging that *"perception of such objects is always one-sided"*[46] and that the phenomenological method may yield different results if performed under altered circumstances. Phenomenology aimed, in this regard, to eliminate the presuppositions amassed by the natural sciences about the world and objects of study, so that the phenomenologist could access experience as pure phenomena. In this way, Husserl distinguished between man's involvement with things and the world, which he called the natural attitude, and the phenomenological attitude, which denotes "the reflective point of view from which we carry out philosophical analysis of the intentions exercised in the natural attitude and the objective correlates of these intentions."[47] Husserl, in particular, was "deeply suspicious of attempts to apply the model of the natural or positive sciences to the understanding of human consciousness."[48] The natural attitude "only credits that which is physically given," and in so doing, it "either denies the life of consciousness altogether or else 'naturalises' it as a 'fact' of physical reality." If encountered as objects through the natural attitude, "the phenomena of consciousness are thereby deprived of their essential status as living intentional experience."[49] In order to avoid this misunderstanding, Husserl proposed the suspension of the intentions and convictions that operate in the natural attitude by something he called the phenomenological *epoche*.

The *epoche* is not a doubt or negation of these intentions, as it was for Descartes, but rather a distancing required in order to allow the phenomenologist to contemplate their structure. The method by which one achieves the *epoche* or suspension and moves from the natural attitude to the phenomenological attitude is called the phenomenological reduction, and it is, perhaps, the most salient feature of Husserlian and subsequent phenomenologies. The reduction is to be understood as "a 'leading back' from natural beliefs to the reflective consideration of intentions and their objects."[50] In the words of Mary Warnock, the reduction "consists in putting on one side (in brackets) all that is known, normally assumed, about the objects of perception or thought in order to *describe* and, later, analyse them as pure phenomena."[51] Bracketing-out and description are crucial for unobjectified access to experience, which theories of the natural sciences could not obtain. What, though, remains behind once the reduction has been carried out and the *epoche* or suspension has occurred? John D. Caputo suggests that "by the reduction the phenomenological investigator is, according to Husserl, carried back from the hitherto naively accepted world of objects, values and other men, to the transcendental subjectivity which 'constitutes' them."[52] Bracketing the world in this manner shows "how the ordinary objective world is dependent upon the perceiving and thinking subject." In other words, what has been thus far taken for granted as existing independent of any act of perception is "shown to be given both existence and intelligibility or sense by my transcendental Ego," which is the self left over after common assumptions previously held have been reduced or suspended. As Warnock claims, the goal of the phenomenological *epoche* "may be said to be transcendental subjectivity" or "consciousness."[53]

Phenomenology as a method, therefore, aims to return to pure phenomena and, through the phenomenological reduction, to access "the generating axis of our intentional experiences before they are overlaid by objectifying constructs," the generating axis being transcendental subjectivity;[54] for Husserl such access to both phenomena and consciousness was important because he aimed to restate the relation between knowing and the world: "the world is an *experience which we live* before it becomes an *object which we know* in some impersonal or detached fashion."[55] This was what attracted Heidegger to phenomenology: its attempt to contest at a fundamental level the subject-object dichotomy and to replace the notion of "substance," as the enduring quality of things or entities, with the category of relation; to show, in other words, that "[m]an and world are first and foremost in relation; it is only subsequently, at the reflective level of logic, that we divide them into separate entities."[56]

Given its attention to things as they show themselves, phenomenology hoped to provide "the scientific ideal of knowledge with a rigorous foundation."[57] It attempted to achieve this by seeking a pretheoretical attitude through which to gain access to life or lived experience. Such access was possible by bracketing out the imposition of "scientific" theoretical frameworks and schemata that prevent things from showing themselves in themselves. For Heidegger, too, phenomenology was the method that conceived of itself as the attempt to investigate originary lived experience, and thus his chosen method for his project of fundamental ontology. He believed, however, that despite the desire to contest dichotomous thinking, the phenomenologists' focus on the transcendental ego

defined the human being as a coherence of experience, a centre of acts unified in an ego: they never raised the question of the sense [meaning] of Being of this, our own Dasein [existence]. Instead, they fell back on traditional definitions dividing man into reason and sense, soul and body, inner and outer, without a sense of what *holds these realities together as a whole.*[58]

After World War I, therefore, Heidegger collaborated with Husserl to implement radical phenomenology, centered on "explicating life as it presents itself to us in concrete, individual, historical existence."[59] This radicalization "he now regarded as [philosophy's] highest and deepest possibility,"[60] but it would eventually lead Heidegger away from Husserl's phenomenology, despite their close working relationship throughout the early postwar years.

### Radical Phenomenology

Acknowledging the numerous limitations of phenomenology eventually led Heidegger toward an interpretive approach; yet it was, in fact, Heidegger's response to Husserl's critics that led to his departure away from the dominant Husserlian assumptions.[61] While investigating how to access lived experience, Heidegger engaged with the prominent objections to Husserlian phenomenology put forward by the philosopher Paul Natorp, a member of the reigning philosophical movement of neo-Kantianism, proponents of which also included Wilhelm Windelband and Heinrich Rickert, Heidegger's doctoral supervisor.[62] Heidegger made it his task to "expose the primacy of the theoretical attitude"[63] in the methodology of neo-Kantianism and in the philosophy of values in general. He argued that "the true essence of philosophy is something quite unique beyond any connection with ideology, worldview, and teachings about the ultimate destiny and meaning of human living." Moreover, philosophical thinking ought to be "more rigorous, more primordial than scientific knowing; it is more radical, more essential than the exploration of nature and life by the theorizing attitude of the sciences."[64] This was the programmatic call of Husserl himself that phenomenology be able to both grasp and also "articulate the pretheoretical realm of life in a pretheoretical way, and so to achieve the unique status of a pretheoretical science."[65] With Husserl, Heidegger intended to establish that "philosophy is not a theoretical, speculative science at all; it is a way of disclosing (living) experience."[66] Heidegger took phenomenology into a new direction by focusing on the need to look at the origin, the *Ur-sprung* or "the *origin* of the factic life"[67] and did not think that this could be achieved within the frameworks of the human and natural sciences, which investigated factic life by dividing it into separate disciplines.

How could phenomenology be radicalized to access "the pretheoretical realm of life in a pretheoretical way"?[68] Theodore Kisiel notes, "The problem of a pretheoretical science thus ultimately becomes a problem of language: how to approach and articulate the dynamic, and thus elusive, facticity of life?"[69] It is while struggling to find his own way toward philosophically accessing life that Heidegger encountered Paul Natorp's objections. Natorp had argued that phenomenology could not fulfill its desire to attend to living experience as it showed itself. He maintained that "the 'stream' of living experience is brought to a halt by reflection: 'there is no immediate grasp (hold) of living experience.'"[70] This criticism challenged both Husserlian phenomenology and Heidegger's own attempts to use phenomenology as the method for accessing lived experience for restating the question of Being. There were two specific objections raised by Natorp, the first of which argued that phenomenology could not have "intuitive access to its chosen subject-matter." This objection amounted, Kisiel suggests, to asking, "How is the nonobjectifiable subject matter of phenomenology to be even *approached* without already theoretically inflicting an objectification upon it? How are we to go along with life reflectively without deliving it?"[71] The second objection voiced the doubt that, in addition to the first concern with accessibility, phenomenology would be furthermore unable to *express* its purported access to its subject matter. Kisiel explains,

> Phenomenology claims to merely describe what it sees. But description is circumscription into general concepts, a "subsumption" under abstractions. The concrete immediacy to be described is thereby mediated into abstract contexts. There is no such thing as immediate description, since all expression, any attempt to put something into words, generalizes and so objectifies.[72]

Natorp insisted that reflective analysis always already transformed, or even deformed, the living experiences on which it reflected. Specifically, in expressing its description and analysis of the perceptual object, phenomenology unwittingly generalized and created theoretical concepts with which to convey phenomena. For Natorp, this amounted to a "devastation" brought on to experience that could only be undone, he claimed, by his own method of "reconstruction," according to which "analysis and interpretation can 'regain' (reconstruct) the 'wholeness of the subjective' (the immediately given prior to the analysis) from the primordial life of consciousness 'theoretically.'"[73]

Heidegger, however, denied that Natorp's proposed method of reconstruction could successfully disclose the sphere of lived experience because, despite Natorp's arguments to the contrary, "Even reconstruction is objectification; it consists in construction, in theorizing."[74] For Heidegger, moreover, Natorp's method brought about the "absolutization of the logical" and the "most radical absolutization of the theoretical."[75] With respect to Natorp's objections as such, Heidegger responded by turning away from the transcendental or pure phenomenology of Husserl toward *Verstehen*, or understanding, a school of thought largely influenced by Friedrich Schleiermacher (1768–1834) and Wilhelm Dilthey (1833–1911).[76]

Heidegger's reply to the first objection about accessing life without objectifying it

> pointed to a non-intuitive form of access . . . a certain familiarity which life already has of itself and *which phenomenology needs only to repeat.* This spontaneous experience of experience, this streaming return of experiencing life upon already experienced life, is the immanent historicity of life.[77]

Heidegger cautioned against depending on and searching for "objectifying concepts which seize life and so still its stream" and encouraged the utilization of the kind of access that *life already has to itself,* which "provides the possibility of finding less intrusive pre-cepts or pre-concepts which at once reach back into life's motivation and forward into its tendency."[78] This understanding that life already has of itself "at once repeats and foreruns life's course" and is able to stretch "itself unitively and indifferently along the whole of the life stream without disrupting it."[79] Heidegger's response advocated against the "abstractive objectifying universal" that extracted experience and subsumed it to the universal, which he had likened to the situation of "form subsuming matter." Instead, Heidegger called for a "nonobjective option of a more indicative and intentional universal stemming directly from the very temporal intentional movement of *finding oneself experiencing experience.*"[80]

It is crucial to note that in responding to the first objection of accessibility, Heidegger also provided the answer to the second critique, which had contested phenomenology's ability to *express* immediate experience. By turning to the access that life already has of itself, "[t]he problems of intuition and expression are therefore transposed into the possibility of a (1) nonreflective understanding and (2) the nonobjectifying conceptualization that it [nonreflective understanding] itself provides, that allusive universal called the *formal indication.*"[81] The method of formal indication formulates the understanding that life has of itself into concepts that merely *designate* certain terms in a formal manner to denote the phenomena under scrutiny. These terms act almost as placeholders leaving the analysis and determination of the phenomena to the phenomenological bracketing-out and description. Kisiel explains, "Words like 'life,' 'lived experience,' 'I myself' drawn from daily life pose a danger of objectification in our descriptions; they cannot be taken univocally, but rather must be understood in their *formal* character as *indicative* of certain phenomena of the concrete domain."[82] Heidegger's formal indication thus attempted to avoid the reduction of the phenomena of lived experience to their representative concepts, fearing that this would lead to their inevitable neglect.

Heidegger's reactions and responses to these neo-Kantian objections opened up the way to a pretheoretical solution to the problem of intuition-expression. Heidegger attempted to "find less intrusive, more natural ways to get a grip of its [phenomenology's] subject matter" away from Husserl's and neo-Kantianism's theoretical solution to the methodological problem of access and expression.[83] His suggestion that access and expression have their origin in the "'immanent historicity of life in itself'"[84] meant that Heidegger's radical phenomenology did not have to remain within the limitations of Husserlian phenomenology, whose delineation between intuition and expression resulted in the "immediacy of intuition" becoming lost in the "mediacy of expression" and their initial unity (in the sense that prereflective life already lives reflectively) being interrupted. This nondisruptive entry into the historicity of life emanated from an implicit understanding life has of itself, which Heidegger called "hermeneutic intuition," and which he brought to serve phenomenology methodologically. The hermeneutic intuition could understand "the articulations of life itself, which accrue to the self-experience that occurs in the 'dialectical' return of experiencing life to already experienced life."[85] The departure from Husserl ultimately rested on the need to conduct philosophical questioning that "is not added on and attached to the questioned object, factical life, externally; rather it is to be understood as the explicit grasping of a basic movement of factical life," by that life itself.[86] In other words, the structure of understanding is such that "[a]ll of our experiences, beginning with our most direct perceptions, are from the start already expressed, indeed interpreted."[87] This turn away from Husserlian phenomenology amounted to a "hermeneutic breakthrough," the point at which the method and the subject matter are revealed as united, where "a formally indicating hermeneutics and a dynamically understood facticity belong essentially together in a close-knit unity."[88] Heidegger's answer to Natorp's objections of accessibility and expression was akin to a desire "to let the facts speak for themselves; and at the same time to claim that there are no such things as uninterpreted facts."[89]

Heidegger's response to Naport was also much more than that: it signified his attempt to grasp the presupposed "subject" in nonsubjectivist terms. His turn to hermeneutic phenomenology amounted to a rejection of Husserl's efforts "to isolate the 'transcendental Ego,' the undifferentiated, pure 'I,' who perceives and constructs the world, but is not involved in it."[90] Heidegger's "hermeneutic breakthrough" adhered "more radically than Husserl to the phenomenological demand to attend to the things themselves"[91] by asking "what remains unthought in the appeal to the things themselves."[92] What had remained unthought in Husserl's phenomenology was thinking of Being-thus, of how it is that being appears *as* something.[93] Thinking the unthought led to the search "for an entity both with regard to the fact *that* it is and with regard to its Being *as* it is" (*Being and Time,* 24; emphasis added).

## CHALLENGING SUBJECTIVITY: THE PRIORITY OF FACTICITY

As already argued in the introduction and chapter 1, international relations relies on a subjectivist ontology centered on the "assertive, disengaged self who generates distance from its background (tradition, embodiment) and foreground (external nature, other subjects) in the name of accelerating mastery of them."[94] In Heidegger's view, the modern conception of the subject was infiltrated by the notion of substance (*Being and Time,* 123–31), a Cartesian legacy of the emphasis on the *cogito* to the detriment of the *sum* (131).[95] For Heidegger, grasping the subject as substance was phenomenally inadequate "as a descriptive framework for the fabric of our lives."[96] Heidegger proposed, instead, to abandon the equivalence of human existence to the "I" and to undertake an examination of the structures and "phenomenal content *[Bestand]*" of human existence, which post-Cartesian ontology had obscured (72).[97] Heidegger's hermeneutic phenomenology, it was suggested in the preceding section, became the method for letting lived experience show itself, for ontological examination into what life might reveal itself to be, when it is not grasped by theoretical constructs that pay little attention to the facticity of life.

### Arriving at Dasein: Heidegger's Terminology

Heidegger's early years at Freiburg were spent seeking a way to challenge transcendental phenomenology, whose focus on consciousness resounded with Cartesianism. Instead, Heidegger's radicalization of phenomenology aimed to gain access to "life as it presents itself to us in concrete, individual, historical existence,"[98] and it involved a gradual evolution in the terms that Heidegger used to grasp his subject matter. For example, in the war emergency semester of 1919, the topic is still "amorphously" described as "life in and for itself," changing later to "factic life experience," with Heidegger adopting the term "facticity" from neo-Kantianism; by the summer semester of 1920 he turns to "concrete actual Dasein," more reminiscent of the vocabulary of *Being and Time.*[99] Heidegger used the term "Dasein" in order to avoid the preconceptions that accompany "subject" and to formally indicate the being that we ourselves are in each case. Jean-Luc Nancy notes,

> Dasein—that ordinary German noun for existence, which Heidegger gives as a "title" to humanity and beneath which, for him, humanity and only humanity exists—is the *being-the-there* of being itself . . . the there of being, its taking place, insofar as it is also a ravishment and a distancing (a coming and going of sense), takes place neither anywhere other nor toward anywhere other than the here of this world here.[100]

The term "Dasein," this "intentionally vague, non-descriptive, almost vacuous designation," both avoids presuppositions about what kind of being this is (conscious, having mind and body, etc.) and also unites the search for method with the matter to be analyzed.[101] A look at Heidegger's 1923 course Ontology illustrates how his notion that "life" has the ability to access its own experience had by then been connected to the being that has this ability: Dasein, in each case our own.[102] For Heidegger, then, "Dasein" serves as a "formal indicator," a concept used to designate this being whose primary characteristics have yet to be properly delineated. Importantly, in avoiding the term "subject" or "I" of post-Cartesian philosophy, Heidegger leaves open the question of the "who" of this being while at the same time claiming that in each case "I" am this being. However, Heidegger is not simply proposing any type of inquiry for examining Dasein. He states quite clearly that such inquiry must take the form of what he calls existential analysis. "*[F]undamental ontology,* from which alone all other ontologies can take their rise, must be sought in the *existential analytic* of Dasein [Daseinanalytik]" (*Being and Time,* 34; emphasis in original). The existential analytic, through which Heidegger interrogates Dasein, investigates entities within the world by means other than theoretical construction, examining the structures of existence of Dasein in order to find out *how* Dasein is without assuming in advance and, on the assumptions of traditional ontology, *what* it is. As Heidegger indicated in his rejoinder to Natorp, however, the *how* and *what* are related since there is an "intimate relationship between method and subject matter in ontology," which enables a letting-be-seen of Dasein's constitution as Being-in-the-world.[103]

### Matter and Method: Phenomenology as the Method for Ontology

Heidegger's project of redirecting philosophical thought to the "question of Being" resulted in phenomenology being brought to bear on the "facticity" of entities, rejecting the Husserlian attempt to isolate the pure ego from its perceptual objects. Having received its "fundamental issue" from Greek ontology, his concern with the question of Being moved through its Husserlian phenomenological beginnings to reformulate a radicalized, hermeneutic access to human existence.[104] Phenomenology and ontology became explicitly intertwined because, in interpretative phenomenology, the "perceiving subject" turns to inquire about itself as the perceptual object. Existential analysis of that being that each of us is showed Dasein to be the investigator, as well as that which is interrogated *(das Befragte) (Being and Time,* 24). Hence, Heidegger's phenomenological concern becomes the manner in which Dasein shows "itself to itself" and what "makes possible this showing [of Dasein to itself]."[105]

Heidegger's concern with ontology and his search for a method for ontological examination arrived, therefore, at a convergence, "a point where they are one and the same: a hermeneutics *of* facticity."[106] The genitive "of" is a double genitive. It means that understanding, *Verstehen,* belongs to facticity, and at the same time it means that understanding takes facticity as its object.[107] The hermeneutics of facticity "is simply the operation of philosophy itself that catches hold of life in its activity. . . . [It] is factical life caught in the act of interpreting itself."[108] Caputo argues that "Dasein's understanding of Being is the sole condition under which both ontology and phenomenology are possible."[109] Not only is phenomenology possible solely as ontology, but in the words of Heidegger himself, *"only as phenomenology, is ontology possible" (Being and Time,* 60; emphasis in original). In other words, "[i]t is only under the condition that Dasein understands Being that beings can be experienced as beings (phenomenology) and that they can be understood to *be* (ontology)."[110]

Heidegger's initial attempts to refocus attention on the "question of Being" and on the difference between Being and beings (the so-called ontico-ontological difference that had remained "unthought" by philosophy)[111] entailed also the "destruction" of the ontological tradition. As Heidegger understood it, the notion of destruction or "destructive retrieve" destroys "in the tradition what is philosophically unjustifiable and maintain[s] those primordial experiences from which genuine philosophical insights ultimately flow."[112] Thus the destructive retrieve does not *overcome* a tradition, but rather, searches for and retains its positive possibilities, which are subsequently used to transform the tradition's *problematic* and preserve it as a possible *question.* Derrida notes, "Heidegger recognises that economically and strategically he had to borrow the syntaxic and lexical resources of the language of metaphysics, as one must always do at the very moment that one deconstructs this language."[113] Furthermore, Heidegger's convergence of matter and method meant that destruction was also rendered inseparable from phenomenology because it "is first regarded as a counter to the pervasive tendency of objectification."[114] The task of fundamental ontology is, thus, made possible by destruction, but also deconstruction is now connected to phenomenology:

> The destructive retrieve and the phenomenological method cannot be taken to be independent and unrelated procedures; rather both procedures belong intimately together and the one (hermeneutic phenomenology) cannot possibly achieve its goal without the other (destructive retrieve).[115]

### The Paradoxical Priority of Dasein?

Heidegger wished to tap into the implicit, nonintuitive understanding that existence has of itself (*Being and Time,* 59) because, as was quoted earlier, "*fundamental ontology,* from which alone all other ontologies can take their rise, must be sought in the *existential analytic* of Dasein" (34). For Heidegger, "Dasein" was the being that has some understanding of Being, although this understanding is superficial or at the very least saturated with preexisting theories that occlude proper consideration and sanction neglect of the question of Being. Thus, in order to gain a better understanding of "Being," Heidegger began with an investigation of the existential structures of Dasein, the being to which *some* understanding of Being belongs. Moreover, Dasein has priority in the sense that it is the being that *poses* the question of the meaning of Being; therefore, in order "to work out the question of Being adequately, we must make an entity—the inquirer—transparent in his own Being" (27). In other words, the choice of Dasein is not accidental; at the very least, by posing the question of Being, Dasein launches the inquiry, so to speak.

More specifically, in his consideration of the question of Being, Heidegger discerns three closely related ways in which Dasein has priority. First, Dasein is not merely present in the world: its "presence" has the "*determinate* character of existence" and as such it exhibits ontical priority.[116] Second, Dasein has an ontological priority because Dasein's "existence is thus *determinative* for it" (*Being and Time,* 34; emphasis added). Because Dasein is the being that asks the question of Being, its own existence is an issue for it. Third, "Dasein also possesses—as constitutive for its understanding of existence—an understanding of Being of all entities of a character other than its own" (34). This understanding that Dasein has of entities makes Dasein the being that it is. Its understanding of other entities in the world gives Dasein a priority in that its existence is the precondition for "all ontologies" (34). These priorities are revealed to be related, therefore, to Dasein's factical being as existence, a fact that determines the kind of being that it is—and the being that it is constitutes the possibility of understanding itself and beings other than itself.

In his analysis of Dasein, Heidegger set out to challenge modern subjectivity as the basis for human inquiry in the modern era. Jacques Taminiaux clarifies:

> Heidegger at that time agrees with modern philosophy, from Descartes to Husserl, that philosophical investigation has for its ground the being that we ourselves are. What he disagrees with is not the priority of our own being, but the ontological definition of our being.[117]

He proposed, therefore, that phenomenology "ought to begin by paying attention to the intentional behaviour of man in his concrete and daily life, to the ways in which man actually comports himself to the things of the world"[118] and "must radically disassociate itself from what is often referred to as a worldless Cartesian subject, a *res cogitans* . . . it must avoid a notion of subjectivity in which it becomes a problem to account for how a subject can ever hook up with the world."[119]

For this purpose, Heidegger avoided positing a theoretical account of existence that isolates the self from its world; on the contrary, he wished to show that Dasein's dealings in the world are *always already* infused with meaning, and take place within already existing and other-determined intelligibility. Such availability of meaning, in turn, leads to wonderment: to the question of Being itself. In the words of Robert B. Pippin,

> to deal with objects, other persons, social practices, and so forth, all the "beings" or "entities," is to be engaged in an always disclosed world, familiar and saturated with significance. Any sort of dealing, whether practical or cognitive, goes on "in the light of" such already present intelligibility, and ought to force on us the question of the possibility of such significance itself, or the meaning of Being in general.[120]

Dasein's paradoxical priority, in other words, lies in its capacity to ask the question of Being but at the same time to neglect it, and this led Heidegger to a phenomenological investigation of Dasein. The next chapter will discuss the existential analysis provided by Heidegger in an attempt to discern from it, better, to *retrieve* from it an "optics of coexistence" that locates human existence in its world as a heteronomous and coexistential entity whose structures of existence point to the primacy of *coexistence* evident in the relation to otherness and the other.

## CONCLUSION, WITH AN INTERLUDE

The previous discussion attempted to provide the context within which we can understand Heidegger's analysis of Dasein. Such a context will be invaluable in situating the reading of Heidegger's *Daseinanalytik,* in the next chapter, where an optics of coexistence is retrieved from Heidegger's own account. For the purposes of the forthcoming discussion of the optics of coexistence, it is important to recall that Heidegger's search for the appropriate method for the question of Being challenged the predominance of the subject in modern philosophy. The method Heidegger used for philosophically accessing existence aimed to go beyond the reflective or theoretical attitude. Its radicalization by Heidegger wedded phenomenology to ontology in order to make possible the showing of Dasein to itself.

For critical international theory, it is similarly significant to remember that the status of this account is not one of theoretical construction. Thus, it should not be understood as an account of the subject competing with that of Hobbes or other social theorists, constructed to suit a social environment or to justify certain political arrangements in theoretical terms. Heidegger was primarily concerned with going *beyond* theoretical construction in order to allow lived experience to access itself. Discussing the search for method also clarified that Heidegger's thought was not animated by the specific issue of coexistence, whose neglect within the field of international theory was identified in the introduction. Heidegger was concerned, rather, with reinstating the question of the meaning of Being as a philosophical undertaking; yet, as I will show in the next chapter, it is through the articulation of a radically hermeneutic phenomenological method that Heidegger's analysis showed how existence lets itself be seen as coexistential and heteronomous, how otherness permeates existence and constitutes it. The discussion of Heidegger's search for his method, therefore, also highlights the fact that coexistence cannot be analyzed through the uncritical acceptance of theoretical assumptions regarding the modern subject but must, rather, be sought in its facticity.

In this chapter, I suggested that Heidegger's retrieval of a radical phenomenology is attentive to facticity and lived experience. Such attentiveness makes evident, I argue in the next chapter, an optics of coexistence arising out of the existential analysis of Dasein. Before discussing the elements that compose the optics of coexistence, however, it is necessary to examine the prominent critique to the phenomenological method, and to Heidegger's radicalization of it, advanced by Emmanuel Levinas. In his earlier works Levinas was greatly influenced by Heidegger's phenomenology and praised precisely its attunement to facticity of human existence and otherness.[121] After the Second World War, however, his writings became very critical of Heidegger, and of ontology and phenomenology more generally. Indeed, Levinas's critique questions the ability of phenomenology, and in particular the ontological turn given to it by Heidegger, to *respond* to the other in a way that does not reduce her to the same; and as such, an examination of it is crucial for the core concern of this book with the effacement of heteronomy.

### Levinas's Critique

Levinas's prominent and influential critique was that phenomenology and ontology are "incapable of respecting the Being and meaning of the other" and that this renders them "philosophies of violence."[122] Levinas contested the Western philosophical tradition, which he calls Hellenic, and its trajectory toward systematic totalization, which he regarded as violent to otherness. For Levinas, the entire Hellenic philosophical tradition, including phenomenology and ontology, frames engagements with alterity through "ontological totalitarianism,"[123] where a tendency to equate truth to presence is seen to reduce the other to the same. He also wished to supplement this tradition with a Hebraic openness to "the infinite,"[124] which gained him the title of *the* philosopher of otherness.[125]

Despite the pervasive influence of both Husserl and Heidegger on his thought, Levinas attempted to go against the grain of ontological inquiry, and particularly Heideggerian fundamental ontology, by claiming that "ethics is first philosophy." Levinas argued that ethics should precede ontology but "that philosophical distance between ontology and ethics, can itself be understood phenomenologically within the implicit horizon of events in Europe during the years 1933–45."[126] The events of the Second World War, the Holocaust, and also the disenchantment of Levinas with Heidegger after the latter's involvement with National Socialism affected the development of Levinas's philosophy.

Levinas voiced two specific concerns about phenomenology and ontology. The first related to ontology's "capacity to think about the totality of beings as such."[127] For Levinas, totality refers to the reduction of individuals to "bearers of forces that command them unbeknown to themselves. The meaning of individuals (invisible outside of this totality) is derived from the totality."[128] David Wood helpfully calls this "ontological penetration," which results in a "reductive and ultimately destructive scrutiny" and "paves the way for those forms of exploitation and even genocide albeit unintentionally."[129] It is totality's tendency to comprehend "individual human beings in terms of their relation to Being" that brings forth a type of "detachment . . . sacrificing concrete individuality. And does this not *actually* facilitate real elimination, extermination?"[130]

Levinas's second objection, especially pertinent to the discussion of method in this chapter, was that phenomenology and ontology accorded a privileged position to comprehension and knowledge as the predominant modes of relating to the other. For Levinas, this results in the appropriation of the other by knowledge in denial of the ethical relationship with the other that is constitutive, he argues, of the self. Levinasian thought has sought to underline the ethical relation, expressed in the face-to-face encounter with the other, and to explain how this differs from the dominant Hellenic conception of approaching otherness as an object to be known by an I, evident in relationships of comprehension and knowledge. Levinas's conception of the face-to-face relationship, therefore, is not one of knowledge, of encountering the other as an object to be known based on a theme *(arche)* of an already constituted self. The face-to-face relation disrupts the commonplace understanding of alterity derived from the thematization of otherness on the basis of the theme of an independently constituted self. When an I discovers the other and approaches the other as an object of knowledge, an object of comprehension, the other is not ethically involved in the I's constitution. "[B]eing in direct relation with the Other is not to thematize the Other and consider him in the manner one considers a known object, nor to communicate a knowledge to him."[131] Knowledge (of the other) is not social, or ethical, because "knowledge is re-presentation, a return to presence, and nothing may remain *other* to it"; the other has been freed, through the I's knowing it, of its otherness.[132] Moreover, "the most audacious and remote knowledge does not put us in communion with the truly other; it does not take the place of sociality; it is always a solitude."[133]

Levinas argued that despite its attention to "facticity," Heidegger's project of restating the question of Being is tied up nonetheless with comprehension, and as such entails a certain violence toward the other:

> To affirm the priority of *Being* over *existents* is to already decide the essence of philosophy; it is to subordinate the relation with *someone* who is an existent, (the ethical relation) to a relation with the *Being of existents,* which, impersonal, permits the apprehension, the domination of existents (a relationship of knowing), subordinates justice to freedom.[134]

Tina Chanter explains, "Levinas is concerned to show how philosophy's preoccupation with positing knowledge as the fundamental relationship between the subject and the world has obscured a more original and archaic responsibility, from which the knowing subject's relation to its world, and the subject/object dichotomy that underlies and informs this relationship, is derivative."[135] Therefore, "Levinas reads Heidegger's philosophy as repeating, at some level, the epistemological trope of rendering the world knowable, thereby eradicating any possibility of radical alterity."[136] For Levinas, the other's alterity is irreducible to a theme of my consciousness, "the other is infinitely more than I can ever know"; indeed, the other is "absolutely" and "infinitely" other.[137] Phenomenology and ontology are understood by Levinas to be "philosophies of violence" in a specific sense that has to do with their relationship to comprehension: violence, hence, has to be understood as "the violence of my freedom to try to understand, grasp, contain and hold the other within my conceptual categories."[138] While Levinas rightly acknowledges that "[i]n Heidegger coexistence is, to be sure, taken as a relationship with the Other irreducible to objective cognition," he is concerned that "in the final analysis it also rests on the relationship with *being in general,* on comprehension, on ontology."[139] Thus, the other becomes an object of comprehension engulfed within the framework of the "knowing self," as described in the first two sections of this chapter.

In Levinas's thought, by contrast, "subjectivity is structured as *the other in the same,* but in a way different from that of consciousness. Consciousness is always correlative with a theme," whereas "*the other in the same* determinative of subjectivity is the restlessness of the same disturbed by the other."[140] Levinas argues that the face-to-face encounter with the other is *constitutive* of the self, that it is where subjectivity is exposed and uncovered to itself, not as a possession of the autonomous "I" but as heteronomy. This understanding of subjectivity does not assume an already constituted "I" who is in relationship with the other. Rather, the other's face summons the self into consciousness and constitutes it as subject.

In sum, Levinas attributes to phenomenology and ontology the kind of obsession with knowledge and comprehension that was the sign of neo-Kantianism as discussed earlier. It is possible, however, to question whether Heidegger's turn to *Verstehen* is tantamount to comprehension in this same sense. While *Verstehen* is customarily rendered by "comprehension,"[141] the term refers, as discussed in light of Kisiel's investigations, to the kind of understanding that life has of itself, an understanding that belongs to facticity and that, at the same time, turns toward facticity as its subject matter. This kind of understanding arguably employs a different attitude than the kind of comprehension toward grasping life and the other as an object of knowledge. In casting Heidegger's ontology as comprehension, Levinas proposed that, on the contrary, his own philosophy was informed by a "phenomenology of nearness"[142] that claims to avoid the ontological totalitarianism of the Western philosophical tradition and describes a relationality to the other beyond knowledge and instrumentality. Is this not misleading? How can Levinas accuse phenomenology and ontology of "violence" while at the same time utilizing so extensively "Husserl's essential teaching" in terms of paying attention to experience and in the notion of intentionality, as Derrida so rightly points out?[143] At the very least, argues Derrida, "Levinas' metaphysics in a sense presupposes—at least we have attempted to show this—the transcendental phenomenology that it seeks to put into question."[144]

For the purposes of the discussion here, Levinas's critique must be understood with its specific particularities. First, as Robert J. S. Manning points out, it is problematic to consider Levinas as working outside of philosophy, or to ignore his debt to phenomenology and its resources. Levinas's own work is "unimaginable without the two Greeks named Husserl and Heidegger."[145] Thus, his critique of Heidegger has to be contextualized within his debt to Heidegger's philosophy and framework, as well as Heidegger's radicalization of phenomenology and the attention to facticity this very framework enabled.[146]

Second, Levinas's ethics as first philosophy has in the last twenty years been called into question both by his restatement of metaphysical humanism[147] and also by his political statements, prompting the need to reexamine the limits of the face-to-face relationship and particularities of his own political relationship to the State of Israel.[148] Such statements have questioned whether the face-to-face ethical relation is one that can sustain the multiplicity of others, of the social.[149] Therefore, Levinas's own insights can be used to problematize the limits of his thought.

Third, and most important for the discussions within this book, it is unproductive to assume that Levinas's critique of Heidegger amounts to a dismissal. Levinas never stopped expressing his admiration of *Being and Time* while exploring its limits and ambiguities; such admiration is quite distinct from "almost juvenile enthusiasm"[150] and must be understood as a critical but productive engagement with the paths that Heidegger's thought opens. In other words, Levinas's work cannot *but* be seen as one of the most substantive engagements with Heidegger, to rival that of Jacques Derrida and other French philosophers. In light of this engagement, Levinas's concerns about phenomenology and ontology and the "violence" to otherness ought to prompt his readers not to dismiss Heidegger but to turn, or better to *return,* to him and critically reengage his work in light of the question of otherness posed by Levinas. This book's concerns with coexistence, the role of otherness, and the effacement of heteronomy, in which the subjectivist commitments of international relations result, are not only parallel with Levinas's own concerns but are inspired by the concerns he voices about otherness and heteronomy. It is in this light that the "optics of coexistence" is explored in the next chapter, taking normative inspiration from the Levinasian critique with which to supplement Heidegger's concern with accessing facticity. Through Levinas, the turn to Heidegger assumes a critical tone, as well as an excavational attitude, which seeks to retrieve from his thought the coexistential and heteronomous aspect of existence.

# 3

## An Optics of Coexistence: Dasein's Radical Embeddedness in Its World

The previous chapter outlined Heidegger's critical engagement with phenomenology and traditional ontology in search of a method that would access lived experience while, at the same time, avoiding the prevalent assumptions related to the modern subject. It also examined the critique of Emmanuel Levinas that phenomenology and ontology are "philosophies of violence," part of the Western philosophical tradition in which the other is reduced to the same. The remaining chapters of the book are all specifically motivated by Levinas's critique; rather than dismissing Heidegger, however, they (re)turn to his thought critically and explore the ways in which such a critical rereading can retrieve *from* Heidegger's hermeneutic phenomenology an account of coexistential and heteronomous selfhood that is radically embedded in the world. The present chapter, in particular, retrieves certain elements found in Heidegger's thought that attest to the coexistential heteronomy of the self and the constitutive role of otherness for existence at the most fundamental level. By examining the substantive existential analysis of Being-in-the-world found in Heidegger's *Being and Time,* this chapter makes possible an account of the primacy of relation and sociality of existence *(Dasein).*[1] Whereas a "subject" has been traditionally understood as an assertive, masterful, and largely disengaged self,[2] the interrogation of Dasein's existential structures illuminates an account of existence as coexistence, as permeated through and through by otherness.

Specifically, Heidegger's account of Being-in-the-world diverges substantially from previous Cartesian and post-Cartesian articulations of subjectivity. Whereas such accounts tend to posit the subject as an isolated and self-sufficient being,[3] Heidegger's existential analytic begins, instead, from the premise that it is misleading to assume that the answer to the question "who is Dasein?" is the "I." Heidegger's phenomenological analyses suggest, moreover, that the theoretical positing of Dasein as subject is phenomenally inadequate at the ontological level.[4] Importantly, avoiding the assumptions of modern subjectivity and using existential analysis to "unwork" it enables Heidegger to attend to existence in its facticity. By reading his discussion with Levinas's concern with otherness in mind, the chapter reveals in his thought an "optics of coexistence"—a host of elements that attest not to subjectivity in its autonomous and nonrelational sense, but rather to a coexistential heteronomy. These elements are best referred to as an *optics* because they enable a different *seeing* of the phenomena of existence. The chapter uses the Levinasian critique, examined in the previous chapter, as a call to return to Heidegger and to explore anew the ways in which his thought can be read as a *heterology,* a discourse about *to heteron,* the other.

Specifically, there are four distinct, but related, elements in Heidegger's existential analysis that highlight not only the fact of the self's constitution by otherness, but also the ways in which this is manifested in the self's everyday life. First, Dasein initially and primarily *(zunächst und zumeist)* finds itself immersed in the world.[5] Understanding Dasein as existing primarily in the mode of "engaged immersion" helps to shift emphasis away from reflection and "knowing" as the definitive modes of human relationality. In other words, Dasein's main relationship to other entities cannot be assumed to be one of knowing; Dasein does not initially and primarily encounter entities and the world as "objects" of comprehension. Rather, Dasein is immersed continuously among things and other beings of its own character in a more fundamental and immediate way, allaying some of the fears about phenomenology's reliance on the knowing and perceiving subject.[6] More important, challenging the reflective relationship of comprehension and, therefore, of objectification, which the modern subject has toward other beings and the world, allows the disclosive character of existence to be brought to the fore. This illustrates clearly how Dasein discloses the Being of other entities while at the same time existing prereflectively and "outside of itself" among the things and beings that constitute it.

Second, Dasein's dealings (or "comportments") while immersed in daily activities disclose a different conception of the world as such. Thinking of existence as engaged immersion brings to the fore a notion of the world as a web of involvements with other beings, as a background of meanings against which existence makes sense of itself *prereflectively*. Revealing the world as a totality of meanings, references, and relations also illuminates that this is a web that is not created by Dasein alone. Rather, Dasein's way of life and the norms and rules that help it go about its business in the world are structured by others and are only shared by Dasein. This dependence that Dasein has on other-created meanings and understandings signifies that Dasein has an ontological relationship to the world.

Third, Dasein is Being-in-the-world *with others*. For Dasein, existence is already coexistence; Being-there is always Being-with, to the extent that Dasein is indistinguishable from others. Selfhood is coexistential in its constitution, where such an understanding of "coexistence" is not tantamount to the uniting, composition, or copresence[7] of completed and autonomous subjects. Finally, Dasein is fundamentally attuned to the world in which it exists, and its understanding of itself and other entities is affected by this attunement. Its attunement shows it to be an entity *thrown* into its world; at the same time, its understanding of itself as possibility indicates that it also projects itself toward the future. Taken together, the aspects of Dasein's fundamental attunement and situated understanding indicate that its world matters to it; in other words, Dasein is an entity better understood as *care*.

When viewed together, these four elements of the optics of coexistence, retrieved from Heidegger's phenomenology of everydayness, elucidate Dasein's coexistential heteronomy and, thus, contest the presuppositions of modern subjectivity. The following four sections explicate each of these elements in greater detail, highlighting the need for close attention to facticity within international political theory, an emphasis that lets the primacy of relation, of coexistence, be seen in the structures of existence.

## DASEIN'S ENGAGED IMMERSION IN ITS WORLD

As already discussed in chapter 2, Heidegger was writing at a time when the prominence of neo-Kantianism, on the one hand, and Edmund Husserl's concern with the transcendental subject, on the other, signaled the dominance of the modern subject. The centrality of the reflective subject in Western philosophy since Descartes, and the resulting emergence of the theoretical attitude, created rigid dichotomies between subject and object. It led to the perception that "as individual humans we are individual subjects and egos, and what we represent and mean are only subjective pictures which we carry around in us"; holding onto this understanding of the subject meant that "we never reach the things themselves."[8] Understanding the world in such subjectivist terms could not be surpassed by a mere shift to the consideration of collective "things," "by talking about 'we' instead of 'I' and by taking into account the community rather than the individual."[9] Heidegger attempted, therefore, to "advance an anti-individualist and anti-mentalist account of the general possibility of any sort of meaning, of anything being intelligible at all."[10]

Heidegger's thinking about the question of the general intelligibility of the world, the question of "Being" as he called it, sought to divert attention from the detached subject of post-Cartesian philosophy. In fact, as the previous chapter argued, he wished to call into question the primacy of relating to beings as mere objects of reflection and representation, whose very existence could be doubted by a "subject."[11] The Western philosophical tradition, he claimed, had been concerned either with "explaining deliberate action (Aristotle) or with assigning moral responsibility (Kant)."[12] Refusing to restrict human comportment to these two modes, Heidegger focused attention on the more primary,[13] but neglected, perspective of everydayness, in order to elucidate a prereflective and nondeliberative type of comportment and relationality in the world, which forms the first element of the optics of coexistence. Hubert Dreyfus usefully refers to this mode of everyday relating to beings as "ongoing coping" in order to emphasize its nondeliberative aspect, while Slavoj Žižek suggests the term "engaged immersion" to highlight the character of being *within* the world of activity.[14] Both terms, used here interchangeably, highlight that Dasein initially and primarily finds itself immersed in the world and relates to others and the world in

AN OPTICS OF COEXISTENCE · 61

the mode of average everydayness. Everydayness is "a positive phenomenal characteristic" of Dasein that enables the examination of
Dasein's prereflective relations by offering a perspective quite distinct from the privileged position of disinterested gazing at objects
of comprehension (*Being and Time*, 69).

Engaged immersion is presented here as the first element of the
optics of coexistence because it calls into question not only the su-
premacy of disinterested knowledge toward objects and the world,
but also the reduction of Dasein as Being-in-the-world to "a single
exemplar—knowing the world" (*Being and Time*, 86). Whereas the
"relation of subject to object is initially conceived as a knowing
relation," this is due to the prior determination of both terms as
"knower and known."[15] The suggestion that Dasein exists in its
world in the mode of ongoing coping shows this prior determination
to be phenomenologically distorting.[16] The examination of such a
type of comportment toward beings reveals "that all relations of
mental states to their objects presuppose a more basic form of being-
with-things which does not involve mental activity."[17] Prior to reflection, "Being-in-the-world, as concern, is *fascinated by* the world
with which it is concerned" (88; emphasis in original), in other
words, "[o]ur dealings with the world typically absorb or fascinate
us; our tasks, and so the various entities we employ in carrying
them out, preoccupy us."[18] Even when Dasein refrains from nondeliberative, nonreflective activity such as "producing, manipulating, and the like," it is still not reflective as such; rather, "it puts itself into what is now the sole remaining mode of Being-in, the mode
of just tarrying alongside [amid] *[das Nur-noch-verweilen bei]*"
(88). The mode of going along in the midst of other entities may be
the very condition of possibility of deliberate reflection about entities, but also shows that reflection is not the primary and initial way
in which Dasein comports itself in its world.

The first element of the optics of coexistence, then, refutes the
Cartesian assumption that reflection and knowing are the primary
modes of relating with other entities, rendered as objects to a subject.
On the contrary, engaged immersion shows that Dasein does not
encounter entities as objects of *theorein* (see, gaze, or observe), but
rather as equipment, stuff, or gear available in its world of activity
and work. Ongoing coping in the world of work usually takes the
form of using and manipulating available things (equipment, tools,

etc.).[19] When Dasein is shown to relate initially and primarily in a nondeliberative, engaged mode, the world and other entities cease to be grasped as objects for a reflective subject and come into view as themselves constitutive of Dasein. Moreover, and more important, in going about its concerns in everyday life, Dasein discloses the Being of other entities, and of the world itself, while at the same time revealing and highlighting the role of otherness in what Jean-Luc Nancy calls the "layer of everyday experience."[20]

### Engaged Immersion and Dasein's Disclosive Character

Dasein does not, initially and primarily, encounter entities within the world as a knowing subject; how then does it relate to entities? In other words, what does engaged immersion really mean? Let us discuss an example that Heidegger gives in the context of the world of work to bring into view the character of ongoing coping. While working, Dasein most probably uses and manipulates equipment or tools. Heidegger gives the example of a hammer, but one could also imagine Dasein similarly using all kinds of equipment, such as industrial machinery or computers. In his example, when a carpenter uses a hammer she is absorbed in this activity. She is not thinking "what is a hammer?" or reflecting on it as an object to be known. She primarily uses the hammer without reflection. But while hammering, it becomes apparent that she has an implicit and prereflective understanding about the character and use of a hammer as a piece of equipment and that she has "appropriated this equipment in a way that could not possibly be more suitable" (*Being and Time*, 98).

Although being absorbed in the activity, engaged immersion in the form of using a tool, such as a hammer, makes manifest the kind of Being that equipment has. It is the handling of equipment in the most appropriate way that reveals its Being: "the less we stare at the hammer-Thing, and the more we seize hold of it and use it, the more primordial does our relationship to it become, and the more unveiledly is it encountered as that which it is—as equipment" (98). It is by using the hammer for what it is intended, for hammering, that "uncovers the specific 'manipulability' *[Handlichkeit]* of the hammer" and shows its Being as readiness-to-hand (availableness) (98). John Haugeland suggests, "Availability is the *way* of equipmental being."[21] Dasein's directed activity to get something done in its work world, then, affirms that equipment or gear is not merely occurrent in the world ("present-at-hand," in Heidegger's term) but is *available* ("ready-to-hand") for Dasein to use in its everyday work and activity.

Furthermore, engaged immersion shows that equipment does not occur singularly in this world of work. Rather, it belongs and functions as part of an equipmental whole, which endows it with meaning. A hammer is only a hammer in relation to nails, wooden boards, and so on. "Equipment—in accordance with its equipmentality—always is *in terms of [aus]* its belonging to other equipment" (*Being and Time,* 97; emphasis in original) and this equipmental totality invokes the "concrete circumstances or context" of using the equipment.[22] In addition to disclosing the concrete context of use, however, Dasein's engaged immersion with available equipment in the world of work highlights its proper function, which, in turn, "presupposes something *for which* it is usable, an end-product."[23] In other words, the Being of an available thing becomes manifest when one considers its role. Thus, the role of the hammer might be to drive nails into wooden boards: disclosing the function of equipment enables the relationship of a specific piece of equipment to the equipmental totality to be understood as a role relationship. The highlighting of the referential assignment of a piece of gear indicates that, with each available entity, "there always belongs a totality of equipment, in which it can be this equipment that it is" (97). The "specific functionality," the assignment, of a piece of equipment within a whole set of references "makes the thing what it is."[24]

It should be noted, moreover, that Dasein's initial involvement is not with the things (equipment or gear) themselves. "On the contrary, that with which we concern ourselves primarily is the work—that which is to be produced" (*Being and Time,* 99). The work for which the equipment is assigned a specific function also presupposes other relationships, for example, that raw material is available or that the final product or service is intended for people to make use of and their requirements and interests affect the work being done. Thus, the work is assigned a "towards-which" reference that refers to the "end-points we use in making sense of a flow of directed activity."[25] The final end of the chain of "towards-which" assignments is Dasein itself, because "Dasein exists in the manner of being-in-the-world and as such *it is for the sake of its own self.*"[26] This assignment of work and gear "for-the-sake-of" Dasein is not conspicuous in everyday work, however (116). Yet it is this latent "self-interpretation" of directed activity that "informs and orders all [of Dasein's] activities."[27]

The example of how Dasein encounters tools and equipment illustrates that Dasein's worldly Being is "always already outside of itself, dwelling amidst objects in all their variety"; at the same time, while working or coping in its daily activities, entities show up for Dasein "in the full specificity of their nature," and this ability to disclose entities as they are "in their what-being and that-being" makes Dasein the "clearing."[28] There are two issues to note here. First, that while dwelling among other beings, Dasein becomes constituted by them, through using them and having its own role within the totality of meanings and references that make the work or activity possible. Second, by the fact of its *being-in* the world, Dasein has the ability to disclose other entities. It does not do so by reflecting about them as objects of knowledge and comprehension, but rather by being engaged within them, absorbed and fascinated by them; in this mode of engaged immersion in the world, Dasein discloses the Being of entities and Dasein's Being is constituted by its *disclosedness* (*Being and Time*, 171).

Moreover, Dasein's involvement with equipment in the work world discloses that existence operates according to a totality of references and assignments. The work itself "bears with it that referential totality within which the equipment is encountered" (*Being and Time*, 99). The referential assignments that map how, and for what reason, activity occurs, make the work world meaningful and comprehensible for Dasein, who exists in it prereflectively absorbed in its daily activities. As such, the work world is a micro example of the surrounding world *(Umwelt)* that Dasein's disclosive character brings to the fore. This understanding of the world, as a totality of involvements, references, and meanings, is examined in greater detail as the second element of the optics of coexistence in order to show its essentially coexistential and heteronomous character. Prior to this discussion, however, the role of reflective deliberation deserves further analysis in order to dispel its assumed primacy and to suggest its proper place in human existence.

### The Role of Reflection

Heidegger's suggestion that Dasein's everyday mode of being is engaged immersion, importantly, is not intended to denigrate reflection or knowing. Focusing on ongoing coping does not mean simply wishing "to make practical activity primary"; rather, it suggests "that neither practical activity nor contemplative knowing can be understood as a relation between a self-sufficient mind and an independent world."[29] Engaged immersion was "meant to show that the traditional epistemic situation of a mind distinct from objects, *whether observing or acting upon them,* is a deficient mode of being-in-the-world."[30] For Heidegger, knowing, in the sense of disinterested knowledge, can only be regarded as a "founded mode" of Being-in-the-world, "a mode which can subsist only when connected with something else," that is, in this case, the mode of engaged immersion (*Being and Time,* 86, note 1). Theoretical reflection, then, is not primary for Dasein's dealings with entities in the world; rather, Dasein engages in reflection when this is called for by situations that thrust it outside of its prereflective mode of engaged immersion.

Let us examine the role of reflection for Dasein within the context of the work world. The tools and equipment, as well as the equipmental totality, are not noticeable while Dasein is immersed in its everyday activity because as a user of equipment, Dasein is focusing on the particular task at hand and on the end result it wants to achieve. In this way, the equipment itself and the totality of which it is a part are subsumed in the task and become transparent and invisible. The user is not explicitly aware of any specific traits that a particular piece of equipment may have while using it or how it specifically functions within the equipmental whole. In other words, Dasein is not reflecting on the equipment or the raw materials as objects of comprehension; it is merely using them in the most appropriate way.

The inconspicuousness of equipment continues throughout the normal, unproblematic functioning of everyday directed activity. Deliberate reflection toward available (ready-to-hand) entities is only called for when a breakdown or disturbance in the referential totality occurs. When nondeliberative engaged immersion is no longer possible, the user turns to reflection and deliberation in order to restore the referential totality to its normal state. Knowing is required as a mode of relating to entities when there is "a *deficiency* in our having-to-do with the world concernfully" (*Being and Time,* 88; emphasis in original). The specific situation of breakdown in Dasein's ordinary immersion in the world of work calls for new modes of encountering entities and of being-encountered that are not, as it was shown earlier, part of Dasein's initial and primary involvement with entities in the world.[31] Such disturbances reveal Dasein as a being capable of reflection and deliberation when it is called for by a deficiency in everyday comportment. Switching to a reflective relationship with things in situations of disturbance, however, establishes that disinterested reflection is not the primary or initial mode of relating to the world and other entities. Rather, the world and available equipment are related to primarily through everyday dealings in the mode of ongoing coping, making Dasein's constant and extensive involvement in practical activity a novel starting point for existential analysis (102). As the situation of breakdown illustrates, Dasein is both capable and inclined to engage in theoretical reflection; to focus from the start on the reflective subject, however, is to obscure how reflection comes about and to occlude Dasein's primary relationship to its world as one of immersed involvement. The knowing subject that "encounters present-at-hand objects on to which he then projects his aims, and exploits them accordingly," Žižek clarifies in this regard, "falsifies the proper state of things: the fact that engaged immersion in the world is primordial, and that all other modes of the presence of objects are derived from it."[32]

The phenomenological observation, therefore, that Dasein's engaged immersion is the primary mode of relating to entities within the world forms the first element of the optics of coexistence. Understanding human existence to be immersed in its world in an engaged manner counters the proposition that the subject is first and foremost involved in a relation of reflection and objectification with things and the world. Furthermore, Dasein's everyday comportments, in the form of ongoing coping, help to disclose the Being of entities as either available (ready-to-hand) or present (present-at-hand) and the world as a referential totality of meaning and relations.[33] It also points to Dasein's disclosive character, which suggests that, as an entity, Dasein has an ontological relationship to the world. In fact, it can be argued that "solipsism is an ontological impossibility for Dasein since Dasein occurs only in disclosive relations."[34] Such disclosive relations show that Dasein is constituted by the things and entities in which it is absorbed in its everydayness, and also by the meanings, references, and relationships within the equipmental whole in which it is initially and primarily immersed. The constitutive role of otherness for Dasein, therefore, becomes clearer when reflection and knowing are accorded their proper place as "founded modes" of being in the world. This role is further elaborated when the second element of the optics of coexistence, that of the world as a referential totality in which Dasein makes sense of itself and the ontological relationship that this signifies, is explored.

## THE WORLD AS A SHARED WEB OF MEANINGS AND RELATIONS

Two equally important insights emerge from the previous discussion of engaged immersion to form the second element of the optics of coexistence. First, that engaged immersion is indicative of a more basic state of immersion, one that Heidegger calls "Being-in-the-world." This state of radical embeddedness reveals, as this section analyzes, that Dasein has an ontological relationship to the world and, as such, it is not merely contained in the world spatially as a disembedded "subject." Second, the conception of the world that arises from the discussion of engaged immersion as the initial and primary mode of Dasein's comportment is not nature, or even a "container" of other entities; rather, the world appears as a totality of references and assignments, a set of relations and sense (meaning) according to which Dasein orients itself. Both aspects, Being-in-the-world and the world as a referential totality, related as they are, serve to establish a context of inner-worldly belonging that gives Dasein a worldly character and becomes, together with the primacy of engaged immersion, the bedrock of the optics of coexistence.

The disclosive character of Dasein's engaged immersion in the work world has crucially illuminated that Dasein can be understood as Being-in-the-world and that this denotes a range of involvements within the world, such as "dealing with the world; tarrying alongside it in the manner of performing, effecting and completing, but also contemplating, interrogating, and determining by way of contemplation and comparison"; taken as a whole, it can be argued that "Being-in-the-world is characterized as concern."[35] However, Dasein's everyday praxis does not only indicate that Dasein is Being-in-the-world; it simultaneously discloses the world as a totality of meanings, references, and assignments in which Dasein makes sense of itself (as existence).

To suggest that Dasein "has a world" leads to an understanding of "world" as the referential background that enables Dasein to make sense of its environment.[36] Referred to in this manner, "world" designates something other than a spatial container of all entities, an object, or even nature. For Dasein, whose Being is Being-in-the-world, this world can only be understood as "an 'environment' within which man dwells with the things he uses in a circumspective manner. The worldliness of this world is defined . . . as a meaningful totality of references."[37] The references by which Dasein locates itself in the world, and according to which existence becomes both possible and meaningful, are all connected in such a way that the totality is also a "web of assignment relations."[38] One assignment is related to another, and to the referential whole, in a chain, or rather a web, such that the referential totality is also a "relational totality," which Heidegger calls "significance" (*Being and Time*, 120). It is this connectedness of signifying assignments that makes the whole meaningful. Because it is meaningful, the world is "a web of socially or culturally constituted assignments *within* which entities can appear as the particular types of object that they are."[39] Furthermore, Dasein has an existing familiarity with the world as a totality of assignment relations and this familiarity is the ontical condition for entities to show themselves as they are in themselves (120).[40]

Making assignments, completing the chain, enlarging or altering the web of references, all are part of Dasein's Being as Being-in-the-world. Therefore, the totality of involvements helps to substantiate that within it "lurks an ontological relationship to the world" (*Being and Time*, 118). Dasein's general absorption in its everyday dealings reveals "the world as familiar in such a way that there is no separation between Dasein's disclosing comportment and the world disclosed."[41] Dasein's familiarity with the referential totality and its readiness and capacity to do what is appropriate, in other words, to cope in each concrete context, is constantly active. This relationship to the world is so familiar that Heidegger "simply calls it *being-in-the-world*."[42] "On the face of it," John Haugeland notes, "this structure looks like a relation: being-amidst as a relation between self (agent, who) and world"; yet, Being-in-the-world is more properly understood "as a single entity with two interdependent structural aspects: self and world."[43] In other words, Dasein is worldly from the start and as part of the kind of being that it is. "In clarifying Being-in-the-world," Heidegger notes, "we have shown that a bare subject without a world never 'is' proximally, nor is it ever given" (152). Moreover, "Dasein in so far as it is, has always submitted itself already to a 'world' which it encounters, and this *submission* belongs essentially to its Being" (120–21; emphasis in original).

What is the character of this world in which Dasein is always already absorbed? The world, understood as a referential totality, primarily includes references, norms, and meanings assigned and altered by *other* Dasein. The multitude of Dasein's activities and its use of equipment and other things "*presuppose* the disclosure of one *shared* world."[44] This is because the web of other-created, shared references "must therefore always be laid out . . . in advance of any particular encounter with an object."[45] Without this shared "web," this "common institutional framework," behavior would not be intelligible; the web works tacitly and holistically, and against this background Dasein's roles, norms, and praxis "make sense in relation to one another and as a whole."[46]

Dasein's initial and primary comportment toward entities and other Daseins is in the mode of average everydayness. In everydayness, Dasein operates according to already existing meanings, rules, and norms within the referential and equipmental whole. The functioning of the whole requires a certain *average* or undifferentiated way of acting and behaving into which Dasein has already been socialized. "Averageness," however, does not suggest that ways of behaving and acting are identical among Daseins. On the contrary, Dasein goes about its concerns by *uniquely appropriating* these shared meanings, norms, and practices that add up to the referential totality. This appropriating relationship that Dasein has with respect to the shared web of meanings and relations is what Heidegger calls "mineness." The interplay between averageness and mineness enables Heidegger to say about Dasein that "in each case, *I* am this entity," while at the same time, Dasein is Being-in-the-world, a basic state of being that indicates an ontological familiarity and submission to the world. The relationship between averageness and mineness is quite distinct from the subjectivist "conception of Dasein as an occurrent [present-at-hand] subject," which "isolates Dasein."[47] Dasein's absorption in the world means that it participates in, and is moreover constituted by, averageness, but this immersion can "have its unique appropriations."[48] Only then can averageness appear as "the ontological source of the familiarity and readiness that makes the ontical discovery of entities, of others, and even of myself

possible,"[49] which lends meaning to Dasein's comportment toward
other beings without contradicting the possibility of mineness in the
form of unique appropriations of average meaning and behavior.

When the world is understood as a shared, already given, web of
references, Dasein itself is illuminated as "shared social activity"[50]
uniquely appropriated, in each case, through mineness. This unique
appropriation that Dasein *is* does not result, however, in the return
of the autonomous self of Cartesian thought.[51] Conceiving Dasein
as "a 'living' way of life," that is, a way of life currently being lived
out, allows mineness (in each case *I* am myself this entity) to be reconciled with averageness ("Dasein is shared practices") in order to
arrive at Dasein being a uniquely appropriated way of life.[52]

This second element of the optics of coexistence, then, provides
an understanding of the world as a relational totality of meaning
and involvement to which Dasein has an ontological relationship.
This element rescinds completely the relationship of disinterested
distance that the modern subject is purported to have to the world,
taken as its object of reflection. On the contrary, not only is Dasein
Being-in-the-world, but also the world is accessed by Dasein as a
web of relations and references already given in advance as the background against which Dasein orients its activities and behavior and
makes sense of its existence. The world, formed by otherness, is only
ever shared (and, occasionally, appropriated in a distinct way) by
Dasein. The way the assignments of meaning are connected shows
that Dasein's world is fundamentally relational; it is shared with
other Daseins and therefore coexistential, but it is also already and
primarily created by others in an average way and, as such, it is
heteronomous. This specific relationship that Dasein has with other
Dasein is the third element of the optics of coexistence.

## BEING-THERE IS BEING-WITH

The analysis of engaged immersion has already argued that conceptualizing Dasein as a *knowing* subject would not be "phenomenally
adequate," while the conception of the world as a totality of meaning has indicated that Dasein is not an isolated subject, but rather
has an ontological relationship with the world. Robert Pippin has
argued that this is "immediately suggestive of *some theory of sociality,* rather than subjectivity in the Cartesian sense."[53] Following the
discussion of Dasein's engaged immersion and the worldly context in

which its comportments with other entities unfold, this section now turns to the third element of the optics of coexistence, which sets out the precise relationship that Dasein has with others as well as its ontological significance. This third element focuses on Heidegger's discussion of Dasein as Being-with, which refutes most directly the phenomenological adequacy of the modern nonrelational subject. Heidegger's existential analysis calls into question the assumption that the (self-sufficient) "I" is the answer to the question "who is Dasein?" and suggests, instead, that Dasein is essentially Being-with and, as such, is indistinguishable from others. The exposition of Dasein as fundamentally constituted by its capacity to be with others within the world dispels further the understanding of coexistence as mere copresence, which the ground of modern subjectivity imposes on ontology and also on international relations as a social science reliant on modern ontological commitments. As such, this third aspect of the optics of coexistence becomes, perhaps, the most important but also the most contentious element in the "unworking" of modern subjectivity.

### Withness as a Prior Capacity of Dasein

The discussion of engaged immersion in the world suggested that "Dasein finds itself proximally in *what* it does, uses, expects, avoids—in those things environmentally ready-to-hand [available] with which it is proximally *concerned*" (*Being and Time*, 155; emphases in original). Others, therefore, "are encountered from out of the *world*, in which concernfully circumspective Dasein essentially dwells" (155; emphasis in original). Chapters 1 and 2 have already discussed how post-Cartesian thought traditionally viewed the other as either an object of comprehension or a copresent subject. Existential analysis, however, shows that in the mode of average everydayness, Dasein encounters others "environmentally" in its surrounding work world in the course of its everyday dealings.[54] For example, the available equipment that a particular Dasein uses is not designated specifically for it; rather, equipment is available for all others, who are disclosed by their usage of it. More specifically, the equipmental totality highlights the importance of the other because equipment bears not only "in-order-to" (e.g., perform a task) assignments, but also "towards-which" (e.g., for this end) and "whereof" (e.g., the origin of the ready-to-hand) ones. These "towards-which" and "whereof" references "of equipmental totalities relate the work-world to other people."[55] When Dasein is at work producing something or performing a task, this is always oriented with reference to the others for whom the task is performed or the thing is produced, in other words, to its future users or consumers. When Dasein is using material, its suppliers or producers are encountered as to whether they do their supplying or producing well. Even on the mode of "tarrying amidst," various entities show themselves as belonging to others, being used, serviced, maintained, sold, or bought by them. In the surrounding world of praxis, then, "along with the equipment to be found when one is at work *[in Arbeit],* those Others for whom the 'work' *[Werk]* is destined are 'encountered too'" (153). It is in this world of activity where others are initially disclosed by Dasein's everyday praxis.

Mulhall notes that there are three distinct ways in which other Daseins "show up" in the world. First, they are an additional type of entity that is encountered by Dasein in the course of its disclosing engagement in the world. Second, the work Dasein produces and the tasks it performs are generally intended for others, either as consumers or as further producers in the process of completing the work. Third, the available things (equipment) that Dasein uses or encounters are not ready-to-hand (available) for that particular Dasein alone. An available thing is available for every Dasein capable of using it; in this way readiness-to-hand is "inherently intersubjective."[56] The emphasis placed on Dasein's engaged immersion, therefore, means that the "Dasein-with of others is often encountered in terms of what is ready-to-hand within-the-world"; other Dasein are encountered in their own work environment and not as entities that Dasein studies reflectively: "We meet them 'at work,' that is, primarily in their Being-in-the-world," notes Heidegger (*Being and Time,* 156). Although it is within this environmental context of equipment and in the mode of ongoing coping that their Being is disclosed, this is neither readiness-to-hand nor presence-at-hand. Heidegger employs the term "Dasein-with"

> to designate that Being for which the Others who are *[die seienden Anderen]* are freed [disclosed] within-the-world. This Dasein-with of the Others is disclosed within-the-world for a Dasein, and so too for those who are Daseins with us *[die Mitdaseienden],* only because Dasein in itself is essentially Being-with (156).

The others are encountered "in" the work-world in the basic mode of Being-in-the-world, that is, "they are *like* the very Dasein which frees [discloses] them, in that *they are there too, and there with it*" (*Being and Time*, 154). Although the relationship to the other is mediated through the work world, this does not mean that it is not originary, that there is, in other words, a distinction between the with-world and the work world, as if these were separate and distinct. Michael Theunissen has argued, "The environmental kind of encounter of *Dasein*-with does not suspend the circumstance that the surrounding world is itself already a with-world and that thereby all equipment carries 'with-like' traits from the outset."[57]

It is more important to note that others are not encountered in the world "as a 'plurality' of subjects that, thanks to their incarnation, arise as 'person-things-present-at-hand' among other things."[58] The logic of composition, with its conception of others as subjects and of their coexistence as the coming together of self-sufficient subjects, is directly refuted by Heidegger. His reformulation of the "with" beyond composition "unworks" the nonrelational character assumed of the modern subject. "The world of Dasein is a *with-world [Mitwelt]*. Being-in is *Being-with* Others. Their Being-in-themselves within-the-world is *Dasein-with [Mitdasein]*" (*Being and Time*, 155; emphases in original). "With," then, shapes the very Being of Dasein as a worldly entity and cannot be understood as signifying copresence:

> Being-there-too *[Auch-da-sein]* with them does not have the onto-logical character of a Being-present-at-hand-along-"with" them within a world. This "with" is something of the character of Dasein; the "too" means a sameness of Being as circumspectively concernful Being-in-the-world. "With" and "too" are to be understood *existentially,* not categorically. By reason of this *with-like [mithaften]* Being-in-the-world, the world is always the one I share with Others. (154–55; emphases in original)

The claim that "Dasein is essentially Being-with" is not merely a description that "I am not present-at-hand alone, and that Others of my kind occur," nor that "I am currently with others" (*Being and Time*, 156); rather, Being-with is an attribute of Dasein's Being. Heidegger explains, "Being-with is an existential characteristic of Dasein even when factically no Other is present-at-hand or perceived" (156). Even when no Others are present, Dasein is Being-with. Being-alone is possible only for an entity who has Being-with as its Being (157). To say that Dasein is Being-with, then, has little to do with the actual presence of one or multiple others, because "with" is not about spatial proximity. Rather, the "with" is an existential attribute of Dasein. Georgopoulos articulates this quite effectively when he argues that the term "with" cannot be seen

> as designating a relationship that can be noted once there are more than two terms. Rather we have to think of *Mit-sein,* of *Being-with,* or more exactly of the very Being *of* with, of withness. There can be two terms that can encounter one another only if first *there is* withness. That is, only if first there is a primordial structure of commonness, of a with relationship, can a specific type of relationship be instituted.[59]

"Withness," Heidegger suggests, is the existential commonness that makes all actual interactions with, and experiences of, others possible. This "sharing" of the world is a "prior capacity," which Dasein possesses; it is the capacity to-be-with *(mit-sein)* that makes any consideration of, and relationship with, others possible. Coexistence and its multifaceted dimensions rest on this existential structure of Being-with. Michael Gelven notes, "To say that Being-with (or to-be-with) is an *a priori* existential of Dasein means that one cannot be a self unless it is within one's possibilities to relate in a unique way to other Daseins. Hence, to be Dasein at all means to-be-with."[60]

What is this way in which Dasein relates to others, given that its Being is Being-with? "If the world is revealed in concerned dealings, what Heidegger called *besorgen,* so *Mitdasein* (Dasein-with) is originally revealed in what he calls *Fürsorge,*" where this "refers to those dealings by virtue of which the Other appears as another Dasein."[61] Dasein comports itself toward other Daseins with solicitude (*Fürsorge,* commonly meaning "welfare"). Referring to the range of comportment to other Daseins, solicitude is not synonymous with respect. As an ontological claim, comportment in terms of solicitude can take many forms, from being inattentive, indifferent, or hostile toward others to being attentive and caring. While it may be attractive to view solicitude in an a priori positive way, it may be worth remembering that "[i]n average everydayness, however, solicitude, is . . . an absorption in worldly matters of common concern"[62] and that such a concern often finds expression in keeping one's distance and interacting with others with distrust and reserve (*Being and Time,* 219). However, despite the forms in which solicitude is manifested in average everydayness, "[i]n clarifying Being-in-the-world we have shown that a bare subject without a world never 'is' proximally, nor is it ever given. And so in the end an isolated 'I' without Others is just as far from being proximally given" (152).

The phenomenological examination of average everydayness, then, provides an account in which relationality is prior and primary and in which existence is coexistence in its ontological sense. The analysis of Dasein as Being-with goes beyond notions of intersubjectivity, with their basis on *empathetic* relations with Others, because "[o]nly those who cut the I off from the Other must latch onto 'empathy' as that act that is supposed to instate the initially absent bond between I and the Other."[63] Being-there is Being-with, Heidegger claims, to the extent that others "are rather those from whom, for the most part, one does not distinguish oneself—those among whom one is too" (*Being and Time,* 154). Walter A. Davis concurs when he writes of the fundamental relationship with the other: "When the other comes before us it is not to meet an already formed subject which may or may not choose to enter into relationships from which it can always subsequently detach itself. Relationships have 'always already' begun." Dasein's constitution is structured by the other: "Being with and like the others, we are one with the comforts of the commonplace, the already thought, which is not outside us but within, already at work producing an 'identity' which is prior to all subjectivity."[64]

### The Manifestation of Being-with as the "They"

It is not only important to examine "withness" as an attribute of human existence; it is equally significant, as it was for Heidegger, to ask how this existential structure of Being-with manifests itself. According to the analysis of average everydayness in *Being and Time,* Being-with manifests itself in the phenomenon of *das Man,* which has been rather misleadingly translated as the "they," although one cannot assume that Dasein is distinct from the "they" on the basis of this translation. The "they," or the "one," as it is also sometimes referred to, is part of Dasein's constitution. Dasein belongs to others "who proximally and for the most part *'are there'* in everyday Being-with-one-another" (*Being and Time,* 164; emphasis in original). "The 'they,' . . . which we all are, though not as the sum, prescribes the kind of Being of everydayness," notes Heidegger; as the "they," others are not distinct in average everydayness; rather, "any Other can represent them" (164).

To suggest that the "they" prescribes the Being of everydayness is to provide a particular answer to the question "who is Dasein?": the who of Dasein is not the "I" but the "they." This answer asserts the priority and primacy of the others for Dasein in its constitution as Being-in-the-world. As Davis explains, "The 'they' is primary. *We* don't fall into it from a prior self-presence, but are in it and delivered over to it long before any question of independence arises."[65] What does this response to the question of "who" in the form of the "they" signify, however? The "they," it can be argued, rescinds any priority of the self and affirms the primacy of sociality and relationality found in the first three elements of the optics of coexistence:

> We live in the midst of others with their beliefs and values, fears and conflicts already so deeply embedded in us that the initial experience of reflection is the shock of discovering how utterly the voice of the other comes pouring forth whenever I, the sovereign individual, speak, feel, think, or act.[66]

There are two related arguments contained within Heidegger's examination of Dasein's indistinguishability from others in the form of the "they." First, the suggestion that the "they," rather than the "I," may be the answer to "who" is everyday Dasein, an answer that attests to Dasein's immersion in the world with others. Averageness has a norm-creating function. When the "they" is understood to establish and maintain averageness and to contain the whole of shared practices, it can be seen to constitute "one shared world rather than a plurality of individual worlds"; to point, moreover, to the norm-creating role of "withness," which Dreyfus has long called "constitutive conformity."[67] As Herman Philipse also notes, the "they" "is a fundamental structure of everyday life that is constitutive of the cultural public world," and it is, moreover, "the mode of Being in which we live 'proximally and most of the time.'"[68] The notion of constitutive conformity illuminates that Dasein "requires for its Being-in-the-world an expected and normal way of referring to and dealing with others. In this sense the 'I-myself' exists, in significant part, in its conformity to the 'one' or 'anybody' or 'they,' and it shares . . . a commonality of significance," suggests Howard

Tuttle.[69] Heidegger's problematization of the subject's purported autonomy through the designation of the "they" as Dasein's everyday self, therefore, appears to be "the last nail in the coffin of the Cartesian tradition."[70]

Second, Heidegger's discussion of the "they" also contains what appear to be "negative connotations," in order to establish that "our habitual and social self, which is structured by public rules, norms, and roles . . . is not our real or authentic self."[71] What conceptions do we hold of our habitual selves in modernity? As chapters 1 and 2 discussed extensively, post-Cartesian thought assumes that in modernity one's "habitual self" is the sovereign, knowing, and self-sufficient subject. In other words, when Heidegger suggests that our habitual self is not our authentic self, he is referring to the publicly held self-understanding of Dasein as an autonomous and distinct subject, an individualist conception of the self that flourishes within the discourses of the "they," but also within philosophy and the human sciences. When Heidegger claims that average everydayness is an "inauthentic" mode of being that must be called into question, he is referring to the ways in which Dasein understands itself as a sovereign and self-sufficient subject. He thus views the shared world as the place of self-dispersal, where one compares himself to others and where "there is constant care as to the way one differs from them" (*Being and Time*, 163). Whether Dasein feels that it is lagging behind, whether it wants to maintain a certain superiority, Dasein's "Being-with-one-another has the character of distantiality [*Abständingkeit*]" (164).

Yet, distantiality is only possible because "Dasein, as everyday Being-with-one-another, stands in *subjection* to Others. It itself *is* not; its Being has been taken away by the Others" (*Being and Time*, 164; emphases in original). This happens precisely because Dasein belongs to the Others, to "the one" and "enhances their power" so that Dasein is "the one" initially and primarily (164).[72] But in designating them as "the Others," Dasein hides this *fact* of belonging to them. Dasein belongs to "the One" to such an extent that

> Being-with-one-another dissolves one's own Dasein completely into the kind of Being of "the Others," in such a way, indeed, that the others, as distinguishable and explicit, vanish more and more. In this inconspicuousness and unascertainability, the real dictatorship of the "they" is unfolded. (164)

In the safe fold of "the one," Dasein takes its pleasures as *one* would, and considers certain things sad, as *one* would, and so comports itself in the world with entities and other Daseins as the "they" would. Heidegger argues that

> the "they" maintains itself factically in the averageness of *that which belongs to it,* of that which it regards as valid and that which it does not, and of that to which it grants success and to that which it denies it. . . . Publicness proximally controls every way in which the world and Dasein get interpreted. (165; emphasis added)

Although constitutive of the shared world, and of Dasein as the "they," for Heidegger "averageness" has a serious repercussion in that it tends toward a "leveling down" of Dasein's possibilities of Being by containing them within the parameters of average and publicly acceptable behavior. In the constant process of adjustment, Dasein "seek[s] in its everyday sense to approximate the public, positive sense of the 'anybody,'" and this renders it too hesitant "to roam too far from public use and expectation."[73] Averageness and publicness affect interpretations of the world and make it appear familiar to all. In this way, "[e]veryone is the other, and no one is himself. The "they," which supplies the answer to the question of the "who" of Dasein, is the nobody to whom every Dasein has already surrendered itself in Being-among-one-another" (166). This surrender, Heidegger argues, can be thought of as a kind of dispersal into the "they-self" such that "Dasein is the 'they'" (167).

But it is not only Dasein's possibilities that are constrained and leveled down; similarly, the other's particularity and singularity is diffused because the other becomes the anonymous nobody, an unnamed no one. Such a dispersed Dasein must be distinguished from the proper self, although the "they," this dispersed self, denotes "who" Dasein primarily is in its average everydayness.[74]

The negative connotations of Heidegger's discussion of the "they" might rightfully prompt the question: why does he shed light on the heteronomous constitution of Dasein only to immediately argue that this is "inauthentic" and call for something translators have called "authenticity"? Dreyfus claims that Heidegger confuses the two aspects of the "they," namely, "constitutive conformity" (the positive and essential norm-creating and socializing function of the "they") and unwanted social conformism. Heidegger's analysis, I suggest, endeavored to prevent the reification of the "they" as the antidote to the "I." Heidegger's description of the "they" aims not to problematize this everyday mode of being toward a recovery of the "I" but, on the contrary, to illuminate that it is *within* the norm-creating ideational resources of the "they" that notions of sovereign subjectivity have arisen and been maintained. Dasein's self can be neither the they-self nor the subject, but must be *proper* for Dasein's Being as Being-with. Being-in-the-world is constituted as radically immersed and embedded within the referential totality and as Being-with. Dasein's Being-with is ontologically manifested in the "they," from whom Dasein does not distinguish itself. Being-lost in the "they" arises from and continues Dasein's self-understanding as an autonomous and self-sufficient subject, unaware of its constitution as a heteronomous self. The negative connotations one might sense in the discussion of the "they" might well stem from Heidegger's desire to unsettle Dasein's acceptance of the public discourse of subjectivity, which is improper for Dasein and its ability to be itself as Being-with.

### Interlude: The Communal Determination of Mitsein and the Heidegger Affair

I have argued that the third element of the optics of coexistence illustrates that Dasein's "factical" coexistence is heteronomous: "the ways in which the other inhabits our being as the subtext that is constantly at work in a vast array of activities that make up the busy business of the day."[75] The "they" is constitutive of both the significance of the world and of Dasein as submitted to the world. Heidegger's discussion of the "they" as the answer to the question "who is Dasein?" also emphasizes, however, that such heteronomy, such "withness," is *not* part of Dasein's everyday self-understanding. In everydayness Dasein entertains conceptions of itself as autonomous, the discourse of autonomy and self-sufficiency being one of the discourses of publicness in liberal modernity. Becoming-proper, as examined in chapter 4, is a movement by Dasein toward a more genuine understanding of its heteronomy and of the way in which this primarily manifests itself. The movement toward an appropriation of one's heteronomy involves, it will be argued, an awareness of Dasein's ability to be itself.

The third element of the optics of coexistence is the most contentious. In part, this is due to the ambivalent interpretations of "inauthenticity" that often lead to a confusion between what Drey-fus has called the "constitutive conformity" function of the "they" and what is often taken as a conservative and dismissive critique of societal conformism in Heidegger's thought, which will be exam-ined further in chapter 4 through an examination of the intricate relation between authenticity and inauthenticity. The third element of the optics of coexistence is also contentious for another, far more serious reason. Its contention arises from the determination that Heidegger gives to Being-with in the second Division of *Being and Time,* which is customarily understood to be tied to a "people" or "community" and thought to be linked to his political involvement with and acceptance of National Socialism in the 1930s. Any in-quiry that claims that in Being-with one finds the kernels of a co-existential heteronomy that enables, along with the other elements of the optics of coexistence, both the unworking of modern sub-jectivity and, more positively, the articulation of a different under-standing of coexistence beyond the logic of composition, cannot but confront the question of how Heidegger determines Being-with in Division II, how this affects the relationship to others and otherness, and, finally, whether this points to a fundamentally fascist thought. Chapter 6 closely investigates this "communal determination" of Being-with and explicitly addresses the question of community, as well as Heidegger's politics.

Let us make two points about this, the first with Pierre Bourdieu that Heidegger's thought is of an "exceptionally polyphonic and polysemic character."[76] By this, Bourdieu did not in any way mean to excuse Heidegger's politics or to refute readings that emphasized the political implications of his thought. On the contrary, Bourdieu analyzed the ways in which Heidegger speaks in multiple registers and fields, which make difficult the drawing of direct connections between politics and philosophy. Therefore, just as the "commu-nal determination" of Being-with can be analyzed as a conservative, some would say fascist, reading of Heidegger, it is also open to a different and sometimes contrary interpretation. But one interpreta-tion is not negated by the other, nor can an authoritative position be ascertained: rather, both interpretations demand attention. As Michael Zimmerman similarly argues, Heidegger's discussion of Being-with in Division II can be read profitably without regard to their political implications, but they can and should *also* be read in terms of those implications. His thought cannot be reduced to the level of an ideological "reflex" of socio-political conditions, but on the other hand it cannot be regarded as wholly detached from such conditions.[77]

The second point arises with the question whether authorial interpretations of a text, especially ambivalent and polysemic ones, ought to be given a privileged position. Should Heidegger's own interpretations be given greater weight than those of his many readers? Can one not retrieve from Heidegger's existential discussion of Dasein as Being-with the parameters of a coexistential heteronomy that he reveals (in the sense of phenomenologically illuminating), even if he himself does not acknowledge this or may in certain contexts appear to diminish or, at worst, dismiss it? Raising these two points does not provide a definitive answer, if such an answer is at all possible; these points merely preface the discussion here in order to proceed with the fourth and final element of the optics of coexistence, while allowing a return to this concern in chapter 6 where it will be situated more appropriately within the greater analysis of coexistence and community.

Dasein is immersed in an engaged manner into its everyday world of praxis and has an ontological relationship to the web of meanings and references that is its world, in which it is essentially Being-with others, such that it cannot, ontologically, be distinguished *from* others. Collectively, the first three elements of the optics of coexistence have already fundamentally challenged the understanding of human existence as "subject" in three ways: first, they have called into question the acceptance of a primarily reflective subject that encounters other entities as merely copresent with it and toward which it has a relationship of comprehension; second, as a subject that is disembedded from and masterful of its world; and, finally, as an autonomous and self-sufficient being, distinct from others within the world. Out of these three elements of the optics of coexistence, a certain "coexistential heteronomy" has emerged that illustrates that attention to the facticity of existence denies the determination of coexistence according to the logic of composition predicated on modern subjectivity, with its resulting effacement of the self's heteronomy. On the contrary, otherness constitutes Dasein in a multiplicity of ways, seen in the ways in which available entities absorb and concern Dasein prereflectively in its everydayness; by always already providing a world of meaning, norms, rules, and practices that help Dasein orient its existence and everyday interactions and to which Dasein is already "submitted"; and, in the primary form of the "they," by making Dasein indistinguishable from the other Daseins that provide the social context that comforts Dasein while socializing it into common practices and ways of life, so that Dasein is essentially Being-with, a kind of Being made possible by the fundamental "withness" of Dasein. The fourth element of the optics of coexistence reinforces the aspects already discussed by highlighting Dasein's worldly attunement and understanding, which illuminate that the Being of Dasein is "care."

### DASEIN IS CARE: THROWNNESS, PROJECTIVENESS, FALLENNESS

The final element of the optics of coexistence is perhaps the most illuminating of Dasein's radical embeddedness in the world of publicness and otherness: this is the discussion of Dasein as care, evident in its attunement and understanding. Attunement and understanding provide a detailed account of Dasein's radical embeddedness in the public and other-generated world; their consideration illustrates, for Heidegger, the constitution of being the "there"—how Dasein is its "there" in an "everyday manner" (*Being and Time,* 171). Whereas the previous elements of the optics of coexistence were derived from an analysis of Being-in-the-world that focused mostly on the world, attunement and understanding explicate the Being-in of Dasein. These two ways of being-in are co-originary (Heidegger calls this "equiprimordial" [172]): attunement accompanies and affects understanding, while attunement "maintains itself in a certain understanding" (203); that is, attunement is meaningless without the understanding of how Dasein finds itself in the world. In Heidegger's terms, "a state-of-mind [attunement] always has its understanding, even if it merely keeps it suppressed. Understanding always has its mood" (182). This can only signify, Davis argues, that Dasein's "anxious attunement to . . . [its own existence] is the ultimate basis of any act of interpretation."[78] These interrelated aspects of embeddedness, of Being-in, show Dasein to be a radically *thrown* being, yet one that *projects* itself outward into the world.

## Attunement, Moods, and Throwness

Heidegger's term *Befindlichkeit,* which Michel Haar appropriately translates as "attunement,"[79] refers, Mulhall suggests, to "the capacity to be affected by the world, to find that the entities and situations it [Dasein] faces matter."[80] In other words, the public world, with its entities and circumstances, matters to Dasein because Dasein, contrary to the discourse of the modern subject standing in mastery over the world, is already submitted to the world. Heidegger calls this radical attunement Dasein's "throwness," and it is, perhaps, best illustrated by the phenomenon of moods.

Moods are often portrayed as mental states, but, Mulhall explains, they are more appropriately considered to be "affective inflections of Dasein's temperament that are typically experienced as 'given,' as states into which one has been thrown."[81] These dispositions make it evident that what goes on around Dasein affects it. Dasein's moods disclose that it is fundamentally attuned to the "world" (both as surrounding world, *Umwelt,* and as with-world, *Mitwelt*) as a being thrown into the world of activity and of others and that it is in such a state of throwness without being explicitly aware of it. To understand moods in this way is to deny that they are individual mental states and to regard them instead as social, as a product of publicness, by which Dasein is affected. The phrase "public mood" is used often to describe how "membership of a group might, for example, lead to [Dasein] being thrown into a mood that grips that group, finding herself immersed in its melancholy or hysteria."[82] Heidegger suggests, moreover, that moods are necessary for publicness: "Publicness, as the kind of Being which belongs to the 'they,' not only has in general its own ways of having a mood, but needs moods and 'makes' them for itself" (*Being and Time,* 178). The social aspect of moods also "implies that an individual's social world fixes the range of moods into which she can be thrown."[83]

Moods are interesting to look at here because they are indicative of Dasein's fundamental attunement to its public and other-created world. This chapter has already looked at the world as a totality of sense, assignments, and relations, already laid out in advance of, and indeed enabling, Dasein's activity and interactions with entities and things. Dasein's attunement, of which moods are the best example, signifies "a disclosive submission to the world, out of which we can encounter something that matters to us" (*Being and Time,* 177). Moods disclose Dasein to itself "prior to all cognition and volition, and beyond their range of disclosure" (175) because what they ultimately reveal is Dasein as the kind of entity for whose own Being is an issue (180). Specifically, moods show Dasein to be that entity that is "Being-delivered-over to the 'there'": that Dasein *is* means that it is "thrown in such a way that, as Being-in-the-world, it is its 'there'" (174). The ease with which bad moods, in particular, are recognized by Dasein is related to its being a thrown entity. Moods "disclose Dasein in its thrownness, and—proximally and for the most part— in the manner of an evasive turning-away" (175). Yet, the disclosure of such fundamental attunement to the world and to others can also be seen as the "existential kind of Being in which Dasein constantly surrenders itself to the 'world' and lets the 'world' 'matter' to it in a way that somehow Dasein evades its very self" (178). The everyday manifestation of Dasein's witness in the "they," where Dasein is indistinguishable from others, led Heidegger to argue that Dasein is lost in its everydayness, and this "lostness" is sustained by this publicness of moods. Moods, therefore, disclose Dasein as a thrown being and, simultaneously, affect how Dasein comports itself to its world, whether in relation to other entities or to possibilities about its life.

### Understanding and Projection

Being-in the world in this radically attuned manner also affects Dasein's understanding. This means that attunement and moods radically shape Dasein's understanding of the world and situations within the world: "The world does not exist neutrally, or as a clear and distinct object. Instead the world must always remain an object of possible interpretation."[84] Beyond this, however, Heidegger examined understanding as constitutive for Dasein's Being-in. As Heidegger suggests, "understanding something" usually refers "to being able to manage something, being a match for it, being competent to do something" (*Being and Time,* 183). However, when understanding is constitutive of how Dasein is "in" the world, how it is the "there," this competence "is not a 'what,' but Being as existing": Dasein is not merely competent for this or that task, rather "it is primarily Being-possible. Dasein is in every case what it can be, and in the way in which it is its possibility" (183). But what is the meaning of "possibility" here? It does not mean merely something that has yet to take place, that is not actual but "merely possible" (183). Understood as an existential attribute, possibility is the most proximate and appropriate characterization of Dasein and its ability to be *(Seinskönnen)* (183). In other words, "Dasein's true existential medium is not actuality but possibility."[85] Understanding, Heidegger suggests, "must be conceived primarily as Dasein's potentiality-for-Being [ability to be]" (210), and this ability to be belongs to its facticity (185).

Where attunement "reveal[s] Dasein as thrown Being-in-the-world, understanding reveals it as carrying forward that momentum"[86] and as "press[ing] forward into possibilities" *(Being and Time,* 184). Tuttle suggests that this means that "human existence is open to the future in such a way that it casts a tendential structure ahead of itself as part of its Being. This structure is Dasein's apprehension of its own possibilities."[87] Understanding, therefore, "corresponds to the active side of Dasein's confrontation with its own existentiell possibilities."[88] As Being-in-the-world, Dasein is faced with concrete possibilities that are defined and "limited" by the factical situation in which it finds itself thrown. The forward-pressing structure of Dasein's understanding, however, shows that, as thrown, Dasein projects itself "onto one or other existentiell possibility."[89] Heidegger notes that "[a]s thrown, Dasein is thrown into the kind of Being which we call 'projecting,'" indeed, Dasein has *"already* projected itself; and as long as it is, it is projecting" (185; emphasis added). "As understanding, Dasein projects its Being upon possibilities" (188).

Dasein's "attunement" and "understanding," therefore, are constitutive of how it is the "there." Their examination reveals, for the purposes of explicating the fourth element of the optics of coexistence, a radical emdeddedness in the world, which can be best understood as "thrown projection": "Just as thrownness is projective (disclosing the world as a space of possibilities that matter to us in specific ways), so projection is thrown (to be exercised in a field of possibilities whose structure it did not itself project)."[90] Hence, Dasein's Being must be understood as *"ahead-of-itself-in-already-being-in-a-world"* *(Being and Time,* 236; emphasis in original).

Thrownness and projection form one ontological structure that signifies Dasein's radical embeddedness, how it is its "there," as both taking place within the bounds of the world and also taking up concrete possibilities within it. However, given that in average every-dayness Dasein is manifested as the "they," how does this affect its attunement and understanding? Stated otherwise, Dasein's radical embeddedness in the world, its thrown projection, must be analyzed within the "phenomenal horizon" of everydayness (*Being and Time*, 210). To assess how thrown projection occurs in everydayness, Heidegger therefore examines certain "definite phenomena" that "characterize the way in which, in an everyday manner, Dasein is its 'there'" (219). These phenomena are "idle talk," "ambiguity," and "curiosity," and together they reveal that there is a "basic kind of Being which belongs to everydayness," which Heidegger calls the "*falling*' of Dasein" (219; emphasis in original). Idle talk, ambiguity, and curiosity, then, are interconnected phenomena indicative of fallenness, which together with thrownness and projectiveness, "reveals the essential unity of Dasein's Being to be what Heidegger calls *care* ('Sorge')."[91] Although the terms appear pejorative, they are "far removed from any moralizing critique of everyday Dasein" because they are positive phenomena whose analysis illuminates fallenness (211).

### "Falling Prey" to the World

"Idle talk" refers to the type of everyday understanding and interpreting that lies in the ready significance present in casual, customary expressions, which make claims about this thing or that, but primarily focus on the claim and not on the thing itself. As such, idle talk "does not communicate in such a way as to let this entity be appropriated in a primordial manner, but communicates rather by following the route of *gossiping* and *passing the word along*" (*Being and Time*, 212; emphases in original). Expressions of idle talk "are a way of preventing an honest search for what is real, while at the same time asserting some definiteness,"[92] because "[w]hat is said-in-the-talk as such, spreads in wider circles and takes on an authoritative character" (212). This kind of average intelligibility, however, does not wish to draw a distinction between what might be gossip and what might be an appropriate way of disclosing this or that being. On the contrary, saying something in idle talk "gets passed along in further retelling" and "amounts to perverting the act of disclosing [*Erschliessen*] into an act of *closing off [Verschiessen]*" (213;

emphasis added). When Dasein "closes off," it distorts its proper relationship to "its primary and primordially genuine relationships-of-Being towards the world, towards Being-with, and towards its very Being-in" (214).

Curiosity, moreover, "expresses the tendency toward a peculiar way of letting the world be encountered by us in perception" (214). This tendency shows Dasein to be floating away "from what is ready-to-hand and toward the exotic, the alien and the distant," by searching for new and unknown "objects not in order to grasp them in their reality but to stimulate itself with their newness, so that novelty is sought with increasing velocity."[93] Dasein acquires a spectator's attitude toward the world, but this is concerned less with marveling at things than with "abandoning itself to the world" (216). Comporting itself curiously toward the world, Dasein "remains in a state of concealed indifference; it seems observational yet is neutral in its relation to the world. In its search for distraction and novelty, it is blind to the actuality in front of it."[94] The effects of both idle talk and curiosity make it "impossible to decide what is disclosed in a genuine understanding and what is not" (217).

Finally, in addition to idle talk and curiosity, ambiguity affects not only Dasein's understanding of the world but also its relations to "Being-with-one another as such, and even to Dasein's Being toward itself" (*Being and Time*, 217). "Dasein here sees the world as theory and abstraction, while remaining neutral and passive," explains Tuttle regarding ambiguity.[95] This, however, is "manufactured indifference or theoreticality," which nonetheless "has already established itself in the understanding as a potentiality-for-Being, and in the way Dasein projects itself and presents itself with possibilities" (217). It is important to note that in the ambiguity of how things are interpreted in publicness, Dasein relates to the other on the basis of "what 'they' have heard about him, what 'they' say in their talk about him, and 'they' know about him" (219). There is no effort to comport oneself to the other in ways that might be genuine. Rather, there occurs an "intent watching of one another, a secret and reciprocal listening-in. Under the mask of 'for-one-another,' an 'against-one-another' is in play" (219).

Idle talk, curiosity, and ambiguity are the ways in which the "they," Dasein's ontological manifestation in everydayness, is "the there":

> Idle talk discloses to Dasein a Being towards its world, towards Others, and towards itself—a Being in which these are understood, but in a mode of groundless floating. Curiosity discloses everything and anything, yet in such a way that Being-in is everywhere and nowhere. Ambiguity hides nothing from Dasein's understanding, but only in order that Being-in-the-world should be suppressed in this uprooted "everywhere and nowhere." (*Being and Time*, 221)

These phenomena falsely guide Dasein into thinking that "the possibilities of its Being will be secure, genuine and full" (222). As noted above, they make up the Being of everydayness, which Heidegger calls fallenness, best understood as "falling prey" (219). But again, this ought not to be understood as a disparaging description that implies that Dasein falls "from a purer and higher 'primal status'" or that Dasein becomes *mere facticity;* rather, Dasein falls *into* the world, "which itself belongs to its Being," that is, to which it has an ontological relationship (220). "Falling prey to the 'world' means being absorbed in being-with-another as it is guided by idle talk, curiosity, and ambiguity."[96] If Dasein is an entity thrown into a world, dominated by ways of being-in which are given to it, rather than adapted to it as *that* particular Dasein that it is, then the aforementioned dispersal of its self into the "they" is what occurs initially and primarily for Dasein.

Therefore, fallenness ought not to be portrayed negatively, as though it indicated a less than optimal situation, because this is not the status of the discussion of falling:

> A set of limits can only be thought of as limitations if there exists a possible mode of existence to which those limits do not apply. Since that is not the case, the inherent worldliness of human existence must be thought of as an aspect of the human condition. It is a condition of human life, not a constraint upon it.[97]

This absorption, although initial and primary, accounts for Dasein being-lost, being something other than its proper self, a self that is its proper ability-to-be (potentiality-for-Being). Dasein is an entity thrown into the world, whose norms and practices are not of its own making and "which it did not itself fully choose or determine."[98] In everydayness, this means that it acts, thinks, and feels as *anyone* would; it is, in other words, other-directed and self-dispersed and this affects its understanding of its possibilities and its ability to be.

As Mulhall notes, the prominent characteristic of self-dispersal in everydayness is that Dasein has no awareness of its fallenness, that is, no conception of itself *as* lost.[99] Dasein believes in the fiction of sovereign subjectivity with its assumptions of self-sufficiency and separateness, and comes to view its relationality to others as voluntary.

Dasein begins to become aware of itself as a thrown and fallen entity through anxiety, which is a particular kind of affect. Unlike fear, with which it is often misleadingly confused, anxiety does not arise from the perception of an external entity. Rather, it "plunges Dasein into an anxiety about itself in the face of itself" and reveals Dasein's "existence as essentially thrown projection" into the world, and "its everyday mode of existence as fallen."[100] What Dasein is anxious about is no one but itself: "In anxiety, Dasein is anxious about itself: not about some concrete existentiell possibility, but about the fact that its Being is Being-possible, that its existence necessarily involves projecting itself upon one or other possibility."[101] Georgopoulos also indicates that through anxiety, "attention for the first time . . . is focused on Dasein *as* Dasein" (Being-the-there), thrown, projected, and fallen. As such, Dasein's Being has a three-fold structure, which Heidegger called "care" *(Sorge)*.[102]

In sum, the final element of the optics of coexistence is the disclosure of Dasein as "care." The three elements of the care structure are *thrownness,* as seen in Dasein's attunement, which reveals that the world and other Dasein matter to it; *projectiveness,* as seen through its capacity for understanding itself as futural and possible; and finally, *fallenness,* seen in its being-guided by idle talk, curiosity, and ambiguity, which shows it to have "fallen prey" to the everyday world.[103] The phenomenological description of the three aspects of "care" grasp Dasein's comportment more effectively "than do the categories of 'rational animal,'"[104] contests J. Glenn Gray. These three "belong together," John McCumber suggests, and cannot "be reduced to the others either, and there is no yet more basic unity to bring them together."[105] Care, used here to illuminate the radically embedded way in which heteronomous Dasein is "in" the world, is above all "the unifying origin of the various limits that characterize Dasein's distinctive mode of existence."[106] As the fourth element of the optics of coexistence, "care" serves to reinforce the other three elements, of engaged immersion, of the ontological relationship to the world and of Being-with, by providing the unifying context of embeddedness in the form of thrownness, projectiviness, and fallenness.

## CONCLUSION

Recalling the analyses in the introduction and the first and second chapters, post-Cartesian subjectivity allows the conceptualization of entities as indivisible units.[107] This assumed indivisibility has historically enabled modern political theory to reduce coexistence to the condition of staying-together, requiring an event of union, described astutely by Jürgen Habermas as a "physics of sociation."[108] The implicit assumptions made about coexistence within international relations, too, can be said to be predicated on such subjectivist ontological premises. Coexistence becomes understood as a state that involves composition of subjects with characteristics not amenable to coexistence; the nonrelational and self-sufficient presuppositions about the self as subject render coexistence a tentative and uncertain, though sought-after, condition.

Thus far, the investigation of the optics of coexistence has shown Dasein to be heteronomously constituted, a conception that unworks the reflective, nonrelational, and self-sufficient features of modern subjectivity in the following ways. First, Dasein initially and primarily finds itself immersed in its dealings with the world. Understanding the primary mode of Dasein to be engaged immersion challenges the assumption that reflection and knowing are the definitive modes of human relationality toward entities and the world. Second, Dasein's disclosive character reveals a conception of the world as a background web of meanings against which existence makes sense of itself prereflectively and as a totality of assignments and relations with available things and other beings. This totality is not solely authored or created by Dasein; rather, the practices, norms, and rules that help Dasein cope with its involvements in the world are structured by otherness and already given to it in advance of its involvement. Generally, any access that Dasein has to "itself" is ontologically mediated through otherness. Third, Dasein can be said to be essentially Being-with—withness is an attribute of the kind of being that it is. For Dasein, existence is already coexistence, Being-there is always Being-with. Selfhood is coexistential but this is far from identical to composition or copresence assumed of the completed and autonomous subject of modernity. Withness, furthermore, manifests itself in such a way that, for the most part, in its everydayness Dasein cannot be distinguished from others.

Finally, Dasein is fundamentally attuned to the world and its understanding of itself, and the surrounding world is affected by this attunement. Its attunement illuminates a radical embeddedness that is best described as being-*thrown* into the world, but at the same time its understanding of itself as "possibility" indicates that it also projects itself on possibilities and toward the future. Dasein's embeddedness has the structure of *thrown projection*. The world, and others, *matter* to Dasein: Dasein's attunement is evident in its disposition for moods, from the structure of its understanding, and in its use of language or discourse. In everydayness, the world matters to such an overwhelming extent that Dasein can be said to have fallen prey to the world. Fallenness, thrownness, and projectiveness together suggest that, rather than self-presence and self-sufficiency, Dasein's Being is better understood as *care*.

In the course of its everyday comportments, Dasein's *heteronomy* is manifested in its being other-directed, although Dasein itself is unaware of this and considers itself to be both self-sufficient and autonomous. For the analysis here, Dasein is inauthentic when it is not aware of its heteronomous constitution and its immersion into the "they"; it behaves *as subject,* meaning the autonomous and sovereign subject of mastery. This flight from its heteronomy might be inauthentic for the kind of being that it is, but it is the primary and initial mode in which it is found in everydayness. Inauthenticity is constitutive for Dasein's Being and expresses the primacy of otherness in its existence. Therefore, although the optics of coexistence illustrates the ways in which human existence is coexistentially heteronomous, they do not explain how it becomes aware of this heteronomy. The ontological submission to the world, which the four elements of the optics of coexistence bring to the fore, is manifested in Dasein losing sight of its own ability to be and projecting itself onto possibilities that are not proper for it. When Dasein "falls" into the world, it comports itself in public and average terms, maintaining a self-understanding, which is not proper for a coexistentially heteronomous, fundamentally worldly being.

Becoming its proper self, then, could be thought of as a process of recognizing itself as "already" being-radically-in-relation. Becoming-proper would require that Dasein begin to grasp its heteronomy as the primacy of relation by challenging the discourses of autonomy to which it conforms. Whereas inauthenticity means that Dasein lives its life according to average understandings, unaware of its proper ability to be, in becoming-proper Dasein would open itself up to its self as a heteronomous being characterized by anxiety and care for its Being. The process of becoming-proper, which is the focus of the next chapter, is reinterpreted not as the discovery of some true inner self but rather as the process of relinquishing notions of self-sufficiency and of being resolute toward its coexistential heteronomy. Becoming-proper involves an awareness of its own ability to be a primarily heteronomous entity, whose very Being-there is Being-with and whose world matters to it.

With these four elements, coexistence is revealed as the proximal fact of Dasein's existence. The optics of coexistence offers an account of primary sociality that disrupts the predominance of the nonrelational subject and reveals instead the constitutive role of the other *(heteron)*. Heidegger's phenomenological analysis of Dasein offers a refutation of the subjectivist presuppositions of modern philosophy and human sciences, whose reliance on this assumption leads to the reduction of coexistence to composition. This chapter, in pointing to the optics of coexistence in Heidegger's existential analytic, illustrated the permeating and constitutive role of otherness for Dasein by examining how Dasein is a disclosive being absorbed and fascinated by its relations with other entities, how Dasein is essentially Being-with, and also how otherness structures Dasein's world as well as its attunement and understanding. The discussion of otherness often relied on associated terms such as "averageness" and "publicness." For some the frequent use of "otherness" as opposed to a concrete other might appear insufficiently positive or edifying. Yet, the discussion reads in the self's facticity the undeniable role of otherness and of others in the constitution of the self, a role so pervasive that it questions the taken-for-granted equivalence of self and "I."

This disclosure of Dasein as coexistentially heteronomous and radically embedded in the world renders unstable the terms of sub-

jectivist discourse and has important ramifications for conceptualizing coexistence, beyond the logic of composition, as a question-
worthy issue of global politics. Such conceptualization is examined
further in chapters 5 and 6 after the discussion of becoming-proper
in chapter 4.

# 4

## Becoming-Proper: Authenticity and Inauthenticity Revisited

In the previous chapter I outlined Heidegger's analysis of the existential structures of Dasein in *Being and Time*[1] and suggested that the existential analytic contains a number of elements, grouped together as an "optics of coexistence," which reveal that coexistence is the proximal fact of Dasein's existence. These elements both "unwork" modern subjectivity by challenging its most prominent features and also advance a substantively different account of the self with which to rethink coexistence within politics and international relations.

Specifically, the elements contained in the optics of coexistence exemplify a coexistential heteronomy in a variety of ways: first, in Dasein's mode of "engaged immersion," in which it uses things prereflectively as it copes with its dealings in the world. Second, Dasein's existence exhibits this heteronomy in the ontological relationship it has to the "world," understood as a totality of references, assignments, and meanings that it has not authored and by which it makes sense of itself and its activities. Dasein copes with its everyday going-about-its-business "plugged into" this relational totality, which forms the background of its life. Third, Dasein's heteronomy is evident in its prior capacity for "withness." Dasein is Being-with to the extent that in its everydayness it cannot be distinguished from others. This Being-with, moreover, ought not to be understood as the "with" that unites distinct and self-sufficient subjects but rather as a constitutive existential structure of Dasein. And finally, Dasein's heteronomy can be seen in the way in which it is a being *thrown* into the world and which understands its existence as possibility. Dasein's modes of being-in the world, namely, its attunement and understanding, reveal that Dasein's "factical life is disturbed by everyday concerns," that its world, in other words, matters to it.[2] It is attuned to the world, and its self-understanding is always already affected by this attunement. When Dasein is indistinguishable from others, its "there" is manifested in language in terms of idle talk, curiosity, and ambiguity, such that the Being of this everyday self is "falling." Heidegger regarded the fallenness of Dasein as the very Being of everydayness, the initial and primary way that Dasein is "in" the world.

However, as an everyday public self indistinguishable from others (for which the ambiguous term "they" is used, though it must be remembered that in everydayness Dasein *is* the "they"), Dasein is not able to have a proper understanding of itself. Without an appropriate understanding of its Being as coexistentially heteronomous, Dasein cannot project itself onto possibilities that make the most of its ability to be *(Seinskönnen)*. The ontological submission to the world that the four elements of the optics of coexistence have brought to the fore also indicates that Dasein has no awareness of its own ability to be and projects itself onto possibilities that are, for the most part, publicly decided for it by the "they-self."[3] Its self-understanding is determined by the public discourses of "sovereign subjectivity," which lead it to regard itself as self-sufficient and autonomous. When Dasein "falls prey" to the world, it comports itself in average terms that are not proper for its Being as a coexistentially heteronomous and fundamentally worldly entity.

Therefore, the optics of coexistence discussed in chapter 3 illustrated the ways in which human existence is coexistentially heteronomous but did not delineate the process by which Dasein *becomes aware* of its heteronomy or how it takes it up in the unfolding of its existence. The purpose of the present chapter is to discuss precisely this process by examining what has been somewhat misleadingly called authenticity. Here, "authenticity" refers to the process of "becoming-proper," a term offered as a more suitable alternative for capturing Dasein's traversing toward a proper intelligibility of itself as a heteronomously constituted and fundamentally coexistential being. As a process, becoming-proper involves a recovery of its dispersed being as a "self." I argue here that authenticity is only a *modification* of the average, Heidegger would say inauthentic, way in which Dasein relates to its coexistential heteronomy in its everydayness. Understanding authenticity in this way does not mean the discovery or recovery of some true inner and solipsistic self but rather advances a conception of becoming-proper as Dasein's process of relinquishing notions of self-sufficiency and becoming resolute toward its coexistential heteronomy. This process of modification enables Dasein to improve its self-intelligibility by gaining an awareness of its own ability to be as a primarily heteronomous entity, whose very Being-there is Being-with, and whose world matters to it.

Inauthenticity, I noted in the previous chapter, meant that Dasein has no conception of itself *as* lost:[4] it is oblivious, in other words, both to its heteronomy, how it is constituted through and through by otherness, and also how it is dispersed in the "they." In denying its other-constituted and other-mediated existence, Dasein comports itself in the world *as if it were* a sovereign subject, believing in the fiction of autonomy, self-sufficiency, and separateness and viewing its relationality to others as voluntary. How can Dasein reach a genuine understanding of itself and of its possibilities, not as subject but rather on the basis of its Being as "care"? How can it reach an understanding of itself as "already" being-radically-in-relation and recognize this primacy of otherness for its Being? Anxiety, it was noted briefly in chapter 3, brings Dasein back from its falling and "makes manifest to it that authenticity and inauthenticity are possibilities of its Being" (*Being and Time*, 235). In this way, anxiety can be said to individualize Dasein by making evident the way it is lost in the "they" and by signaling that Dasein's Being is an issue for it. Anxiety in itself, however, does not provide the means through which Dasein can break through its dispersal and view its existence as a whole self, as care. Ontologically, this recovery occurs through Dasein's understanding of itself as a finite being, what Heidegger called "Being-towards-death," an exposition of which is given in the next section. This is followed by a discussion of how the modification of inauthenticity affects Dasein's radically heteronomous embeddedness and addresses four specific concerns and objections raised about the notions of Being-towards-death, authenticity, and related concepts such as resoluteness, resulting in a rethinking of the process of becoming-proper itself. The chapter concludes with an examination of the dialogic relation between authenticity and inauthenticity.

## BECOMING-WHOLE: "BEING-TOWARDS-DEATH"

Dasein does not regard itself as whole while lost in the "they"; it is self-dispersed and "insofar as it exists, it is oriented toward the next moment of its existence."[5] In order to be able to recover an understanding of its ability to be as a radically thrown being and to project itself onto proper possibilities for the kind of being that it is, Dasein must grasp itself in all the elements of its care-structure. How, though, can Dasein see itself as a whole self when, at the end of its life, Dasein is no longer able to look at itself as a whole, just as its life has reached its end and can be fully grasped?

According to Heidegger, death brings Dasein to its end and makes it complete, but this completion cannot be grasped, since Dasein does not experience its own death. Although Dasein can witness another's death, this is not tantamount to grasping someone else's life *as a whole*. The other's death is an event that Dasein may find shocking, sad, or frightening but, as an occurrence, it does not afford the outlook of totality that might redress Dasein's understanding of itself beyond self-dispersion. Jacques Derrida notes, "[N]othing is more substitutable and yet nothing is less so than the syntagm 'my death'"; that is because "[e]veryone's death, the death of all those who can say 'death,' is irreplaceable."[6] The inability of Dasein to examine itself as a whole, just when it is "completed," indicates that death is obscured as an issue for Dasein. In everydayness Dasein's being-towards-death is never given proper consideration despite being constantly referred to in gossip and idle talk. Heidegger explains, "death is 'known' as a mishap which is constantly occurring" (*Being and Time,* 296). The everyday reference to death and its designation as a well-known occurrence renders it inconspicuous. Its everyday interpretation as something that will eventually occur to everyone results in postponing an examination of death as something worth pondering: in the present "it has nothing to do with us" (297). "They say, 'Death is certain'; and in saying so, they implant in Dasein the illusion that it is *itself* certain of its death" (301; emphasis in original). In this way, "[t]he 'they' provides a *constant tranquillization about death*" (298; emphasis in original) by making Dasein believe that it has already confronted its own finitude when all it has done is to have evaded such confrontation.

By revoking the everyday understanding of death as a biological act, Heidegger showed that finitude is not merely the physical end or limit of Dasein. It "impends at every moment of Dasein's life" and this has nothing to do with the progression of age.[7] Death is a possibility that cannot be *surpassed,* no matter how young or old Dasein might be presently. When Dasein is forced to consider what its *own* death means for it, it realizes that death is nothing but the possibility of its impossibility (294). Since the other's death cannot afford Dasein this perspective, nor can it unburden Dasein of its own death, it can be said that death is Dasein's ownmost possibility. Once Dasein anticipates its own death, its finitude ceases to hold it in morbid fascination or condemn it to melancholy. Anticipation of its death, readiness for finitude, makes Dasein ready for anxiety; it is in this *anticipatory* sense that Dasein can be said to be "Being-towards-death." Finitude is, therefore, Dasein's ownmost possibility, and as such, it is *unsurpassable* no matter how the "they" try to mitigate against the proper anticipation of death through comforting idle talk. Moreover, facing the possibility of one's death leads Dasein to realize that, despite its fundamental relationality and its embeddedness in its world, death is "a non-relational possibility."[8] Dasein cannot, in other words, share it with others as one would a burden. To this extent, Heidegger argues that "death lays claim to it as an individual Dasein. The non-relational character of death, as understood in anticipation, individualizes Dasein down to itself" (308). Thus, taking the three defining characteristics of finitude: it is "that *possibility which is one's ownmost, which is non-relational, and which is not to be outstripped [surpassed]*" (294; emphasis in original).[9]

There are several significant implications of such an understanding of Being-towards-death for Dasein's existence. When death is grasped as Dasein's *ownmost* possibility, Stephen Mulhall argues, it is accompanied by the realization that its Being is an issue for it. Dasein's existence matters to it, not in its disparate moments but as a whole; it is as a whole that Dasein must question how it wants to live its life, and it is for the whole of its life that it must take responsibility. Taking responsibility for one's life as a whole, furthermore, involves an acceptance that, for the greater part of its existence, Dasein has relinquished responsibility to others and has allowed itself to be drawn into customary practices and ways of living that it had not critically appraised and chosen for itself. When Dasein conceives of its death as a *nonrelational* possibility, moreover, it realizes that the publicly held opinions by which it had oriented and ordered its life, the discourses of idle talk in which it drowned its anxiety, and the curious and ambiguous involvement with available things "are ultimately inessential to the task of being authentically itself"; finally, the impossibility of *surpassing* or avoiding death shows Dasein that its existence is "ultimately to be given up or annihilated, and is utterly contingent, and in no way necessary; from which it follows that every existentiell possibility which makes up that utterly contingent life is itself contingent."[10] Mortality enhances the fact that Dasein has to choose one life to live and, at the same time, forego other possibilities; hence, death elucidates that only Dasein can be responsible for the specific projection it chooses. The radical contingency of Dasein's existence reveals it to be finite and not grounded in certainty, and yet it must project itself, it must cast itself forward onto a concrete possibility. Becoming-proper can begin to be understood, then, as "a projection upon an existentiell possibility in the light of itself as mortal."[11]

## The Call of Conscience

It should then be ontologically possible to grasp Dasein's existence as a whole by invoking a confrontation with one's own finitude. How could such a confrontation come about in the course of everyday life? Since the roots of the existential analytic are found in the lived experiences of Dasein (*Being and Time*, 34), what sort of experience can actually lead Dasein to recover its dispersed self and to view itself as a whole? Heidegger suggests that the phenomenon of "the call of conscience" performs precisely this task of rousing Dasein out of its "lostness" in the "they" and bringing about a consideration of itself as a contingent, yet whole, entity. The phenomenon of the voice of conscience, speaking to human beings from within, had been historically discussed in spiritual, mystical, religious, and moral terms. Heidegger, however, wished to see whether the voice of conscience could be seen as a *call* to Dasein's ownmost ability to be, without becoming reduced to an aspect of spirituality or morality. In order for the call of conscience to be effective in this sense, it must not be similar to the kind of discourse in which Dasein participates in the folds of the "they." It must not voice the things Dasein wants to hear, as with idle talk, nor should it fuel Dasein's curiosity about everyday activities and events. Heidegger maintains that the call of conscience cannot, furthermore, contain a specific directive toward particular possibilities or encouragement for Dasein to follow this or that way of life. Rather the call of conscience "has the character of an *appeal* to Dasein by calling it to its ownmost potentiality-for-Being-its-Self [ability to be]" (314; emphasis in original). "'[N]othing' gets called to this Self," Heidegger writes, pointing to the call's lack of positive content; the call appeals to Dasein's self that is lost in the "they-self" (318).

It is important to ask, moreover, *whose* voice might call Dasein to itself. Heidegger suggests that the call comes from within Dasein and yet from *beyond* it; the voice of conscience itself does the calling. It would appear that the call of conscience is ontologically possible for Dasein only because the Being of Dasein is care. Yet, this apparent indeterminacy of the identity of the caller "does not justify seeking the caller in some entity with a character other than that of Dasein" (321). The caller could not be a being that does not have Dasein's coexistential heteronomy because, Mulhall argues, the

> passive aspect of the voice of conscience suggests that it relates to Dasein's thrownness—that the voice of conscience is somehow expressive of the fact that Dasein is always already delivered over to the task of existing, placed in a particular situation it did not choose to occupy, but from which it must nevertheless choose how to go on with its life.[12]

The primary reason for the prevalent understanding of the call of conscience in religious or moral terms lies with the nature of the call, which often appears to accuse Dasein, to address it as guilty, and to call it to accept responsibility. Dasein's everyday comportment in the world, however, does not make it guilty according to a body of law or a certain moral code. The discussion of guilt and conscience, therefore, should be understood not in a moral but rather in an ontological sense. In fact, Heidegger notes, "'*Being-guilty*' . . . is a kind of Being which belongs to Dasein" (328). Dasein can be seen as Being-guilty because it is responsible for a lack, not as something present-at-hand that ought to be there but is not, but nevertheless as something which has the "not" as its basis. "This 'not' belongs to the existential meaning of thrownness" (330). Conscience, for Heidegger,

> calls Dasein forth to the possibility of taking over, in existing, even that thrown entity which it is; it calls Dasein *back* to its thrownness so as to understand this thrownness as the null basis which it has to take up into existence." (333; emphasis in original)

Significantly, the discussion of finitude and guilt in some way can be seen as a return to the discussion of "who" is Dasein. The process whereby Dasein recovers its dispersed self brings-forth something even more destabilizing for modern subjectivity: it reveals "authentic" Dasein as a being whose basis is the "not," nothingness, whose existence is utterly contingent. Therefore, the attempt to understand its being-there as a whole, and for which Dasein is responsible, requires that Dasein take "on one's finitude, if . . . finitude is characterized by groundlessness *(Grund-losigkeit)* or by the concealment of the ground *(Grund-verborgenheit)*."[13] Becoming-proper, therefore, is not about the adoption of particular lifestyles or attitudes, and this is confirmed by the lack of specific content in the call of conscience. On the contrary, "the response it [the call] seeks is responsiveness, the desire to have a conscience," which can be understood as the desire to be a self; in this vein, "the particular form of self-disclosedness that the voice of conscience elicits in Dasein is a reticent self-projection upon one's ownmost Being-guilty in which one is ready for anxiety."[14] This self-projection encouraged by Dasein's responsiveness to the call of conscience is what Heidegger calls "resoluteness" (in the sense of having resolve). Taking over death as Dasein's ownmost possibility can only mean, François Raffoul argues, "taking over and making oneself responsible for or making oneself the basis of this 'not' or absence of basis."[15] Jean-Luc Nancy makes the connection between nothingness as the ground of Dasein and the deconstruction of "certainty" as the ground of modern subjectivity quite explicit when he notes that "[a]ll of Heidegger's research into 'being-for (or toward)-death' was nothing other than an attempt to state this: *I* is not—am not—a subject."[16]

For historical reasons—whether they are as specific as the frequent reading of Heidegger through the work of Jean-Paul Sartre or whether they are as general as the attempt to grasp a text that unsettles modern subjectivity through subjectivist terms, translations, and understandings, or even whether they are fueled by the difficulties of Heidegger's neologisms—authentic Dasein and its resolute response to the call of conscience have often been interpreted as a return to an individualist, decisionist, and isolated subject that rejects the "inauthentic" world for authentic solitude and fortitude. If the optics of coexistence is to be useful in rethinking coexistence in international relations beyond the composition of self-sufficient subjects, however, these conceptions of authenticity and Being-toward-death must be discussed and refuted.

## READINGS AND MISREADINGS OF BECOMING-PROPER

There are a number of concerns and objections voiced against Heidegger's account of Being-towards-death and authenticity. In this section I examine three such concerns in order to better delineate, through their consideration, the critical and coexistential reading of Heidegger's existential analytic that was undertaken in the previous chapter.

The first concern is associated most prominently with Emmanuel Levinas, who questions the privileged site afforded to Being-towards-death in the process of becoming-proper. Levinas wonders what repercussions such a prioritization of finitude has on the ability of Heidegger's thought to privilege the other-constituted character of existence, i.e., coexistence. Like the second and third objections examined later on, it too entails concerns about the relationship between authenticity and forms of individualization. While Levinas is interested in the repercussions the perspective of finitude has for the relationship with the other, the rest of the concerns ask whether the discourse of authenticity harbors within it the radical individualization of Dasein, which inadvertently returns Dasein to an individualist/decisionist, inward-looking, and isolated selfhood that is reminiscent of the modern subject. Simon Critchley and Peter Dews ponder precisely such a set of concerns when they write:

> Although, in its authentic existence—through the experience of angst, death, and conscience—*Dasein* becomes individualized and resolute, that is, it becomes a Self, this conception of authentic selfhood cannot be confused with metaphysical conceptions of subjectivity. *Or can it?*[17]

Critchley and Dews's question exemplifies the at best ambivalent, at worst subjectivist, reception of authenticity. These concerns suggest that, if read as just such a return to a radically individualist subject, Heidegger's discourse of authenticity negates the phenomenal descriptions of both Dasein's worldly engaged immersion and also its Being-with, which Heidegger painstakingly provided in Division I of *Being and Time* and which formed two of the elements of the optics of coexistence as described in chapter 3. These concerns will be examined, arguing that although Dasein becomes individualized through its understanding of itself as Being-towards-death, this is not the kind of individualization that revokes the radical embeddedness of Dasein or its capacity for withness. In the reading presented here, the process of authenticity is a process of becoming-proper, which seeks to unsettle the ontological manifestation of Being-with in the form of the "they," and to suggest that Dasein's coexistential heteronomy can be taken up properly. This somewhat confusing claim can be placed into perspective by recalling that, while indistinguishable from the "they," Dasein does not understand itself as heteronomous. Rather, it has an understanding of itself given to it through the public discourses of the "they" that regard the self as subject, in other words, as self-sufficient, autonomous, and largely nonrelational. Becoming-proper, it is suggested, involves a taking up of the radically embedded, heteronomous, and relational self that Dasein is.

### Death and the Ethical Relation to the Other

Levinas's reading of Being-towards-death and becoming-proper calls into question the "celebrated Heideggerian analyses of *being toward death*."[18] He rightly argues that "[t]he way in which Heidegger goes toward death is entirely dictated by the ontological preoccupation."[19] For Levinas, "Heidegger is not interested in the signification of human existing for itself"[20] because death is primarily of interest to Heidegger only as it constitutes an ontological relation to Being. In taking up death as its ownmost possibility Dasein is able to grasp herself as the being whose Being is an issue for it; in other words, as "finite, in question and contested."[21] When Dasein achieves this kind of intelligibility about itself, it is able to ask the question of Being, to which Dasein is "bound or obligated" but which is also "in man's charge."[22] Therefore, Being-towards-death, which is an ontological relationship toward Being, "develops *esse* or being in its proper sense, according to its proper meaning."²³ Two related concerns can be discerned in Levinas's critique here. The first is that Dasein's concrete embeddedness in all its manifestations is of no consequence *other than as a signification of the question of Being.* And does this not signify a reduction of "the entire human adventure" to "being as Being"?²⁴

More important, the second concern is that though arriving at a previously ungraspable relationship to Being fills Dasein with awe and readies it for anxiety, is it not the case that "those neutral ontological relations to being that invite wonder consign the ethical relation, the relation to the other person, to secondary significance?"²⁵ Levinas wishes to highlight and eventually disrupt the actual impact this has on relations to the other. If Being-towards-death "is to be capable of a possibility marked by its untransferable, exclusive and unsurpassable character," Dasein's death has the character of mineness: "[i]n dying, the ontological structure that is mineness, *Jemeinigkeit,* reveals itself."²⁶ Mineness, according to Levinas, is revealed because death is the "most proper possibility, exclusive in regard to an other, isolating, and extreme or unsurpassable as a possibility"; such a possibility is isolating because it "cuts all my ties with other men."²⁷ Heidegger, Levinas suggests, phenomenologically arrives at Dasein's radical embeddedness through "thrownness" and "fallenness" (as well as the other elements that the optics of coexistence has highlighted within the *Daseinanalytik*), only to negate this achievement through the discussion of authenticity and the isolating individualization of Being-towards-death. In *Time and the Other,* Levinas also tied this to freedom by arguing that Dasein's realization of its ownmost possibility "makes possible the very feat of grasping a possibility—that is, it makes possible activity and freedom."²⁸ The "abyssal thought"²⁹ of Being-towards-death questions, importantly, the ability of Heidegger's philosophy to privilege the other-constituted character of existence, i.e., of coexistence.

Tina Chanter's pioneering work on Levinas's critique of Heidegger suggests that, at the very least, there is an ambiguity within Heidegger's analysis between Dasein's solicitude for others and the individuation brought about in the process of becoming-proper (examined in the next subsection), which Levinas tends to ignore completely.³⁰ Heidegger does return to consider authentic solicitude, though Chanter is concerned that "this idea is still mediated by the insistence that Dasein must *first* be itself."[31] In other words, for Chanter too, Dasein's becoming-proper does privilege individualization and makes secondary the ethical relationship to the other. In chapter 5 this relationship between ethics, the other, and the self is recast in order to highlight the ways in which (what one might call) *proper* solicitude is associated with the recovery of an ethical self that understands itself as an opening to alterity.

Regarding becoming-proper as the very possibility of freedom, Levinas's assessment is largely correct. Yet, does this freedom return radically embedded and thrown Dasein to a "mastering, controlling, virile author of its own meaning"?[32] How can such a reading be supported when Dasein exists in a referential totality of other-determined significance, a world where meaning and all sense is first and foremost created by others and, at best, modified and uniquely *appropriated* by Dasein, as was discussed in chapter 3? If mineness is possible only as a unique appropriation of other-created meaning and practices, then otherness can never be "cut off" or "cast-away" by Dasein as Levinas seems to suggest—without it there would not be a "world" (of meaning, relations, and references), and as such Dasein would not be understood as Being-in-the-world. "Appropriation," used as a sign of Dasein's mastery by Levinas, can instead be seen as precisely *affirmative* of otherness and its constitutive role, because rather than unlimited freedom, Dasein's mineness consists only of a unique appropriation of other-created meanings, norms, and practices. Despite the potential for confusion brought about by the discourse of individualization associated with Being-towards-death, it must be recalled that withness is constitutive of Dasein and that averageness and publicness are what constitute Dasein as a Being (who is Being-with).

To suggest that becoming-proper is a kind of isolating individualization is to deny the structures of the existence of Dasein, made apparent through existential analysis, as initially and primarily co-existential and heteronomous, in the sense of both other-constituted and other-mediated. Heidegger's argument that "authenticity" (and here it is particularly lamentable that this translation of the term *Eigentlichkeit* hides the sense of what is "proper")[33] is but a modification of "inauthenticity," and that "inauthenticity" is only possible because of authenticity, must be understood in this sense: that becoming-proper as Being-towards-death is not a denial or denigration of the constitutive primacy of the other(s). Indeed, I will argue in the next section, becoming-proper is nothing if *not* the taking up and taking on of inauthenticity as heteronomous existence. Therefore, "freedom" within the notion of Being-towards-death does not mean the uncontrolled and unlimited freedom of a sovereign subject, but rather has to do with *freeing up*, in the sense of properly disclosing, the proper possibilities for the *kind of Being that Dasein is,* i.e., Being-in-the-world with others. This is the meaning of propriety: the appropriation of one's own being as heteronomous Being-with. When Being-towards-death opens up Dasein to the limit, to the finite, by voicing the "abyssal," it also makes possible Dasein's proper relationship with otherness and the other. As David Wood suggests, responsibility, love, and respect may not be "so very distant from wonder and sacred horror."[34]

Let us now turn to the second concern revolving around the notion of resoluteness, especially as it is articulated by another vocal critic of Heidegger (and Heidegger's politics), Karl Löwith.

### Resoluteness: Countering the Charge of Decisionism

Prominent among the suspicions about authenticity is the charge of decisionism put forward most fervently by Löwith. Decisionism amounts to a serious challenge for the optics of coexistence because it suggests that the authentic self is akin to the masterful and willful subject of decision.[35] Löwith draws parallels between what he calls the "ontological decisionism" of Heidegger and the political decisionism of his contemporary Carl Schmitt.[36] Löwith discerns affinities between the "readiness for death and for killing" that distinguishes Schmitt's concept of the political and Heidegger's ontological analysis of Being-towards-death and resoluteness. Löwith argues that the concern with finitude, "rather than any kind of ordering of the social life as is proper to the primordial meaning of the polis, becomes the 'highest court of appeal'" for Schmitt.[37] In this vein, he also draws a parallel between the "threat to existence," as it serves a justifying role for Schmitt's distinction between friend and enemy and Heidegger's analysis of finitude. Dasein's resolute "'capacity-for-being-a-whole' corresponds in political decisionism to the *sacrifice of one's life* for the total state in the exigency of war," Löwith suggests, because "the principle is the same: the radical return to something ultimate, namely, the naked *that*-ness of facticity."[38]

What is of concern is whether the charge of "decisionism" re-verses the "unworking" of modern subjectivity through the articula-tion of the various elements of the optics of coexistence as outlined in the previous chapter. When the notion of resoluteness is under-stood to have the essence of a *decision,* it would require a sovereign and masterful subject. The linkage of decisionism and resoluteness superficially appears to be an easy one to make. It must, however, *itself* be seen not only as a political reading, but as an interpreta-tion that remains firmly embedded within a subjectivist location.[39] In this vein, Richard Polt rightly points out that "any discussion of Heidegger as a 'decisionist' should note that he does not view decisions as springing from the will of the subject as understood in modern philosophy."[40] Joanna Hodge concurs by noting,

> The critique that the enquiries in *Being and Time* are decisionist, voluntarist and fatalist presupposes a humanist, subjectivist read-ing. . . . They all fail to take into account Heidegger's questioning of the Cartesian break, through which Heidegger displaces the modern assumption that the starting point of enquiry is the thinking of an individual human being, a *res cogitans.*[41]

In addition to the subjectivist presuppositions about the subject of resoluteness, readings of resoluteness as "mastery of self" fail to rec-ognize that "[r]esoluteness has little to do with a determined seizing of our freedom to act; it is closer to a *steadfastness* in the face of the vicissitudes of circumstance."[42] For Miguel de Beistegui, too, reso-luteness "is the way in which Dasein comes back to itself, back to its original site, from the dispersion in everydayness into which it is for the most part thrown."[43] Finally, the equation of resoluteness with a decisionist disposition is also unsustainable because, for Heidegger, resoluteness cannot be understood as "an unqualified call to action." Since there is no encouragement to any one particular option, politi-cal, social, or otherwise, "Dasein's resoluteness remains empty" of content and cannot be seen to represent any one social or moral per-spective.[44] Rather, resoluteness can only embody "a reticence which makes us ready for anxiety. Our acceptance of anxiety does not lead to a frenzied state but is the basis of our composure and calm open-ness *(Gelassenheit)*."[45] Next, the kind of transcendence entailed in Dasein's becoming-proper is examined alongside the concerns that it necessitates a flight from worldly embeddedness indicated by the optics of coexistence in chapter 3.

## From "Inwardness" to Transcendence toward the World

The third concern that arises from the ostensible reassertion of sovereign subjectivity in the process of becoming-proper purports that Dasein's transcendence of its inauthenticity leads to a form of isolating inwardness. Understood in this way, authenticity is regarded as an isolation or removal of Dasein from its world, as a return to some inner self, which is more proper for it than its worldly immersion. Is it appropriate, however, to equate authenticity to Polonius's call "to thine own self be true"?[46] Does the call of conscience draw Dasein away from its lostness in the "they" in order to return it to a fixed self that is there to be discovered within? The answer to the urging to be true to one's self ("I am who I am" was Yahweh's answer) is "an answer of self-sufficiency."[47] Thinking of authenticity in this manner, it would seem, transforms becoming-proper into pure introspection and misleadingly confuses Dasein's search for propriety with inwardness and isolation from its world; this is not unrelated to Levinas's concern that authenticity results in the "cutting of ties to other men" and the denigration of the constitutive relations with the other person.

On the contrary, I argue, becoming-proper requires the realization that one's self is Being-in-the-world, disclosed and constituted by its relations within its world. Any inwardness or introspection brought about by the call of conscience has the intention of precisely highlighting the constitutive importance of the world in which Dasein is thrown Being-with others. Becoming-proper turns Dasein toward the world, therefore, and cannot be interpreted as an isolating individuation. The resoluteness of propriety is, indeed, a return from self-dispersal, yet "such a coming back, such gathering is not an inward movement whereby Dasein would cut itself off from the world so as to enjoy the peace and depth of some precious inner life," Beistegui argues; "[r]ather it is a movement of disclosure, of clearing, where Dasein authentically ek-sists its own essence, and this means confronts its own facticity. In coming back to itself, Dasein comes back to its own ecstatic yet finite essence."[48]

According to Dasein's constitution it is, contrary to the charge of inwardness, inauthentic to flee in the face of its worldly character. The call of conscience, therefore, aims to awaken Dasein to the realization that "in its fall it seeks tranquilization and distraction through the concealments of worldliness."[49] Worldiness is inescapable, however, because Dasein's Being *is* thrown projection. No transcendence can ever rescind thrownness, since Dasein cannot exist without a world: "[w]orld belongs to a *relational* structure distinctive of Dasein as such, a structure that we called being-in-the-world."[50] Authenticity seeks to bring out the propriety of Dasein's worldly anxious existence, so that becoming-proper is a finite transcendence, "a surpassing in the direction of world," where the world is understood neither as belonging to Dasein as something subjective nor as something objective related to natural entities or their totality.[51] Dasein's transcendence and its thrownness in the world are linked: "[t]o transcendence belongs world as that toward which surpassing occurs."[52] Transcendence belongs to the very fact of Dasein's being-the-there.[53] Inwardness, then, does not negate the heteronomously coexistential character of Dasein. On the contrary, the struggle for authenticity cannot be reduced to radical, inward-looking individualization because "the only inwardness that the existential subject has is that which plunges it into the world; an inwardness thrown and initially lost and ever only as good as its labor"; if this understanding of transcendence as an anxious movement of Dasein toward the world is obscured, then "the reification of the subject is a foregone conclusion."[54]

The proposition that Dasein transcends its everydayness, not away from but *in the direction of the world,* suggests that becoming-proper is predicated on a distinction between, on the one hand, a "naïve everyday, understood as unproblematic and not in need of clarification, an everyday in which the uncanny experienced as anxiety takes place," and "an everyday rendered strange by being subjected to analysis," on the other.[55] Dasein attempts to transcend its inauthentic self by moving from a flighty (curious, ambiguous, gossipy) immersion in its publicly comprehended everyday toward a resolute engagement with a world that can be subjected to critique. Its everyday world becomes luminous, and its ontological relationship to it is taken up in a steadfast readiness for anxiety. However, if becoming-proper is interpreted as an achievement that is complete, that can be fully actualized, this distorts the understanding of everydayness as that which "both is and is not a simple structure; that the everyday both is and is not aporetic and paradoxical."[56] The everyday world is that which is most familiar for Dasein and yet that which simultaneously harbors uncanniness. Dasein discovers in the midst of familiarity something that shatters its self-perception as a distinct and autonomous subject. It discovers that what distinguishes it from the "they" is *not* innate autonomy but, *in each case,* a critical internalization (in the sense of unique appropriation) of the shared practices and norms of its world, formulated in a way unique for its factical situation.[57]

If Dasein does not become a "subject" once it strives to become-proper, then what is the result of its transcendence toward the world? According to Michael Gelven, becoming-proper discloses Dasein to itself as thrown projection, projecting itself on its possibilities. In his view, "authentic existence is awareness of possibilities."[58] However, I argued earlier that Dasein's *ownmost* possibility is its finitude: how, then, can propriety and death be thought together? Charles Scott argues that "[w]hen dasein's *eigenste Möglichkeit* (most proper possibility) is named death, the meaning of *most proper* or *ownmost* or *most essential* is thus interrupted."[59] Becoming-proper cannot be determined as a specific way of being according to an essence of Dasein, because "[a]uthenticity for Heidegger is not a matter of self's actualizing itself."[60] Rather, it can and should only be thought as a proper readiness for the "improper" being that Dasein is. Seizing Dasein's ownmost possibility means that Dasein "exposes itself as Being-guilty, to its Being-towards-death, to its thrownness, in short, it exposes itself to its own finitude and to its 'own' inappropriable."[61] When Dasein is "lost" in the "they," it is unaware of its constitution as Being-in-the-world and understands itself as self-completing and unencumbered, voluntarily participating in relations with others. In becoming-proper, an interruption of the myth of the "I" reveals Dasein to itself as Being-in-the-world. Thus, becoming-proper tears Dasein away from its passive subjection to the "they" only to return Dasein back to a recognition of its fundamental relationality and embeddedness in the world. In becoming-proper, one's understanding of the separation from others as a sign of selfhood gets disrupted by Being-towards-death.[62] Dasein's recognition of its contingency and finitude, as well as its openness to its factical possibilities, tear Dasein "from the meanings and values by which it makes its way in its society."[63] In the process of becoming-proper, it "is torn from its inherited interpretation of itself as self-founding" and self-sufficient, and brings about a recognition of otherness as constitutive for it; as Scott argues, Dasein "comes into its own by disowning its selfhood in the way it is a self."[64]

Taken together, these related arguments counter the charges of decisionism and isolating individuation. They gesture, moreover, toward an understanding of becoming-proper as a *modification,* and not a negation, of the coexistential heteronomy that the optics of coexistence outlined in the previous chapter. In the following section, the relationship between authentic and inauthentic modes of being concludes the exploration of becoming-proper.

## AUTHENTICITY AND INAUTHENTICITY—
## A DIALOGIC RELATIONSHIP?

I now examine the ways in which *both* becoming-proper (authenticity) and inauthenticity are modes of Dasein's existence "grounded upon that state of Being which we have called '*Being-in-the-world*' (*Being and Time,* 78; emphasis in original). It is important to illustrate that the two modes of being are not separate but rather constitute one another dialogically. Dasein comports itself toward its Being even in the mode of average everydayness, "even if it is only in the mode of fleeing *in the face of it* and forgetfulness *thereof*" (69; emphases in original). Since Dasein flees from a confrontation with the fact that its Being is an issue for it, Heidegger designates everydayness as inauthentic. However, there can be no transcendence of *everydayness,* and therefore of inauthenticity, as such. The proper comportment to one's Being and to entities and other Daseins within the world occurs when Dasein appropriates its average practices, norms, and values in a unique way and has an awareness of its ability to be. Propriety and appropriateness are thus connected and, moreover, they are connected at the point where Dasein arrives at a capability to ask the question of Being as such.[65] Thus, it is not everydayness that is transcended, but the inauthentic relation to one's Being in which Dasein finds itself initially and primarily *(zunächst und zumeist).* This is the meaning of the statement "Inauthenticity belongs to the essential nature of factical Dasein. Authenticity is only a modification but not a total obliteration of inauthenticity."[66]

Moreover, transcendence does not mean "to overcome" or "to go beyond" the world and other beings, as was noted earlier. Rather, transcendence is more appropriately reformulated for Dasein, whose basic constitution is Being-in-the-world, as a going toward the world, toward facticity, a movement through which the shared world is uniquely appropriated *in each case.* "Mineness belongs to any existent Dasein, and belongs to it as the condition which makes authenticity and inauthenticity possible" (78). Dasein's appropriation of its factic coexistence launches a process of becoming-proper for itself as a being that is a radically contingent, foundation-less, death-bound possibility. Becoming-proper demands recognition of one's being as "Being the basis of a nullity" (329), not in a morbid attempt to urge Dasein toward a taking-leave of the factical world but precisely to urge an appropriation of this worldly and other-constituted existence in a unique way. The recognition of finitude and its appropriation as one's ownmost possibility do not rid Dasein of its impropriety. On the contrary, Raffoul argues, "by resolutely projecting my Being-guilty, I appropriate the inappropriable as inappropriable. *I must be the improper (inauthenticity) properly (authentically)."*[67] When authenticity is understood in connection with Dasein's relation to itself as contingent and groundless, "Dasein comes to dwell in familiarity with its mortal temporality."[68] This is the primordial sense of mineness, namely, "giving oneself to what is other and being this givenness (which is at once a reception, a hearing, a corresponding, a hearkening, a belonging) authentically."[69] Although Dasein is *"in each case mine"* (67; emphasis in original), "mineness" is not a property but a reiteration. The singularity of Dasein is taken anew in each *case.* Nancy insists,

> [T]here is no being apart from singularity: each time just this once, and there would be nothing general or common except the "each time just this once." This is how we must understand Heidegger's *Jemeinigkeit* [mineness], Dasein's "each time as my own," which does not define the subjectivity of a substantial presence of the *ego* to itself . . . but which on the contrary defines "mineness" on the basis of the "each time."[70]

This kind of "mineness" "does not imply the substantial permanence, identity, or autonomy of the 'ego,' but rather implies the withdrawal of all substance."[71] Relation is primary, since mineness cannot be understood as Dasein's property, substance, or even its possession of itself.

The ambivalent content, tone, and language in which inauthenticity is approached have often led Heidegger scholars either to denigrate such an "inauthentic mode" or to rush toward a defense of inauthenticity.[72] Yet both camps of the inauthenticity/authenticity debate rest on a distinction that was not intended to establish and maintain a rigid dichotomy between inauthentic and authentic modes of being. Rather, Heidegger invoked this distinction to call for a rendering-*strange* of the everyday average manifestation of Dasein. A dichotomy is not ontologically possible because the mode of "averageness" cannot be transcended, as it constitutes the shared world of significance, understood as the relational totality of involvements, references, and assignments, as was discussed in chapter 3. If by "transcendence" is meant the overcoming of averageness, then this is a phenomenal impossibility because the structures of shared existence are constituted by it. Lawrence Vogel notes in this regard, "There is no pure authenticity but at best an authentic appropriation of the inauthentic."[73] This is not merely an indication of the limitations of the process toward propriety; rather, it is meant to highlight that "authenticity is nothing but inauthenticity seized *as such.*"[74]

Furthermore, transcendence in the conventional meaning of "going beyond" is not only *impossible* but also *unnecessary* because of the dialogic relation between these two modes. Joan Stambaugh argues, "We are both at once, usually without realizing it."[75] In this vein, setting up a dichotomy between inauthenticity and authenticity obscures the fact that there is never a complete severance between them. "Inauthenticity characterizes a kind of Being into which Dasein can divert itself and has for the most part always diverted itself; but Dasein does not necessarily and constantly have to divert itself into this kind of Being" (*Being and Time,* 303). In this way, Heidegger's paradoxical statement "inauthenticity is based on the possibility of authenticity" can be better understood as a dialogical interaction between the two modes (303). Within inauthenticity can be found the very possibility of its modification, authenticity; but at the same time, inauthenticity is only possible for a being who has the capacity to be authentic (proper) within its everyday possibilities. Their interconnection reveals that "if authenticity is always manifested by inauthenticity, authenticity is itself in some sense inauthentic," belonging, that is, in some way to the everyday and its possibilities.[76]

Thinking of authenticity as a modification of inauthenticity also transforms Dasein's relation to otherness. Dasein's submission to the world and the "they" is modified so that it becomes Dasein's understanding of the primacy of *relation* for its Being-in-the-world (*Being and Time,* ¶27). Dasein is both singular (unique) *and* fundamentally related, it's "singularity of the self which knows itself as opening to alterity."[77] Authenticity modifies Dasein's self-understanding so that it comes to consider its heteronomy as being-radically-in relation. Becoming-proper, therefore, involves a transformation of Being-with from lostness in the "they" to the critical appropriation of one's shared way of life. Propriety is an awareness of the heteronomy of Dasein in its concrete situation, as well as a response to it that is unique. It is the recognition, in other words, that "[e]xistence exists in the plural, in the singularly plural."[78]

Thus, discussions of authenticity and inauthenticity must "be understood at the philosophical-hermeneutic level of whether an implicit self-interpretation appropriately articulates and discloses the being proper to Dasein or not."[79] This enhanced intelligibility involves, ultimately, Dasein relinquishing perceptions of selfhood as "merely self-consciousness, self-possession, or self-control" and no longer comporting itself toward beings as a self-sufficient subject; higher intelligibility enables Dasein to "appreciate the meaningfulness of all beings" and to *be* "the maintenance of creative openness to the significance of what is, to the difference it makes that there are beings rather than nothing."[80] Becoming-proper involves, therefore, a disclosive enhancement of relations with others and available things. The dialogic relationship between inauthenticity and authenticity serves to highlight, also, Dasein's relation to itself. It aids the questioning of the assumptions of the modern subject and signifies the unstable process of "the deconstruction of Dasein, Dasein's making itself tremble" by which "Dasein is its own deconstruction."[81]

## CONCLUSION

To conclude, the optics of coexistence, discussed at great length in chapter 3, has sought to unwork the characteristics attributed to modern subjectivity. Acting both as a means of accessing the facticity of existence and as an analysis of the structures of Dasein (being-there), the optics of coexistence reveals that, far from being an innately autonomous and sovereign subject, Dasein is coexistentially heteronomous. This means that its existence is coexistence: in the proximal and average way in which it finds itself in the world, Dasein is radically embedded Being-with, although it flees in the face of this worldiness. By bringing to the fore the ways in which heteronomy permeates and constitutes Dasein, the various elements of the optics of coexistence have rendered untenable both the sovereign and preconstituted subject and the conception of coexistence as the copresence of such already constituted and self-sufficient subjects. In this chapter, on the basis of the optics of coexistence, I examined Heidegger's discussions of Dasein's efforts to become proper for its Being; I discussed the ways in which Dasein can properly take up this radical and coexistential embeddedness and allow it to define Dasein's ability to be. In so doing, I explored some of the more prevalent concerns with Heidegger's articulation of "Being-towards-death" and the concepts of resoluteness and authenticity, arguing for a modified understanding of authenticity as processual, involving a "ceaseless" attempt to properly take on its "inauthenticity," which is constitutive for its Being. The continuous interaction between the proper and improper manifestations of Dasein points to a dialogic relationship between the two that is less certain, not guaranteed, than accounts of resoluteness may, at first glance, suggest. This dialogic relationship between Dasein's proper and improper manifestations unworks subjectivity as the ground of international political inquiry. This unworking is neither a closure nor the replacement of "subject" by another ontological certainty; rather, it is the unraveling of ossified assumptions, which creates the possibility for thinking of coexistence beyond the logic of composition.

How might a new understanding of coexistence be articulated if it can no longer be conceived as mere copresence? To think of coexistence on the basis of coexistential heteronomy is to seek its articulation in ethical and political terms as inspired by the unworking of the modern subject undertaken herein.[82] The turn to ethical and political selfhood is necessary because, as illustrated in the introduction, thinking about coexistence takes place implicitly within various discourses of international political thought. Primary among these are, on the one hand, cosmopolitan discussions of a global ethics, where relationality to the other is articulated in terms of extending human rights, and on the other hand, concerns about the expansion of political community, where the focus on the other relies on "extending the we" beyond the schema of the sovereign state.[83]

In chapter 5 I reflect on coexistence by engaging with the appeal to a global ethics based on the extension of the international human rights regime as proposed recently by prominent works with a cosmopolitan intent. I call ethics *itself* into question and propose a relationality to the other that traverses a different path, away from universalization and codification of legal entitlements and through the recovery of an ethical selfhood that understands itself as an opening to otherness.[84] In chapter 6 I turn to the concern of articulating a *political* thought of coexistence. In my attempt to avoid the articulation of coexistence according to the logic of composition, I engage with the charge that the thought of Martin Heidegger leads to the opposite danger, that of an essentialist determination of coexistence and community along nationalist, some would say fascist, lines. In this sense, I return to the concerns already raised in chapter 3 about the communal determination of Being-with and discuss these within the context of the still-raging debate on Heidegger's politics. Using the recovery of the ethical self outlined in chapter 5, I work toward retrieving out of Heidegger's discussion on Being-with a mode of critical belonging that attempts to escape *both* the logic of additive composition and *also* the determination of community according to an essence.

# 5

# Recovering the "Ethical" Self:
# Global Ethics in Question

*[Q]uestioning was the piety of thought ... piety should from the start have been understood as the docility of listening, thus making the question ... into a modality of reception, a trusting attention to what gives itself to be understood rather than—or prior to—the enterprising, inquisitional activity of a request or inquest.*
    JACQUES DERRIDA, "A NUMBER OF YES (NOMBRE DE OUI)"

The optics of coexistence, discussed in chapters 3 and 4, has sought to unwork modern subjectivity. Returning to Martin Heidegger's phenomenological investigations of the facticity of existence in *Being and Time,* the elements of the optics of coexistence illustrated that, far from being an innately autonomous and sovereign subject, Dasein is coexistentially heteronomous. Its existence is coexistence: in the proximal and average way in which it finds itself in the world, Dasein is radically embedded Being-with, although it flees in the face of its worldliness. Dasein's efforts to become proper for its Being are but negotiations of how to take up this radical embeddedness and allow it to define its ability to be. By bringing to the fore the ways in which otherness permeates and constitutes Dasein, the various elements of the optics of coexistence have rendered untenable not only subjectivist presuppositions about the self, but also the conception of coexistence that such assumptions tend to dictate. The optics of coexistence, in other words, denies the restriction of coexistence to the copresence of already constituted, masterful, and self-sufficient

subjects according to the logic of composition. The optics of coexistence also call into question the effacement of heteronomy—the
multiple ways in which other beings and otherness constitute and
make possible existence, as well as the ways in which human existence is other or strange to itself—which is the irrevocable result of
this logic.

Such a disruption of the logic of composition allows the question
"If not as copresence, how can coexistence be rethought?" Given
the concerns presented at the outset of this volume, any rethinking of coexistence undertaken after the exposition of the optics of
coexistence must avoid suppressing heteronomy. How can an understanding of coexistence be articulated in which heteronomy is adequately reflected, otherness acknowledged for its constitutive role,
and the other not reduced to the same? In this chapter I return to
this necessary rethinking of coexistence and pursue it as a *question*
for world politics.

Given the lack of direct examination of coexistence within international relations, posing this question must take place within related discourses. Therefore, I turn to coexistence within the space
opened up by recent cosmopolitan proposals about the possibility,
at least implicitly, of engendering a normative or ethical kind of coexistence by creating a global ethics through the vehicle of human
rights. Such cosmopolitan proposals, of which Ulrich Beck's articulation is taken to be representative, refer to a set of ideas and ideals
that have become quite influential among institutionalist as well as
critical international relations scholarship because they offer a much-
needed normativity for international politics in a global era.[1] IR discourses critical of realist interstate accounts of international politics
are attracted to the creation and promotion of humanitarian and
other progressive norms, such as those extending and strengthening
the existing international human rights regime, because they expect
such increased normativity to lead to a mediation of the *an-archic*
nature (here understood as unprincipled) of the sovereign state system.[2] Important for the rethinking of coexistence, calls for such a
global ethics are, in many ways, similarly motivated by a desire to
protect others beyond "our" borders. The ethical construction of
universalizable norms and, equally important, the codification of
such norms, usually in the form of human rights instruments and
norms regulating the use of armed intervention, is thought to make

possible such protection of otherness and to engender a different kind of coexistence.[3] Cosmopolitan proposals almost exclusively associate the achievement of a global ethics of inclusiveness—an ethics regarded as suitable for this era of globalization—to the creation of cosmopolitan law for a universal humanity.[4]

Based on the analysis offered in the preceding chapters, the following discussion must contest the appropriateness of ethical construction of such norms and principles, as well as the overwhelming reliance on the legalization of such principles, for preventing the effacement of heteronomy and encouraging inclusiveness of the other. Beyond the reliance of human rights on a subjectivist ontology—well-documented by human rights critics and supporters alike[5]—and while acknowledging other prominent critiques of neoimperialism and selectivity, to mention but two,[6] I ask whether the accordance of human rights to an increasingly globalized humanity is sufficient to inaugurate a global ethics attentive to otherness. Can one simply assume that an ethics of inclusiveness is achievable by universalizing and legalizing principles developed in particular parts of the world, within particular communities? On the contrary, might not an inclusive global ethics require a different openness to the other, an openness that is not necessarily brought about through the mere bestowal of legal entitlements such as human rights? Furthermore, could it be that ethical construction and codification of human rights instruments, with which one seeks to regulate morality and protect others, merely overlay such instruments on the structure of already existing communal norms and morality, which remain closed off to the other?[7] In posing this set of questions, I challenge such cosmopolitan proposals and contend that the bestowal of human rights does not necessarily or directly lead to an ethics of inclusiveness. While the assumption that "we" all belong to a universal humanity and that each of "us" ought to hold specific legal rights and entitlements by virtue of such belonging may appear as an appropriate means of extending ethical regardedness to all others and preventing the effacement of the self's heteronomy, this does not immediately follow from such a universalist legalist gesture.

Attempts to articulate a truly inclusive ethics must instead begin by considering the distinct ethical formations of the local public group, the community in which the self is radically embedded and which always already contains within it a xenophobic element by the very fact of its distinctiveness. Rather than assuming that the creation of ethical codes and the ascription of rights are sufficiently attuned to, and protective of, the self's heteronomy and to otherness in general, in the following discussion I propose an alternative path. The sense of selfhood and identity arises within a public group, seen in the ways in which Dasein is constituted as a heteronomous being within the "they," as discussed in chapter 3, such that openness to others requires cultivation. In this chapter I call for the recovery of an "ethical" selfhood, "which knows itself as opening to alterity."[8] Such an opening to otherness cannot come from the imposition of a legalist perspective, cosmopolitan or otherwise; rather, it requires a radical confrontation of the xenophobic element inherent in the morality and ethics of the public group. The recovery of an "ethical" selfhood open to otherness takes place by extending and appropriating, in a suitable manner, the discussion of Dasein's ceaseless attempts to become-proper for its Being, as outlined in chapter 4. Pursuing coexistence through the recovery of an "ethical" selfhood, however, affects not only the articulation of coexistence beyond copresence but also the consideration of ethics within international political thought more generally.

Coexistence becomes manifest, as will be shown, through the "ethical" self's attitude of liberating solicitude toward the other.[9] This disposition helps disclose the other to its otherness, helping the other understand herself as strange, rendering coexistence as a mutual process of disclosing one's own and the other's otherness, of helping the other become aware of her own heteronomy, and of critically confronting the effacement of heteronomy within publicly prevalent discourses. The elaboration of the "ethical" self can be understood not as a replacement of the modern subject, but precisely *not* as its replacement, manifesting coexistence through a disposition or attitude to others that places heteronomy at its center. The "ethical" self's disposition of liberating solicitude constitutes the very ethicity of what is ethical, such that coexistence itself becomes its manifestation.

Moreover, the recovery of an "ethical" selfhood subverts what is normally designated as ethics for it requires a movement beyond the supposition that ethics is solely ethical construction, i.e., the elaboration of rules that are intended to moderate relations between subjects who are only voluntarily associated. This kind of reduction, characteristic of modernity, takes ethics as "obligatory principles of conduct, rules that tell you what you must do to be blameless."[10] Similarly, the term "ethics" refers to "the body of values by which a culture understands and interprets itself with regard to what is good and bad . . . a group of principles for both conduct and value judgement."[11] These specific definitions of ethics, moreover, resonate throughout ethical theorizing in some Continental and most Anglo-American moral philosophies but also represent the articulation of the great majority of normative theorizing within the discipline of international relations. In fact, the literature on normative theories within international relations is dominated by the traditional conception of ethics as ethical construction.[12] The majority of international ethical approaches, which call for an inclusion of normative questions among the concerns of the discipline, are, to date, formulated largely in the manner of universalizable theorizing or the application of existing ethical theories to specific issues, such as refugees, societal exclusion, intercultural critique, universal human rights and their political success in non-Western parts of the world, and so on. Even for those discourses that strive for a "thoroughgoing anti-foundationalist ethics," such as that of Molly Cochran, "[b]y definition, an ethic is understood to be universalizable" in the sense that it is "interested in seeking convergence on ethical principles."[13]

In a radically different vein, the proposed recovery of an "ethical" selfhood encourages a movement away from both the construction of moral principles and the legalization of such principles in a global juridical and institutional framework. Such an "ethical" selfhood should be understood as a stance, an attitude of heteronomous selfhood aware of itself as open to the other. Naturally, this is not the first call for a reconceptualization of ethics. A number of critical discourses have already emerged within international ethical theorizing, calling for a rethinking of traditional conceptions of ethics.[14] The present discussion merely joins forces with such discourses, whose animating spirit arises from attestations of otherness and suffering that ethics conceived as ethical construction is said to unwittingly occlude. As with the authors of these discourses, I am troubled by the possibility that the reduction of ethics to ethical construction and global rule making might not be sufficiently open to otherness and might, in fact, occlude the very suffering it is meant to banish. In this way, the reconceptualization of coexistence in terms of "ethical" selfhood forms part of an existing critique against traditional understandings of ethics and simultaneously contributes to a rethinking of ethics itself. What occurs is a "destructive retrieve" of ethics in the sense of a double movement of destruction and retrieve, which calls into question the assumptions that hinder its full potential while bringing about a recovery of the "ethical" self as a possibility within ethics that is worth reclaiming and enhancing and that has positive implications for ethical theorizing in IR. This chapter contributes to the critical reevaluation of the very possibility of a global ethics and considers whether a more fruitful direction for ethical theorizing might not be found, instead, in an exploration of coexistence through the articulation of an "ethical" selfhood informed by heteronomy.

Specifically, I contest ethics as ethical construction by examining the linguistic trajectory of the word *éthos* and linking it to the Heideggerian analysis of Dasein's average socialization in the "they." This combined perspective enables the questioning of ethics by showing how the discursive creation of moral norms is both crucial for, and inseparable from, communal processes of socialization and normalization. It is through this connection between normalcy, normalization, and *éthos* within conventional conceptions of ethics as moral rules that the occlusion of suffering and of alterity occurs.[15] The veiling of otherness and suffering points to the urgent need to turn away from a restricted notion of ethics as ethical construction and to seek other means of access to the ethical that adequately reflect the heteronomy disclosed by the optics of coexistence. Hence, ethics itself becomes radically redetermined, beyond rules and norms until it reaches an "unrestricted conception of ethics concerned not just with human beings, but with human beings in relation to difference and to otherness."[16]

## CALLING ETHICS INTO QUESTION

The lack of explicit theorization of ethics by Heidegger discouraged using Heideggerian thinking for normative concerns,[17] leading some critics to claim that his thought, in fact, hinders thinking about ethics and ethical relationality.[18] The discussion of everydayness found in *Being and Time* and, more specifically, the analysis of everyday rules, norms, and social practices under the heading of the "they" *(das Man)* can be read as offering a forceful critique of modern conceptions of morality and ethical construction, indicating that, contrary to widely held perceptions, Heidegger *did* have a lot to say about ethics. Charles E. Scott, for example, argues that the *question* of ethics is "functioning with exceptional force" within Heidegger's thinking, while Joanna Hodge similarly regards that "the question of ethics is the definitive, if unstated problem of his thinking."[19] Recalling Heidegger's discussions of averageness and publicness, the discussion here points to a forceful critique of ethics conceived as moral norms and morality.

The constitutive function that conformity and mimesis have for Dasein's worldly existence is evident in his description of the everyday ontological manifestation of the "who" of Dasein as the "they." As can be recalled from chapter 3, Heidegger acknowledges conformity as positively constitutive for Dasein but also offers a critique of conformism that suggests, at the very least, that shared social practices must be evaluated and uniquely appropriated.[20] The critique challenges public morality insofar as morality and rule making are important modes through which Dasein is socialized into the mentality of the "they." Slavoj Žižek calls this "the inauthentic ontic morality of 'this is how *it is done,* how *one does it*'"[21] such that ethics as rules of conduct can only arise in the context of the "they." If by "ethics" one understands the emergence of a code or of a set of norms expressive of locally acceptable and expected behavior then, Scott argues, "the possibility of ethical thought and action is found in traditional 'normalcy' and its history."[22] The reference to normalcy indicates that the construction of norms usually arises within habitual behavior, which tends to have a normalization effect. Dasein is socialized by adjusting its dealings in the world toward what becomes average practice (averageness) through infinite and minute adjustments. It is through such normalization that norms develop, in the sense that historical and local habitual practices tend to coalesce into customary ways of doing things.[23] Norms, then, are representative of current average practice that is attained through processes of normalization of behavior and the power of habituation.[24] As such, they are undeniably public.

Some of these ways, or practices, also ascend to the level of moral rules, which generally refer to locally desirable ways to regulate action toward others. That such a body of rules exists need not involve the explicit individual choice of those specific rules as such, nor does it signify each Dasein's conscious agreement to obey them. On the contrary, the everyday value judgments and moral acts of members of the public group involve recourse to such rules without reflexive choice (*Being and Time,* 164–65). Moral rules derive from acceptable and desirable practices; indeed, they are called "moral" because they have been historically accorded value within a locally specific public group. Some of these rules might have been gradually and/or officially codified.[25] This connection between expected behavior and ethics can still hold even in references to universal ethics, which can be seen as the universalization of rules arising within a particular public group.

### *Éthos, Ethe,* and Ethics

A linguistic excursion might help to illustrate the relationship between the customary and the moral, as well as the transition from one to the other. Charles Chamberlain's research in this area shows how in the fifth century BC, the word "*éthos* can usually be understood and translated as 'character'" but that this was not true in the case of earlier writers; on the contrary, the term had the prior signification of "animal haunts" or "dwellings" and was usually used in its plural form, *ethea.*[26] Gradually the term became commonly used regarding humans and came to mean "the arena in which people or animals move; further, this essence, whether in an animal or a human being, resists the imposition of outside influences."[27] Similarly for Scott, *éthos* has to do with customary dwelling and the behavior or manners that one exhibits in such a homestead. In *éthos* one finds a particularist drive that encompasses its own "ordering, identity-giving, and nurturing force"; *ethea* were places of belonging, but the term connoted a certain disposition to recalcitrance and resistance to "civilizing" influence.[28] Furthermore, it can be established that the term, where it referred to humans, initially did so to barbarians, indicating that these "are subject to a principle of order, a *logos* all their own . . . off the scale of 'normal'—that is, Greek—expectations."[29]

In the fourth century BC, however, the term's meaning as a place of belonging was reconfigured, and *éthos* became located in the soul and was occasionally used in conjunction with *tropos* (way or manner). It is from this configuration that the connection to character develops as that which evidences one's manners. The spatial sense of the term persists, however, and "now refers to the peculiar characteristics which citizens of a *polis* acquire as part of their civic heritage . . . *ta éthé* in particular are often mentioned in connection with *trephó* and *paideuó*, that is, with the socialization of children."[30] Customary habits become gradually codified into rules and laws, that is, *nómos*. *Nómos* can be seen as the movement to codify into standardized rules, and perhaps promulgate, that which belongs to a particular habitual order.[31] *Nómos* raises particular manners to the level of principles, by which the recalcitrant *ethea* are also "civilized." The movement toward codification and ordering, in this regard, necessarily involves struggle between free and differentiated habituation on the one hand, and the desire to impose an external but principled order on the other. *Éthos* derived from the Indo-European *Swedh*, meaning "one's own," signifies both a person's character and the "way we are of our own" as a distinct group: *éthos* nurtures, socializes, and provides the identificatory processes by which one is one's own self.[32]

What is more, the connection between customary ways of life and ethics is constant and ever evolving through infinitesimal changes, a process that is historically bounded and undeniably local. One cannot but perceive "of laws and principles for thought and action as regional, as a group of claims characteristic of one cultural and historical segment."[33] The derivation of the term *ethics* from *éthos*, from customary ways of life, does not refer only to the mores of small secluded communities, tribes of anthropological interest, or assumed closed cultural groups. It could similarly refer to Western culture, Western civilization, or European *éthos* as a historically enlarged group with its specific ways of being. In this light, the norms, rules, and moral practices, such as human rights, normally associated with the West, as well as the legal manifestations of these rules and norms, are shown to be situated in processes of habituation and socialization of the particular public group or culture, despite their universalist aspirations. When the insights of the historico-linguistic development of the term *ethics* are allowed to inform ethical inquiry, the universality of such rules and norms is increasingly called into question.

### Ethics, Morality, and the "They"

The particular location and basis of ethical construction and codification of customary ways of behaving bring to the fore the relation between ethics and habituation and recall Heidegger's discussion of average everydayness as the initial and primary way in which Dasein finds itself as Being-in-the-world. The historical development of the term *éthos* as a way of life and behavior characteristic of a habitual dwelling place underlies the analysis of how Dasein is embedded in the world. It informs the phenomenological investigation of Being-there amidst others in the form of the "they" in a specific cultural tradition. Bringing the two analyses together shows us how communal éthos is constitutive of the meanings, references, and norms by which Dasein lives its life. Dasein, I argued in chapters 3 and 4, has no essence for Heidegger: rather, it is groundless, an amalgam of shared practices and, as such, finds itself in a world infused with sense already created by others within its historical public group (the "they") and only partly authored by its own practices.[34] Dasein is *thrown* into a world through its dealings with available entities (such as equipment) and its solicitude toward other Daseins, and this thrownness is indicative of its *coexistential heteronomy,* a term that signifies its constitution by and absorption in (Heidegger suggests "subjection" to) others in its world.

Recall, however, that the intelligibility that Dasein has within the "they" is average and as such restricts Dasein's modes of relating to other beings. Conditioned through the practices, beliefs, and perceptions of the "they," Dasein relates to beings, be they tools and equipment available within its work world or other Daseins, as merely present (occurrent or present-at-hand).[35] The average solicitude toward other Daseins as present-at-hand is particularly problematic for a discussion of ethics because it does not disclose other Daseins in their Being but rather as manifested presence. Inasmuch as something or someone is accorded moral significance, it requires the assignment of value as the expression of positivity.[36] As regards itself, moreover, Dasein is ignorant of its heteronomy and entertains conceptions of autonomous selfhood and action free from constraint bestowed on it by an assumed innate autonomy within the discourses of the "they." This average kind of comportment and intelligibility lead to a leveling-down of Dasein's possibilities for Being, but also involve a lack of recognition of this leveling-down and a flight from Dasein's own anxious ability to be. Insofar as morality socializes Dasein within its group, enabling its flight away from its proper self and keeping it within this average and constricting level of interaction with others, morality is a product of the "they." For

Heidegger, then, ethics encloses Dasein in commonplace and average comportment. The moral subject is, despite its purported autonomy, the subject of averageness, publicness, and conformism, unquestioningly remaining within traditional and customary bounds of behavior. Morality, therefore, is part of the average intelligibility through which the world and beings within the world are disclosed; yet, in belonging to averageness, it also forms part of the process by which Dasein is constituted within its group. Ethics, then, arises within the folds of the "they" and sustains the average intelligibility and inauthentic comportment toward others and the world: "the ethical moment is typically a moment of loss of self-questioning."[37] Becoming-proper as discussed in chapter 4, therefore, must involve a critical examination of and, indeed, a calling into question of ethics.

This brief discussion of ethics has a number of critical implications for universalist ethical construction[38] within the discipline of international relations and for the international political practices of states and international institutions.[39] The questioning of ethics, as contained within a prevalent communal éthos, enables the contextualization of scholarly ethical work within its particularist location, which in the case of international relations scholarship is mostly Western. Such locating contests its universal claims and reveals its situated roots.[40] As Silvia Benso remarks, "*Mores* . . . is the theme of ethics as it has been constituted in the history of Western metaphysics."[41] Seen in this light, the aspirations of universalist or cosmopolitan ethics are disclosed as particularist drives of socialization that seek to spread beyond their particularity. Indeed, the present discussion speaks to the most popularly articulated and well-rehearsed charge against universalism, that of imperialism; nevertheless, charges of imperialism should not be the sole, or even the primary, reason why global ethics cannot merely assume a universal perspective from the start.[42] Rather, the hesitation to follow the universal path to global ethics must come from questioning whether such universality leads to an ethics that is attuned to the other, enabling an openness that transcends the legal aspects of cohabitation. A global ethics that is open to the other requires precisely the calling into question both of one's embedded particular ethical practices and also of the very claim of their universality. No matter how valuable such universalism is considered to be for the international and global concerns that the discipline of international relations and global actors wish to address, such locating suggests that universalized customary norms and rules are not the most appropriate response to these concerns. Explorations of coexistence, as well as ethical theorizing, in international relations might greatly benefit from relinquishing ethics understood as ethical construction and legal codification and seek openness to the other in a radically different kind of "cosmopolitan" disposition.

## Turning Away from Ethics

Based on the previous discussion, it has become clear that if ethics arises within the folds of the "they," the call to becoming-proper (or authenticity) amounts to a "turning away from ethics as we know it."[43] To call its ethics into question, based on the group éthos as these are, Dasein must confront its customary practices and their assigned values, no matter how nurturing and comforting they may be or how much value has been previously accorded to them. In this way, becoming-proper, delineated in the previous chapter as the process of properly taking up Dasein's coexistential heteronomy, entails a fundamental reconsideration of the commitment to socially constructed ethical norms. Such a critical reevaluation of ethics, however, is hard to pursue because it disrupts the everyday comfort and safety that Dasein seeks in the "they." Specifically, we can discern three distinct but related difficulties that hinder a critical reexamination of customary normativity.

The first difficulty is that such questioning of ethics is checked by the power of habituation. Since it challenges that which has been most revered by a particular public group, "[w]e cannot believe that our recognition of wrong, our commitment to right, our worship of God, our love of just laws, and our respect for human beings have as part of their fabric the inevitability of what we most abhor."[44] Leaving "what we most abhor" for later consideration, it should be noted that what is required in such a turning away from ethics is not to proclaim that this or that rule is faulty or that another may be better suited to the moral judgment at hand. Rather, the notion of value must itself be brought under scrutiny since it contributes, through its assignment, to the concealment of our average intelligibility and ways of behaving toward others. The habitual obedience to communal moral norms misleads Dasein into believing that it is morally dutiful, a belief that is reinforced by the approval that Dasein receives within the "they," while failing to ensure that one's éthos is open to the other. Therefore, habituation ensures that Dasein remains closed off to the *question* of ethics, to the question of how *it* might be "ethical" beyond ethical rules.

The second difficulty relates to the assumption of sovereign subjectivity that the "they" have created and maintain. The rupture involved in the calling of ethics into question brings Dasein face to face with the impropriety or inauthenticity of its average everydayness, which involves its masterful and controlling comportment with others: turning away from ethics "is nothing less than a twisting free of a body of selfhood that is given in its investment in not knowing its being or its propriety vis-à-vis its being."[45] The interruption of ethics arrests Dasein's self-conception as autonomous subject and throws it back into anxiety by reminding it that it is the being whose Being is an issue for it. Dasein, having no definite and determinate substance or nature, is called to itself by "being called to a being whose meaning is mortal temporality and thus has no intrinsic, determinate meaning at all."[46] Questioning ethics, then, is inseparable from reflecting on the subjectivity that Dasein posits for itself and the relation that ethics has in sustaining it. The indeterminacy and contingency of Dasein's Being reveals ethics to be the ossification of a communal and shared web of rules for a being it wills itself to be in its flight from its radical contingency.[47]

The final and most important difficulty arises from the realization that for all "our" rules and, what is worse, *because* of them, "we" have permitted and covered up that against which "we" purport to construct all moral rules: suffering.[48] Enclosed within the "they," Dasein comports itself ambiguously toward the world and, prompted by curiosity, it moves from one topic of interest to another without relating to others in a way that would let them be in their Being. Average solicitude reduces communication to idle talk and treats other Daseins as merely present in the world alongside Dasein, occluding in this way the paramount role of others and otherness for Dasein's constitution. Morally secure within communal norms and sets of rules set out according to the being it *believes* it is, Dasein drowns out its anxiety in the volume of idle talk and the speed of its curiosity. Avoiding anxiety makes Dasein's own suffering invisible: the truly other to Dasein is that which is most familiar: itself. Dasein's existence is rendered commonplace by the subjectivist assumptions it holds about itself in the publicness of the "they." The invisibility of anxiety reduces suffering to the occurrent, the recognizable, "real violence," as it were. Other Daseins are reduced to mere copresence and are rendered voiceless in the endless transmission of things of interest. Additionally, the noncommunal other, and her suffering, remains inaudible.

Questioning ethics, therefore, reveals a tension between the affirmative nurturing and socialization provided by one's own éthos, on the one hand, and that which the éthos makes inaudible, namely, the suffering and very voice of alterity, on the other hand. Ethics, located within normal and habitual behavior, is deaf, both to the suffering and voice of the other and also to the suffering and voice of Dasein as a radically thrown and contingent being that flees its anxiety in search of safety within the discourses of sovereign subjectivity. In this way, "[t]he interruption of ethics provides an opening to hear what is inaudible in our ethos."[49] Is there a way to open up one's communal éthos to the voice and suffering of the other? Can suffering be made audible without isolating oneself from one's own identity-giving group and practices? How can Dasein's own anxiety for its Being be acknowledged? In other words, how can an "ethical" self, which understands itself as an opening to otherness, be recovered without a severance from its identity-giving éthos?[50]

## HEARING AND SILENCE

Calling one's communal éthos and ethical constructions into question, it was suggested, might create an opening for Dasein to confront its deafness to its own and the other's suffering. The "they" absorb and nurture the self; at the same time such absorption also affects the self's openness both to the other and to its own existential otherness. Even if it is possible to conceive of being called away from the morality and habitual practices of one's particular public group, this still does not address the question of how the self can *hear* such a call. Henry Golz asks,

> Do we create the opening by wilfully moving beyond our situation and even beyond ourselves? Or do we, from the beginning and unknowingly, stand in the opening which is *granted*?[51]

How might everyday morality be questioned? The discussion of the call of conscience, outlined in the previous chapter, and particularly a recent modification to it suggested by Stephen Mulhall, might offer a way to make the other's and Dasein's own suffering audible and enable Dasein to be called to its mortal possibility. Mulhall proposes that the call of conscience, which is the way in which Dasein confronts its radical contingency, ought to be voiced by a third party, quite plausibly, a friend.[52] For Heidegger, the call comes within Dasein and yet from beyond it, signifying in this way that the voice of conscience "does the calling." This apparent indeterminacy "does not justify seeking the caller in some entity with a character other than that of Dasein," since the call of conscience is only ontologically possible because the Being of Dasein is "care" (*Being and Time*, 321).

Mulhall proposes that the call has to come from an authentic friend, one who by her example shows Dasein that its everyday way of being is not proper for it. The authentic friend has already differentiated herself from the they-self, and Dasein witnesses this. The authentic friend does not mirror Dasein in its actions and withholds the affirmation that the "they" usually grants Dasein for its perpetuated absorption in average comportment. Furthermore, the friend does not accept any inauthentic relation with Dasein. Thus, the "undifferentiated mass of the they" is disrupted: "[f]or Dasein could mirror another who exists as separate and self-determining, and who relates to others as genuinely other, only by relating to her as other and to itself as other to that other."[53] The mode of existence that the friend exhibits helps Dasein appropriate its own life properly. Rather than vocalizing the call, the friend disrupts Dasein's lostness in the "they" by example. Her very mode of existence awakens "otherness in Dasein itself; Dasein's relation to that other instantiates a mode of its possible self-relation (a relation to itself as other, not as self-identical)."[54] The mimetic processes by which Dasein is socialized in the "they" lend some support to Mulhall's contention: the proposal concurs with the phenomenal attribute of the call of conscience, which Heidegger suggests is "silent," and recalls, moreover, that the notion of "catching-up" with other Daseins is part of Being-with (*Being and Time*, 164). This type of "mimetic competition" involves Dasein in catching-up with the friend. Once an opening is made by this type of inauthentic catching-up, Dasein may see that its everyday existence is not proper for it and begin the struggle of becoming-proper. In this way, Dasein's own *capacity to hear* the other might be enhanced.[55]

This still does not address the question of *how* Dasein can hear the call, even if voiced by a friend. The problem might not be the source of the call as such, but rather the inability of Dasein to recognize itself as inauthentic while immersed in the "they": "lacking any conception of being other than it is, Dasein conflates its existential potential *(Seinskönnen)* and its existentiell actuality, and represses its uncanniness."[56] This is reinforced by publicness and by the location of Dasein's absorption and fascination with others in its ontological structure as Being-with. If, as Mulhall concedes, the lostness in the "they" arises primarily from Dasein's inability to recognize itself *as lost,* then the chances of hearing the call, *irrespective of its source,* are limited. In other words, even if the other calls to us, is the problem not the inability of the self to recognize both itself as immersed in the normative structures of the community and the exclusion of the other that this entails? The voicing of the call by a friend is not *in itself* sufficient to rouse Dasein from its absorption, nor does it offer any guarantee that the call will penetrate through Dasein's immersion in the "they." Therefore, it is necessary to ask about the "conditions of audibility"[57] of the other and to reflect on how they might be improved. In the following discussion I suggest that the ability to hear and the very conditions of audibility have to be understood as a stepping away from the idle talk of the public group into silence.

### The Conditions of Audibility

In what way can the conditions of audibility be improved, and how could the transformative process begin by which one's own éthos might open up to otherness and suffering? Is all that is required "a simple ontological [or otological?] operation, a small puncture through Dasein's ears so that it could for a moment at least escape the deafening sounds of 'they' drowning out the question of (its) Being"?[58] Heidegger traces such a possibility to the existential structure of discourse.[59] "Hearing is constitutive for discourse," he notes, because the ability to listen discloses authentically that Dasein is Being-with others *(Being and Time,* 206). Having more than a disclosive function, moreover, "[l]istening to . . . is Dasein's existential way of *Being-open* as Being-with for Others" (206; emphasis added). "Da-sein hears because it understands. As being-in-the-world that understands, with the others, it 'listens to' itself and to

*Mitda-sein,* and in this listening it belongs to these."[60] Hearing is an aspect of Dasein's attuned understanding that highlights its state of being thrown into the world *(Geworfenheit).* For Heidegger, Dasein is born into discursive relations, so to speak, but it is specifically "listening to" that enhances the coexistential character of existence. He notes, "Being-with develops in listening to another" (206). Dasein's heteronomous constitution is made concrete through hearing; Dasein lives according to its heteronomy when it listens to the other. When "Dasein is, or rather exists, *hearingly,*" it is brought into communion with itself as Being-with.[61]

Yet, what could make Dasein hear out of its lostness? How could the "conditions of audibility," to use Mulhall's term, be created? The possibility for hearing is related to keeping silent, because silence "is another essential possibility for discourse" *(Being and Time,* 208). Indeed, Miguel de Bestegui argues, silence "seems to occupy a . . . privileged position" in Heidegger's thought, and is regarded as a pivotal link in the relationship between discourse and otherness.[62] "In talking with one another, the person who keeps silent can 'make one understand' (that is he can develop an understanding) and he can do so more authentically than the person who is never short of words" (208). In this regard, "[k]eeping silent authentically is possible only in genuine discoursing" because "[t]o be able to keep silent, Dasein must have something to say—that is, it must have at its disposal an authentic and rich disclosure of itself" (208). In this way, silence cannot be associated with an inability to speak or be considered "a negation nor a privation"; on the contrary, silence should be thought of as "a positive possibility, indeed speech in its most proper sense."[63] As with hearing, with which silence is aligned, "silence is essentially *Mitteilung,* communicating and sharing" because "[i]n silence, Dasein has an ear for the Other, it is 'all ears,' as it were."[64]

As a constitutive part of discourse *(logos),* hearing belongs to everyday comportment in the world; yet, through hearing "Dasein is open, disclosed to itself, to the world and to others in the most authentic way."[65] Hearing, then, "constitutes the primary and authentic way in which Dasein is open for its ownmost potentiality-for-Being—*as in hearing the voice of the friend whom every Dasein carries with-it*" *(Being and Time,* 206; emphasis added). This is an extremely important passage, as it is the only one in *Being and Time* that makes this explicit reference to the other-as-friend, carried within, carried as otherness "in the mode of a voice, a purely phonic presence."[66] Such a "phonic presence" is not uncanny or ghost-like but ought to be understood as constitutive for Dasein as a speaking being. Jacques Derrida remarks, "This voice is an essentially understandable voice, the possibility of speech or discourse."[67]

The sort of presence invoked in Heidegger's quote is not representational: "[t]hrough its voice that I hear, I hear the friend itself, beyond its voice but in that voice"; it is almost an echo of Dasein's withness, where "I hear and carry the friend with me in hearing its voice. . . . Dasein carries it, one might say, in the figure of its voice, its metonymic figure (a part of the whole)."[68] It is a reminder that otherness is not external, in other words, it is not that from which Dasein distinguishes itself. Dasein has no choice with regard to its relation to otherness because, as Being-with, Dasein carries its otherness within it. This discussion of otherness and the facilitating role of hearing and silence oppose subjectivist understandings of relations as *voluntary:* relations can only be taken as voluntary on the basis of an ontological account of subjectivity that denies and obliterates Dasein's heteronomy, its constitution by otherness, and that refutes the other's constitutive role in Dasein's world.

The other-as-friend, whose voice Dasein carries within it, is the specificity of this otherness while at the same time it is Dasein being made aware of the internalization of otherness. "What defines 'the voice of the friend,' then, is not a quality, the friendly characteristic, but a belonging."[69] In this regard, the belonging also says more about the constitution of Dasein, its internal relation to otherness that is part and parcel of its thrownness, than about the friend, who is there as a voice to be heard without choice within Dasein:

> Through its voice, Dasein carries the friend with it, whether it wishes to or not, whether it knows it or not, and whatever its resolution. In any case, what matters here is not what the friend's voice says, not its said, not even the saying of its said. Hardly its voice. Rather what matters is the hearing *(das Hören)* of its voice.[70]

The ear to which the hearing refers, however, does not point to the organ ear but alludes instead to "the ear of and for one's self," attuned not to some inner life but the disclosedness of Dasein as projected outward and ahead of itself, "its very ek-sistence."[71] It is what renders the familiarity of one's own "self" strange. It is significant for becoming-proper that the voice, which Dasein carries within it, is the voice of the other-as-friend: "this hearing could not open Dasein 'to its ownmost potentiality-for-Being,' if hearing were not first the hearing of this voice, the exemplary metonymy of the friend that each Dasein bears close to itself *(bei sich trägt)*."[72] Beistegui, too, insists that propriety and silence are related, because "silencing reveals existence to itself, a call that can only be heard in the withdrawal of language."[73]

Derrida's earlier claim that what is significant for the "conditions of audibility" is the act of hearing, rather than the actual content of the other's voice, touches on two important concerns. First, it helps to dispel the assumption that listening to the other has only positive connotations. As Heidegger explains, it "can be done in several possible ways: following, going along with, and the privative modes of not-hearing, resisting, defying, and turning away" (*Being and Time*, 206–7). Similarly, it cannot be assumed that the voice of the other is a priori positive, as Derrida confirms: "The voice is not friendly, first because it is the voice of a friend, of someone, of another Dasein responding to the question 'who?'"[74] And yet, this is embedded in a different kind of positivity, which pertains to all modes of hearing. The incessant relation between discourse, hearing, and otherness encompasses opposition, resistance, and the possibility of turning away. Derrida suggests:

> [T]here is no essential opposition between *philein* and *Kampf* . . . these negative modes could still determine the hearing of the voice of the friend. To be opposed to the friend, to turn away from it, to defy it, to not hear it, that is still to hear and keep it, to carry with self, *bei sich tragen,* the voice of the friend.[75]

The second concern revolves around the question of how exemplary the figure of the friend is. The crucial question, Derrida argues, is whether the friend is used in those passages of *Being and Time* as any other interchangeable example ("why not sister, brother, father?" asks Derrida) or whether the concept of the friend is in itself crucial to audibility and propriety. Could it be possible that

> exemplarity functions here in another sense, not in the sense of the example among other possible examples, but of the exemplarity that gives to be read and carries in itself *all* the figures of *Mitdasein* as

*Aufeinander-hören*? All the figures of *Mitsein* would be figures of the friend, even if they were secondarily unfriendly or indifferent.[76]

Taking exemplarity in this exceptional way, understood not as interchangeable but as emblematic, suggests that the existential presence of the voice of "the friend" brings forth the possibility of transforming Dasein's selfhood and comportment to its world. This is a crucial and much-debated point that centers on the complex issue of Dasein's constitution as a self. As I noted at length in chapter 3, the self is constituted through and through by otherness in that its world is a web of meanings, assignments, and norms largely constructed by its public group, or community. It is this absorption into the "they," into otherness, which prompted Heidegger to suggest that the answer to the question "who is Dasein?" is not "I" but the "they." Yet, such immersion is not equivalent to openness to the other because the "they" perpetuates a discourse of autonomy and sovereignty of the individual, obstructing in this way Dasein's understanding of itself as heteronomous, as constituted by others. Hence, although embedded through and through in the "they," indeed, being the "they," Dasein considers itself autonomous and sovereign (see *Being and Time,* 368). The example of the friend indicates that the possibility for openness exists within this heteronomy; selfhood manifests itself as heteronomous and at the same time open to the other under conditions of silence and genuine hearing. By choosing to listen less to the idle talk of individuality sustained by the "they," Dasein radically questions itself and begins to hear the voice of heteronomy, that is, of the other within. It is on the basis of this heteronomous self-understanding, of hearing the voice of otherness within Dasein, that the concrete other can also be heard. Importantly, in the absence of a radical questioning about one's selfhood and about the role of otherness within the self, any others in the world can only be heard within the contours of communal éthos, by the rules and norms of customary practice, without a question of how it is that they are implicated in our self-constitution.[77]

In the space created by silence and hearing, there is a possibility of reformulating the communal and public éthos so that it is open to otherness, to the internal and permanent recollection of the voice of the friend, which Dasein carries with it. "[B]y developing what one would call an ontology of friendship or an ontophilology, Heidegger seems to provide the space for a rethinking of ethics."[78] This is because silence "makes dangerous the values by which we give ourselves common lives and establish the rules within which we are constituted" and, in this way, instigates the questioning of public norms and morality.[79] In the wider silence of Being/time Dasein's "reticence [Verschwiegenheit] makes something manifest, and does away with 'idle talk'" (Being and Time, 208); thus, "[h]earing in this silence [of Being/time] is finding oneself in the question of ethics."[80]

## TOWARD A RECOVERY OF AN "ETHICAL" SELF

The previous exploration suggests that the voice of the friend, exemplary of otherness, is carried within Dasein. However, Dasein's flight from the most fundamental otherness, its own, renders it deaf to the cry of the other. The conditions of audibility might be enhanced when idle talk (Gerede) is interrupted, perhaps by the example of a friend, as Mulhall has suggested. In the space of this suspension, there is silence, in which the voice of the other calls Dasein into question and is heard. Heard in silence, the voice is genuine communication and enables a "wrenching motion," by which Dasein "recoils" from its inauthentic practices and "puts itself in question by the values it holds."[81] Heidegger's critique of ethics and morality as a product of the "they" reveals that becoming-proper involves a "twisting free," not only from traditional ways of life but also from conceptions of selfhood that are not proper to it.[82] What become interrupted in this radical recoiling movement are not the worldly relations Dasein has with others, but rather the understanding of its existence in terms of subjectivity and self-sufficiency. The recoiling movement, described by Scott, enables an understanding of propriety as the placing of oneself in question, of questioning the adequacy of thinking of oneself as a subject:

> Heidegger thinks in the interruption of the meaning of our lives by the mortal possibility of living and finds in owning the being's interruption of our lives we may disown the theoretical and existential sufficiency of our selves for defining our being or ability to be.[83]

Therefore, becoming-proper is tantamount to becoming-other or strange to oneself.[84] This estrangement leads to a self-relationship where otherness is what Dasein becomes and how it relates to itself. Once this process is set into motion, Dasein's heteronomy is made apparent to it, enhancing in this way the possibility of listening to *"the voice of the friend whom every Dasein carries with it"* (*Being and Time,* 206; emphasis added).

Thus, the turn away from ethics is entailed in Dasein's own "destructive retrieve," where its selfhood is placed into question. Moreover, through sustained critical engagement with the shared past of its tradition, Dasein is able to discern its own "factical" and "repeatable possibilities,"[85] which are worthy of reconfiguration, but also to distance itself from possibilities that obscure its ability to be *(Seinskönnen).* Seen in this light, the turn away from ethics brings Dasein to face itself as being-guilty-as-the-basis-of-a-nullity (331), and discloses the difference between Dasein and the customary ways of living within its public group: "the call itself discloses not the power of an ethos but the difference of human being, in its being, from traditional ways of life."[86]

To find oneself in the "question of ethics," to use Scott's phrase, is to attempt a recovery of the "ethical" self, which is open to itself as strange and to the voice of the other as always within it.[87] The process of attaining this "ethical" kind of selfhood is not universal but unique to each struggle for propriety; its achievement is never assured or static; one cannot phenomenally speak of completion because what is defining of authenticity is the effort to achieve it.[88] The struggle, the ceaseless movement toward propriety, can be thought, Walter Davis argues, as "the 'ethical' relationship one is living toward oneself."[89] Thus "the ethical" is not universal; on the contrary, it is particularist because it refers to "the primary relationship which underlies all the positions and attitudes one adopts toward the world."[90] How one relates to others on the basis of this self-relationship is not given in advance nor can it be collectively dictated since this would mean a fall into the (constitutive yet inauthentic) public and habitual practices that make up one's éthos within the "they." Yet, in the absence of the relationship one resolutely assumes toward one's own existence, it is impossible to have any proper relationship toward others.

Of course, it can be argued that this self-relationship is not ethical in any common sense of the word but ontological. In "Letter on Humanism," Heidegger refers to ethics as the dwelling in the nearness of Being.[91] The term *éthos* is modified with propriety in mind[92] so that it now means abode, dwelling place. The word names the open region in which the human being dwells. The open region of his abode allows what pertains to the essence of the human being, and what in thus arriving resides in nearness to him, to appear.[93]

There might be an intimate relationship, therefore, between "propriety" and something like "ethicity," which is, according to Derrida, that which makes ethics ethical.[94] The movement to propriety is "ethical" then in the sense that it indicates a struggle expressive of a self-relationship that brings Dasein to reside closer to its Being. In this way, Dasein's genuine appropriation of its heteronomous existence, the *agonistic* relationship it sustains with itself, might be compared to Michel Foucault's Heidegger-inspired ethics as "a practice; ethos is a manner of being."[95] The "ethical" self, then, would embody its propriety toward its finite being as a *techne tou biou,* or a technology of the self.[96] Only on the *ground* of such a self-relationship can an ethical attitude arise toward other beings. It is only on the ground of itself as finite transcendence and unique appropriation of customary and commonly available possibilities that authentic Dasein can ask the ethical question "who am I; what shall I do?" and find an answer in its concrete situation.[97]

## SELFHOOD AND RULES OF PROPER CONDUCT

The recovery of the "ethical" self refers to the "ethicity of propriety," where propriety is the self-relationship that enables Dasein to take up its heteronomy *properly* and to hear the voice of otherness that it carries within. By developing such a self-relationship, the voice of the other can also be genuinely heard. Returning to the discussion of coexistence, within the larger debate about cosmopolitanism's call for a global ethics, how might the recovery of the "ethical" self facilitate a reconceptualization of both ethics and coexistence? How does this recovery cohere, if at all, with the cosmopolitan suggestion for rethinking coexistence appropriately for this era of globalization? Does the recovery of an "ethical" self, which understands itself as an opening to otherness, necessitate relinquishing the construction of ethical rules and moral (and juridical) codes, as called for by recent cosmopolitan thought, as inauthentic, as a remnant of a subjectivist ontology? Or could the "ethicity of propriety" form the basis for minimalist ethical construction that could join cosmopolitan discourses in their search for global ethical norms and rules?[98] This possibility of utilizing the recovery of the "ethical" self as a ground for ethical construction is critically examined next.[99]

### The "Ethical" Self: On the Impossibility of a Renewed Ethical Foundationalism

There is a tension between the affirmative nurturing associated with the socialization processes of a communal éthos and the impropriety of average intelligibility in which these processes result, so that the voice of the outsider and of Dasein's own anxiety in the face of its own Being become inaudible to it. One cannot do away with éthos, since the averageness it generates is constitutive for the totality of meaning in which Dasein orients its existence. Socialization is intimately connected to "belonging," Jean-Luc Nancy notes, and "there is nothing sentimental, domestic, or 'community-oriented' about wanting to say we. It is existence reclaiming its due or its condition: co-existence."[100] Acknowledging that universal ethical rules are embedded in communal *ethe,* Scott wonders whether it would be possible to maintain "a limited field of nurturance . . . a structure that shows itself differently, that shows itself to be outside time and outside ethnic suspicions and conservative provinciality" and, at the same time, delineate on the basis of it "a field of laws and principles, that brings with it, into time, indications, more than hints, but patterns that point to a transtemporal circumscription of the writhing, belligerent interplay of *ethea.*"[101] Is it possible, in other words, to bring into the universal certain limited indications of how to interact among multiple and distinct *ethea*? Such a field of "nurturance," Scott suggests, would effectively maintain the identity-giving and norm-creating characteristics of the local public norms and rules while, at the same time, attempt to provide a minimalist set of principles that would restrain the éthos's resistance to otherness and render it open to the influence and voice of alterity. Put differently, what is at stake in Scott's question is the possibility of universalizing the recovery of the ethical self out of a specific éthos. Four related arguments will be examined as to the impossibility of renewing a universalism grounded on the recovery of the "ethical" self.

The first argument reiterates the impossibility of renewing universalism on the ground of the "ethical" self by examining the conditions under which universalism is possible, specifically in its connection to foundationalism. For Hermann Philipse, suggestions for the introduction of even minimal "indications" for ethical conduct can be taken as merely another "stage in the historical development of ethical foundationalism."[102] If this is indeed so, what is the ultimate ground on which these indicative principles would be based, and does not such a search for a foundation, in and of itself, "lead to an infinite regress unless there are first principles of ethics that are so secure that further justification is not needed"?[103] If one contests, therefore, "the idea that there is supreme moral truth from which rules of conduct could be deduced," then a renewed foundationalism becomes untenable.[104] Andrew Linklater has recently suggested from an "unashamedly" universalist position that "the possibility of occupying an Archimedean standpoint which permits objective knowledge of permanent moral truths which bind the whole of humanity is a claim" that not only has been repeatedly contested but that contemporary theorists "are correct to deny."[105] Yet, surely Scott's call for the introduction of minimal indications is not a suggestion that a secure foundation of moral truth, on which ethical construction can be based, exists. Could, however, Dasein's newly recovered "ethical" openness to alterity, seen in its "self-relationship," *serve* as this foundation for the universal construction of rules? Could one rely, in other words, on the recovery of the "ethical" self as "some kind of ontological commitment" to act as a basis for construction?[106]

This brings us to the second argument as to why the answer is most likely negative. For the "ethical" self to act as the *basis* for even minimalist ethical construction, authentic Dasein would have to be ascribed a substantive essence. In chapter 4, the impossibility of Dasein having an essence was discussed extensively in terms of "Being-towards-death" and Dasein as Being-the-basis-of-a-nullity. Dasein's radically contingent and anxious existence means that Dasein's propriety is found not in permanence but in an abyssal structure that can never act as ground. Derrida notes, "In such a structure, which is a non-fundamental one, at once superficial and bottomless, still and always 'flat,' the proper-ty *(propre)* is sunk."[107] Dasein's groundlessness, therefore, arrests the foundationalist drive from instantiating itself in an ultimate ground: this could only be Dasein's self-relationship, the content of which is that Dasein *has* no ground. In becoming proper, the "ethical" self comes to terms with this groundlessness and into communion with itself as strange. What Dasein has, rather, is a disposition toward itself (it is ready for anxiety) and solicitude toward others. As such, it cannot form the foundation that this kind of ethical construction requires. "Nothing would be more violent or naive," writes Derrida, "than to call for more frontality, more thesis or more thematization, to suppose that one can find a standard *here*."[108] The "ethical" self, engaged in a struggle for propriety, is not an *answer* in the form of a ground, but an awareness that it is itself *questionable*.

A third consideration as to why universalizing the insights gained in the recovery of the "ethical" self is untenable arises from acknowledging that

> ontology can provide ethics . . . only with formal indications of the general characteristics of human existence. In turn, the practical disciplines can be of help to human action only indirectly by providing a rough outline of the practical sphere in question that has to be interpretively concretized in the historical situation of one's own existence.[109]

The role of ontological examination, in other words, is not to dictate explicitly how one ought to act by constructing ethical rules; rather, it "frees the individual for his self-reflection."[110] When, just after the Second World War, Jean Beaufret asked Heidegger why he had hesitated in constructing an ethics, Heidegger's reply could only be that "the question was essentially unanswerable."[111] The responsibility of philosophy was to induce thinking, rather than to impose restrictions or conditions of an ontic nature, as if these were generalizable to each and every person's concrete situation. Hans-Georg Gadamer also notes,

> How can it be the task of a philosopher to construe an ethical system that proposes or prescribes a social order or recommends a new way of molding morals or general public convictions about concrete matters?[112]

Ethical judgments can only be taken on the basis of the factical situation and its specificity. Moreover, as was noted above with the examination of éthos, ethical norms "involve processes of human learning and socialization that are already under way, forming an *éthos,* long before people confront the radical questions associated with philosophy. 'Ethics' presupposes a lived system of values."[113]

Whatever assistance on how to live one's life ethics might desire to provide, it can never replace reflection about and *in* the factical situation by which already existing communal rules of conduct are interpreted. To answer the *question* of ethics with even a minimalist codified morality is to ignore that codification can only be understood as embedded and socialized into a group éthos that resists the "imposition of outside influences" or at best interprets them on the ground of its éthos. To claim that rule making could lie outside one's own éthos, outside of a historical and factical situation, would be to assert that morality requires a kind of reasoning based on logic that everyone is capable of.[114] It is to suggest that reasoning is not embedded within local practices but is universal, yet this might indicate an ethnocentric outlook only thinly disguised as universalism.[115]

Finally, and related to the third argument, it is not possible to encompass universal ethical construction in a philosophy of the limit, such as Heidegger's phenomenology of Dasein, which recognizes that an ahistorical and foundational approach toward proper conduct cannot but fail to do what it is intended to achieve: make the other's voice audible and act in ways that do not occlude the heteronomous facticity of existence. Such a philosophy of the limit responds to, and expresses, the general philosophical crisis in which ethical theorizing finds itself. Universalism "presupposes that there exists an ethics, or at least that an ethics is possible. Now it is probably the case today that neither of these conditions is fulfilled."[116] In this regard ethical contruction

> also suffers from the general exhaustion of philosophical possibilities and manifestly cannot claim to stand outside that exhaustion except at the cost of a certain blindness towards it and its origin: how and from where could one *philosophically* get back beyond Heidegger's delimitation of ethics and humanism?[117]

The ascription of a substantive content to the "ethical" self and the attempt to universalize it is a return to a philosophical humanism whose possibility is limited by the exhaustion of philosophy's own possibilities.[118] What has been called the "end of philosophy"[119] refers not only to "end" as having reached exhaustion or culmination, or even to its goal, but also to the understanding of philosophy as a finite undertaking.[120]

The impossibility of a renewed universalism, however, brings into relief that what currently exists is but "an urgent *plea* for a universal morality."[121] It is questionable whether a set of universal principles could, indeed, bring about a transformation of local *ethe* and provide a design for "interethical" interaction. There is no assurance that what has been inaudible in one's éthos will not be more starkly so if voiced in ways not able to be captured or accommodated by codified norms. The preceding discussion considered that the "ethical" self cannot provide a new foundation nor can its comportment within the factical situation be universalized. Such a refusal, however, does not deny the plea for a global ethics of inclusiveness; it merely suggests that a global ethics might lie, not in ethical construction of universalizable norms and rules, but in a *disposition* or *sensibility* toward the other, which the "ethical" self can cultivate and espouse.

Discussing this disposition, or sensibility, allows a return directly to the reconceptualization of coexistence for international relations and for international ethical discourses that wish to confront and respond to the limitations of universalist and foundationalist thought.[122] The turn to *disposition* is a measured response to the unworking of the modern subject by the phenomenological attentiveness to the facticity of existence; it is a response that heeds, more than ever, the desire to hear the voice of the other, which does not pursue an ethical project that unwittingly obscures its very object of concern.

### The "Ethical" Self's Liberating Solicitude: Coexistence and Ethics

What is *proper* to Dasein, then, has little to do with the moral norms and rules of the public group, or community, in which Dasein is thrown; similarly, it has little to do with norms and rules grounded on a universalized understanding of propriety sought by prominent liberal cosmopolitan discourses. There is no standard of what an authentic human being ought to be; what there is, rather, is the possibility of modifying one's inauthenticity and moving toward propriety as linked to the struggle to render audible the voice of otherness, which Dasein already carries with it. Nonetheless, a mediation among "belligerent *ethea*," which ethical construction wishes to restrain, is still desirable in a world of value plurality and intercommunal conflict.[123] As noted earlier, the notion of the "ethical" self can be understood as an opening to alterity that constitutes the very ethicity of any ethics. Dasein's openness to the other comes from seeing that its ground is nothingness and that no other transcendence is possible but a plunge toward the world of others and other-mediated meaning. Becoming-proper is a constant movement toward the relational totality that is its world, within which relationships with others become reevaluated in their own facticity and thrownness. The recovery of silence and hearing, resulting from the questioning of communal éthos, brings Dasein to face itself as "singularity of the self that knows itself as opening to alterity,"[124] a knowledge that arises from an awareness of itself as strange. "Singularity . . . installs relation as the withdrawal of identity, and communication as the withdrawal of communion," Nancy argues.[125]

The disposition associated with the "ethical" self suggests "that human being can be thought in terms of the clearing or space that it makes for Being, for world, for the realms and regimes of 'truth' or manifestness, for the plurality of cultures."[126] Such a disposition attests to the desire for a different conception of coexistence, one that has moved beyond the logic of composition and is associated with openness and concern for the other. This disposition can be traced to what Heidegger called "liberating solicitude."[127]

Liberating solicitude is, according to Heidegger, one of the two radical manifestations of solicitude (discussed in chapter 3). In addition to privative forms (such as indifference, not caring, neglect), solicitude might take the form of displacing the other. This occurs when Dasein's solicitude for the other "take[s] away 'care' from the Other and puts itself in his position in concern: it can *leap in* for him" (*Being and Time,* 158; emphasis in original). Although still expressive of care for the other, this kind of solicitude does not facilitate the process by which the other uniquely appropriates his shared world and confronts his own radical contingency and groundlessness. *Liberating* solicitude, on the other hand, "pertains essentially to authentic care—that is to the existence of the other . . . it helps the other to become transparent to himself *in* his care and to become *free for* it" (159; emphasis in original). Only the solicitude that "leaps forth and liberates" discloses to the other how his own existence is strange and contingent and allows the other to embark on his own struggle and become-proper. Through this proper kind of comportment, "I call the other to face his own anxious self-responsibility."[128] Liberating solicitude is not only a caring-for the other, it is a *critical* practice that shakes the other out of his own lostness in the communal éthos and enables him to undertake his own struggle for propriety, a propriety expressed as an openness to the other.

It is important to note, however, that liberating solicitude does not only assist the other to face his own Being as care, to recognize himself as heteronomous and strange; furthermore, it is the precondition for the other to become transparent to me as "for who he is."[129] This is most definitely not the disavowal of the other that Levinas accuses Heidegger of; indeed, John Caputo has argued that in this conception of interaction with alterity can be found "an ethics of otherness" based on humility and compassion.[130] It is through such a liberating (in the sense of disclosive) solicitude that Dasein may recognize others in their own groundlessness. Liberating solicitude, far from being a paternalistic attitude toward the other, is the comportment by which Dasein shares the other's basis-of-a-nullity and comports to the other as Being-with.

How does liberating solicitude enable a reconceptualization of coexistence beyond the logic of composition? As the "ethical" self's disposition, liberating solicitude is able to penetrate a particular factical situation, even if this crosses the boundaries of another community. Similarly, Lawrence Vogel claims, it allows the other to do the same because it involves the "recognition of the claim of others who, from beyond 'our' horizon, call into question the parochialism of our tradition insofar as it does not speak for them and who demand that we include their perspectives in the effort to understand ourselves."[131] Such a disposition, furthermore,

> does not involve a subordination of self and others to a common standard that would provide a decision-procedure telling anyone what he ought to do in a particular situation; rather, it involves an attunement to the particularity of others, to others *as* truly other, stemming from an awareness of the singularity of one's own existence.[132]

This is not an impersonal and anonymous perspective; it is an "interpersonal orientation motivated by one's desire not to incorporate others into 'the universal' but, rather, to 'let others be' in their freedom for their own possibilities and to allow one's self-understanding to be informed by theirs."[133] The "ethical" self implies the withdrawal of identity based solely on the nurturing éthos in which Dasein is primarily and initially constituted and socialized, and thus can sustain "a form of coexistence in which one remains attentive to others as centres of transcendence and possibility who are never subsumed by the public projects in which they happen to be absorbed."[134] The "ethical" self liberates the other not by awarding him the badge of a universal humanity, rights, and entitlements, and thus reducing him to sameness, but by calling him to face his own heteronomy and groundlessness.

Moving beyond its reduction to the composition of otherwise unrelated subjects, coexistence can be sustained and renewed by the disposition of liberating solicitude, which does not subsume the other into its sameness but calls him out to his own Being. The liberation comes precisely from the unworking and "releasement" from modern subjectivity that, as has been discussed throughout, is predicated on the denial of heteronomy. This is an active letting-be, a releasement to one's own Being, in which genuine coexistence might be found.[135] Coexistence, then, is a mutual process of disclosing one's own and the other's otherness, of helping the other become aware of his own heteronomy, and of critically confronting the effacement of such heteronomy within publicly prevalent discourses. In other words, the unworking of the modern subject is taken a step further with the elaboration of the "ethical" self, not as a replacement of the modern subject, but precisely *not* as its replacement: a decentering occurs with the ontological consideration of a groundless self whose Being-with, manifested in its solicitude to others, places heteronomy at the center of coexistence. The solicitude of the "ethical" self constitutes the very ethicity of what is "ethical" such that coexistence becomes a manifestation of the "ethical."

For the discipline of international relations this discussion encourages the rethinking of global ethics from being reliant on legal instruments such as human rights toward cultivating a disposition of openness toward the other. This is a proposal that has conceptual merits and goes to the heart of debates about xenophobia, refugees, migration, and so on. However, such a consideration is not a direct replacement of proposals about international institutions and the internationalization of regimes. It is a discussion that alerts scholarship as to the possibility of a different *path* toward global ethics. Furthermore, the attention paid to the questioning of ethics and the cultivating of a disposition toward the other through a reconsideration of how the other constitutes selfhood also means that global ethics is intimately related to the relationship one has with one's own self. As such, it is a continuous process that cannot be fully achieved, in the sense of being instituted once and for all.

## CONCLUSION

In this chapter I examined recent proposals within international relations about constructing a global ethics based on the promotion of human rights as a way of asking the question with which I began the book: how can one think of coexistence beyond the logic of composition? In so doing, I reflected on how coexistence might be rethought in terms of ethical selfhood by undertaking a recovery of an "ethical" self that can assist with the questioning of both coexistence and also conventional conceptions of ethics understood as the ethical construction of universalizable norms and their associated codification and legalization. Through a "destructive retrieve" ethics was called into question, and its meaning was both subverted and expanded. The linguistic trajectory of the word *éthos,* from which ethics is derived, showed that it arises through processes of habituation within distinct, customary ways of life and that it is embedded within habitual and average behavior. Analyzed through Heidegger's discussion of the "they," ethics is shown to be implicated in the processes of socialization and conformity, which are constitutive and nurturing for Dasein as a being whose Being is Being-with. However, these processes enable only an inauthentic intelligibility, which is not appropriate for Dasein as Being-in-the-world: they comfort it into considering itself as subject and encourage it to relate to things in the world as objects and to others as merely copresent. Morality is implicated in this lostness of Dasein and leads it to become deaf to the other and to its own otherness.

Shown to be contained within an éthos, to be a community's own, ethics is disclosed as the codification and promulgation of particularist practices and norms. In this sense, it becomes clear that any claim to the universal must traverse through the particular. Universal aspirations for specific codes remain little more than a *plea.* For international relations, whose initial and primary attempts at ethical theorizing have been dominated by universal theories of ethics, this contextualization locates such attempts within their particularist, almost exclusively Western, locations.

Moving away from ethical construction and codification, the recovery of the "ethical" self, understood as a stance of heteronomous selfhood, "which knows itself as opening to alterity,"[136] forms a different path toward coexistence and ethics. Recovering the "ethical" self becomes possible through hearing and silence, in which the other's voice and suffering can be heard. This "ethical" self, however, cannot be utilized as a basis or foundation for universal ethics. It cannot serve as a deconstructed but reasserted ground for ethical construction; rather, it is a kind of selfhood that is at the heart of the ethicity of ethics. Yet this prohibition against foundationalism and universalism directed the discussion to the articulation of *disposition* or *sensibility* toward the other. For IR, this could become a different path in the effort to work within the limits of Enlightenment thought, at its margins. The turn to the disposition of liberating solicitude is a response befitting an awareness of the limit, which abides by the unworking of the modern subject through the phenomenological attentiveness to the facticity of existence; it is a response that heeds, more than ever, the desire to hear the voice of the other and witness its suffering and pursue no ethical project that unwittingly obscures its very object of concern. The recovery of the "ethical" self as best manifested in its disposition has also come full circle to think coexistence as the sensibility of a heteronomous being who is aware of its disclosive role for itself and the other. In this regard, liberating solicitude is more than an empathy for the other; it is a caring-for (in the sense of *Fürsorge*) that calls the other to his own anxious Being-in-the-world and lets him assume his fundamental mortal possibility.

As was suggested, liberating solicitude, as the coexistential disposition of the "ethical" self, is a critical practice, calling the other to face his own contingency and heteronomy. As such, it assists the final discussion about rethinking coexistence politically in the sense of constituting the community beyond composition and away from essence, which is the focus of the next chapter.

# 6

## *Coexistence, Community, and Critical Belonging*

The theoretic construct of the self-sufficient subject, and its relations of mastery over world and others, presents one of the main obstacles hindering the disclosure of the "irreducibly plural worlds"[1] in which the self finds itself. The recovery of an "ethical" selfhood explored in the previous chapter indicated the ways in which the "ethical" self becomes open to, and in a sense embodies, its innate otherness by cultivating silence and hearing. Its contribution lies in illustrating that it *is* possible to move away from the self-sufficiency of the modern subject and to enable a proper consideration of how a non-self-sufficient, heteronomously constituted, coexistential self can take up its radical relationality. In other words, once the radical relationality of the self is revealed in the disposition of the "ethical" self toward others, possibilities for rethinking *political* coexistence otherwise, and indeed politics itself, can also be properly considered; this is the self-stated task of the critical enterprise of political theorizing, which has called into question its own reliance on traditional categories of politics.

In this chapter I explore how coexistence is to be conceptualized *politically*, given this shift away from the subjectivist discursive domain toward a hermeneutic of non-self-sufficiency as exemplified in the recovery of the "ethical" self.[2] It is, of course, often argued that the act of bringing about a hermeneutic shift in the terms of discourse is itself a political act, which seeks to effect a change in the ways the world, and beings within the world, are to be understood. "[E]very hermeneutical program," argues Stanley Rosen, "is at the same time itself a political manifesto or the corollary of a political manifesto."[3] In part, this is undoubtedly true, and seen in this vein, the recovery of the "ethical" self *is* in itself political, in the sense that it has weighty repercussions for the unproblematic usage of the modern subject in international political theory, rendering the determination of coexistence according to the logic of composition both untenable and unnecessary as a mechanism of articulation of the social. The suggestion that coexistence is implicated in the questioning relation to one's self and to others[4]—a relation best exemplified in the "ethical" self's critical practice of liberating solicitude—is crucial for the task of outlining a *political* thought of coexistence because it represents a hermeneutic shift in the terms of discourse, which enables the conceptualization of a heteronomously constituted, coexistential self for international political theory. The discussion of the "ethical" self is decidedly political in that its recovery avails international political theory of a form of selfhood amenable to nonmasterful relations, which could form the basis for rethinking political coexistence beyond contractarian and additive thinking dependent on sovereign and self-sufficient understandings of the subject.

It is, however, also important to acknowledge that although this "recovery," and the hermeneutic shift it facilitates, is necessary for a political thought of coexistence beyond composition, it is not sufficient in itself because it does not fully address the book's initial concern that international relations does not directly and explicitly discuss the *subject* of coexistence. In the present chapter, a more explicit interrogation of how to think *politically* about coexistence is undertaken: the core question thus becomes, in the words of Jean-Luc Nancy, "What becomes of being-with when the *with* no longer appears as composition, but rather as dis-position?"[5] In what way, to put it otherwise, is the primacy of relation to be theorized politically outside of the additive logic of composition of self-present and self-sufficient subjects?

Any such attempt to articulate a political thought of coexistence must, in general, struggle to avoid an additive (and, therefore, purely procedural) determination according to the logic of composition, as outlined throughout this volume—but this is not the only issue that needs to be confronted. More important, any such endeavor must *also* address the difficult questions of whether it is, in fact, possible to put Heidegger's thought in *Being and Time* to political use, and even if it is possible, whether his thought actually *ought* to be used politically. Is not any political thought of coexistence derived from, or associated with, the thought of Martin Heidegger immediately tainted by his commitment to National Socialism in the 1930s, when he assumed the rectorship of the University of Freiburg in 1933, and his subsequent failure to apologize for, or even discuss, this involvement in the postwar years?[6] The following discussion of the political thought of coexistence, in other words, necessarily takes place within a still-raging debate fueled by increased acknowledgment within the fields of philosophy and politics of his deplorable engagement, which is now familiarly captured by the term "Heidegger's politics."

To put this differently, while critics might accept that Heidegger's thought unworks modern subjectivity and, therefore, can be used to question the reduction of coexistence to copresence, they will certainly wonder whether his thought leads to the opposite extreme, to the determination of coexistence (and more precisely of community) according to a nationalist essence. And is this not the reenactment of the familiar dichotomy between proceduralism and essence, which manifests itself as the debate between liberalism and communitarianism in the fields of international relations and political theory?[7] In trying to discuss coexistence *politically* while avoiding the logic of composition, I examine two objections to the political use of Heidegger's thought. At the same time, I articulate a conception of how community is constituted when *not* determined according to an essence (such as religion, nation, ethnos, language, and so on), a reading that will subsequently enable the emergence of a political selfhood that has a distinct questioning relationship to its historical tradition and, consequently, is able to steer between the extremes of composition and essence.

## HEIDEGGER'S POLITICS AND THE THOUGHT OF COEXISTENCE

The debate on Heidegger's politics has articulated two pertinent objections to the suggestion that one might usefully utilize the recovery of the "ethical" self out of Heidegger's *Daseinanalytik* in order to articulate a political thought of coexistence.[8] The first objection argues that the unworking of the modern subject leaves a gap, a *caesura,* in political thinking that is not addressed in the hermeneutics of facticity one finds in Heidegger's *Being and Time.* The second objection refutes the first and (re)reads *Being and Time* in light of Heidegger's involvement with the Nazis, deeming it to be at best politically vague and thus open to conservative revolutionism, and at worst as determining community along nationalistic and even racist lines and thus wholly inappropriate for a thought of coexistence. This section examines both of these objections in turn.

### An Apolitical Thought?

The contemporary discussion of Heidegger's politics makes it easy to forget that the early reception of *Being and Time* held the view that it was largely an *apolitical* work. Advocates of this position argue that the apoliticality of the phenomenological discussion of *Being and Time* presents a limitation to the work's usefulness for political thought. The argument that *Being and Time* is apolitical arises not only from the lack of explicit discussions about politics in that work, but is also grounded in the purported absence of a positive account of sociality to replace Heidegger's "critique" of the "they."[9] While adhering to conceptions of itself as an autonomous and sovereign subject, the nature of publicness occludes Dasein's lostness in the "they," its behavior of conformity, and the leveling-down of its possibilities, and this results in a generalized consideration of its ability to be *(Seinskönnen).* However, this critique of the "they" has led Dominique Janicaud and other commentators to suggest that "[i]n *Being and Time,* there is thus an especially negative phenomenology of being-with, which at no point introduces a positive phenomenology of political sociability."[10] Janicaud further argues,

> The fundamentally ontological turn given by Heidegger to the phenomenological project . . . reduces the rational city-dweller [of Aristotle] and the political space to the "they" and only leaves open an apolitics, an indeterminate and (in Hegel's term) "abstract" authentic sociability, to *Dasein* concerned with its possibilities.[11]

The purpose of the articulation of the "they" as the everyday manifestation of Being-with was to render strange the familiar accounts of man *as subject,* that is, as autonomous and self-sufficient, giving instead a phenomenological description of the everyday being of Dasein as indistinguishable from others. Heidegger's account of the "they," therefore, is an extensive criticism of humanism's conception "of man as *animal rationale,* and hence on the basis of a preconceived notion of 'nature' or 'animality' or 'objects.'"[12] At the same time, Heidegger's implicit critique sought to avoid reifying the "they" as a preferred "alternative" to the subject.[13] Nevertheless, according to Janicaud, the dismantling of the rational, reflective subject undertaken in *Being and Time* leads Heidegger to ignore *political* socialization. Jürgen Habermas largely concurs when he notes that "[a]ttributing a merely derivative status to *Mitsein* (Being-with-others) he [Heidegger] also misses the dimension of socialization and intersubjectivity."[14] Michael Theunissen lends further credence to this critique when he writes that "individualization is supposed to make being-with-one-another possible, a being-with-one-another that, by comparison with the absorption in the They, is presented as authentic"; yet this purported authenticity, Theunissen argues, only means "[t]hat *Dasein* which is individualized down to itself has equally to be with Others is derived, purely formally, by Heidegger, from the circumstance that authentic being-self remains being-in-the-world and that this latter is still being-with."[15] While other accounts of modernity might corroborate this phenomenological description, in Heidegger, it is claimed, there is no "rehabilitative" discussion of political sociability to provide alternatives for political socialization. In this sense, Heidegger's phenomenological reflections are deemed to be ill-suited for the task of political thought. Indeed, Michel Haar argues, the "absence of political reflection" in *Being and Time* is regrettable, making the "idea of a collective engagement, be it democratic or totalitarian, difficult if not impossible."[16] This absence, moreover, is implicated in the "misinterpretation of 1933": "[f]or it is indeed a misinterpretation, to say nothing of the error of judgement concerning Hitler, to use the categories of *Being and Time* in a collective and political sense."[17]

Such objections to using Heidegger for political thought have not gone unchallenged, however. Other scholars have suggested that Heidegger's focus on practical activity in Dasein's average everydayness (discussed as "engaged immersion" in chapter 3) might not necessarily be a sign of the *apolitical* character of his work at all.[18] Miguel de Beistegui argues, for example, that the nature of the existential analytic might be better captured by the term "prepolitical":

> If *Being and Time* is indeed apparently devoid of political views and
> opinions, if it displaces the terrain of the philosophical investigation
> in the direction of an analysis of being, or of the way in which things
> come to be present for Dasein on the basis of the way in which they
> are granted with meaning, it also acknowledges the essentially col-
> lective and historical dimension of human existence, *prior to* ques-
> tions of organization of this being-in-common.[19]

If his thought is prepolitical, rather than apolitical, it may be possible to put his thought to political use. But in any case, much here
also depends on what one means by "political." Although "prepolitical" in one sense, James Ward suggests that "Heidegger is a
*political* thinker if by 'political' one means, in the manner of classical antiquity, the order of human things."[20] So what for Beistegui is
a prepolitical thought, for Ward qualifies as proper political thought
based on an understanding of the political derived from classical
antiquity. In light of such contrasting opinions, "the seeming apoliticality of the project of fundamental ontology cannot be settled
so easily."[21]

   In fact, as will be shown, both of these related perspectives suggesting that Heidegger's phenomenology is either apolitical or prepolitical may fail to acknowledge that the possibility for political
thought might genuinely exist within his text. In a sense, both views
underplay Heidegger's discussion and the possibility that one could
retrieve a political thought of coexistence from it. In part, this may
derive from a restricted understanding of politics and the political;
for this reason, in the next section of this chapter I illustrate that,
within Heidegger's thought, there exists the possibility for a politics
that is open to the other. To substantiate this claim, the second and
graver objection to his thought, based on Heidegger's own personal
politics, must first be examined.

### A Nazi Thought? Mapping the Debate on Heidegger's Politics

The second objection to using the recovery of the "ethical" self from
Heidegger's discussion for a *political* thought of coexistence, and for
political thought more generally, disagrees with the first contention
that it is an apolitical (or prepolitical) work. It asks, on the contrary,
whether the possibility for articulating an account of coexistence is
impaired both by the apparent determination of authentic Being-

with according to "a people" within the analysis of *Being and Time* and also by the political interpretation of the overall project of fundamental ontology given to it by Heidegger's own subsequent engagement with National Socialism.

At the most obvious level, Heidegger appears to determine Dasein's cohistorizing in a nationalist manner when authentic Being-with *(Mitsein)* is attached to the "community" and the "people" in paragraph 74 of *Being and Time*. Let us quote extensively from this crucial and contentious paragraph, where Heidegger writes:

> If fateful Dasein, as Being-in-the-world, exists essentially in Being-with Others, its historizing is a co-historizing *[Mitgeschehen]* and is determinative for it as *destiny [Geschick]*. This is how we designate the historizing of the community, of a people. Destiny is not something that puts itself together out of individual fates, any more than Being-with-one-another can be conceived as the occurring together of several Subjects. Our fates have already been guided in advance, in our Being with one another in the same world and in our resoluteness for definite possibilities. Only in communicating and in struggling does the power of destiny become free. (*Being and Time*, 436)[22]

Why should Heidegger specifically determine Being-with in terms of a "people"; why does he emphasize such terms as "community," "fate," "destiny," and the historical tradition? And more important, should this discussion about "a people" be read, in light of Heidegger's Nazism, as the emergence of nationalism in his thought? These two questions require greater examination and the response to them is decisive for a critical account of *political* coexistence.

Let us take the second question first, which must be discussed within the context of the continuing debate about the "case of Heidegger."[23] Although few scholars would presently ignore or excuse Heidegger's involvement with the Nazis, three distinct positions exist as to how this affects our consideration of *Being and Time* and his earlier thought more generally. A first group of scholars has argued that Heidegger's thought is inseparable from his politics, and even *Being and Time*, which chronologically predates his rectorship, should be read as a response to National Socialism, as some kind of protofascist text in which the very origins of his politics can be traced.[24] Johannes Fritsche, for example, has provided a rich textual discussion of paragraph 74 of *Being and Time,* which leads him to argue that "the soil of *Being and Time* is völkisch."[25] He castigates most (left-leaning)[26] Heideggerians for having "cultivated this ignorance [of the völkisch character of *Being and Time*] by making procedures of decontextualization their primary tool, and they have been harvesting the sweet grapes of postmetaphysical plurality and recognition of the other as irreducible other from the notion of historicality in *Being and Time.*"[27] Fritsche maintains that it is challenging for non-Germans and especially Americans (where the Heidegger controversy is still raging) "to understand Heidegger's notion of historicality and authentic Dasein. For there could not be a more marked difference than the one between the 'German' rightist notions of Held and fate on the one hand and the 'American' understanding of what it means to be authentic on the other."[28] Fritsche argues that if *Being and Time* is read as Heidegger *intended,* by responding to his own (and Germany's) factical situation, it should become apparent that "*Being and Time* was a highly political and ethical work, that it belonged to the revolutionary Right, and that it contained an argument for the most radical group on the revolutionary Right, namely the National Socialists."[29] All Germans of the Weimar and Nazi eras would have recognized the Nazi agenda in the language of *Being and Time,* he argues. Therefore, "[t]he phenomenology in *Being and Time* can scarcely be saved by screening the nuggets of gold and throwing away the dirt."[30]

A less extreme position is put forward by a second group of authors who acknowledge that there is an ambiguity and vagueness within Heidegger's discussion of these core concepts that may leave them open to a political determination. They argue that it is Heidegger himself who later infuses the analysis of *Being and Time* with political motifs. Philippe Lacoue-Labarthe, for example, calls the communal determination of authentic Being-with "an ontic preference" of Heidegger's, arising presumably from his own conservative revolutionist political persuasions[31] but not made inevitable by the ontological discussion in *Being and Time.* Beistegui adds that the concept of historicality *(Geschichtlichkeit, Geschehen)* is ontologically vague within *Being and Time,* which allows it to be "from the start politically oriented."[32] Jürgen Habermas regards the communal determination of *Mitsein* to be a consequence of the way "understanding" and "sense" are connected to disclosure, which is, of course, collective. He considers that "the historical destiny of a culture or society is determined by a collectively binding preunderstanding of the things and events that can appear in the world at all."[33] Habermas dates the turn to Nazism to 1929, arguing that "from around 1929 on, Heidegger's thought exhibits a *conflation* of philosophical theory and ideological motifs" that amounts, for Habermas, to "the invasion of the philosophy of *Being and Time* by ideology,"[34] made possible by Heidegger's own rereading of his thought. More critically, Simon Critchley calls this communal determination of Being-with the "political fate of fundamental ontology and the *Dasein*-analytic"; for Critchley, thinking about politics and coexistence in the space opened by *Being and Time* would have to avoid the "autarchic telos and tragic-heroic pathos of the thematics of authenticity, where in Paragraph 74, *Mitsein* is determined in terms of 'the people' and its 'destiny.'"[35] Yet Critchley, unlike Fritsche, does allow for the possibility that alternative readings of Being-with may be possible.

There is a third group of scholars who, while still condemning Heidegger's politics as one cannot fail to do, seek to situate his discussion of community and historicality within his broader philosophical preoccupations with the predominance of modern subjectivism. R. N. Newell, for example, suggests that the apparent political orientation of Being-with in the language of the "people" comes from Heidegger's philosophic "concern of how to achieve a cohesive community in a world increasingly dominated by the values of liberal individualism."[36] It is important to highlight that Heidegger avoided any references to "society" *(Gesellschaft)* because he believed that "society today is only the absolutization of modern subjectivity."[37] Indeed, Beistegui also argues that Heidegger's use of the term "community" *(Gemeinschaft)* is made "as much in favour of a specific understanding of the nature of our being-in-common as it is made *against* the view—associated with liberalism, capitalism and intellectualism—which articulates the meaning of communal life in terms of *Gesellschaft* and *Staat*."[38] This point is developed further by David Wood, who argues that "[t]he distinctive function played by destiny . . . is to provide a way of transcending the mere arithmetic addition of individual fates,"[39] to transcend, in other words, the determination of coexistence through what this book has called the "logic of composition." And indeed, the sentence that follows the reference to "community" and "people" reads: "[d]estiny is not something that puts itself together out of individual fates, any more than Being-with-one-another can be conceived as the occurring together of several Subjects" (*Being and Time*, 436).

Yet, does linking the discussion of "the co-historizing of Dasein" to this philosophic concern with liberal understandings of *Gesellschaft* settle the question of "community," as well as its relation to "destiny"? Hardly, for even Beistegui notes that the identification with community is what "gives a political orientation to Heidegger's discussion."[40] Lacoue-Labarthe best articulates the centrality of the issue of community and identification when he argues that the concept of mimesis is the "formidable unanswered, or unformulated, question that continually haunts Heideggerian thought."[41] Heidegger refuses, according to Lacoue-Labarthe, to examine the problem of identification, which is the "German political problem par excellence."[42] A return is called for to the questions of why Heidegger discusses Dasein's cohistorizing in terms of community, and how to understand this discourse of Dasein's historical happening, its cohistorizing, in terms of the historical past of the "community." Is it necessarily the emergence of nationalism in his thought, as Karl Löwith insisted, seen in the "passage from a particular and individual *Dasein* to one that is general, no less particular by virtue of its generality—namely, one of German *Dasein*"?[43] In other words, the crucial question here has to be: is the communal determination of Being-with inevitably nationalistic ("*German* Dasein"), embedded as Fritsche suggested above, in a *völkisch* rhetoric and the "political and ethical" program of National Socialism? An interpretation of this is essential in order to assess whether the thought of Being-with binds the discussion of tradition and community, when seen in light of the horror of the 1930s and 1940s, to a nationalistic determination. The question of community is not a problem for Heidegger *alone*, but is a central problem for political thought and practice in general. Lacoue-Labarthe asks emphatically, "Why would the problem of identification not be, in general, the essential problem of the political?"[44]

This question of identification and its relationship with "destiny" and "the historical past" cannot be ignored. It has to be discussed directly and alongside the related question of whether a nonnationalist, critical reading of authentic Being-with can be given and justified. I examine this fundamental question of identification in *Being and Time* next, in an attempt to retrieve out of Heidegger's discussion an account of how community is constituted without being bound to a homogeneous totality determined biologically, ethnically, or according to other modes of (as)sociation tied to an essence, while at the same time avoiding the determination of coexistence according to the logic of composition. The interpretation that follows would, almost certainly, be castigated by the first group of scholars, who purport that there exists only *one* historically accurate reading of *Being and Time,* one tied to a nationalist agenda. Yet, I offer not a misreading of *Being and Time* but rather a critical appropriation of Heidegger's thought, which is not misplaced, naive, or erroneous; it exists, arguably, within the phenomenology of *Being and Time* as a possibility and can be uncovered and restructured for a political thought of coexistence.

## COEXISTENCE: MIMESIS, COMMUNITY, AND CRITICAL BELONGING

The emergence of Dasein's historicality within its manifested public group (community) and, in particular, the notion of identification, or *mimesis,* are examined here, enabling the recasting of Dasein's cohistorizing in light of the recovery of "ethical" selfhood, outlined in chapter 5, away from a nationalist determination. Heidegger's discussion of Dasein's attitude toward its historical tradition contains within it the possibility of a critical and productive relationship with the community. Such an agonistic relationship toward the historical tradition mirrors the critical relationship of liberating solicitude with which the "ethical" self comports itself toward other Dasein. This is because Dasein's relationship with its tradition similarly displays an agonistic sensibility toward past historical possibilities, uncovering those that can be "repeated" in Dasein's contemporary factical situation, disavowing and discarding others that are not deemed appropriate or productive. Dasein's agonistic attitude recovers "repeatable possibilities," possibilities that are worth recasting, in other words, through a mode of deconstruction parallel to that which Heidegger employs toward the ontological tradition in philosophy.

Interpreting Heidegger's discussion of Dasein's "repetition of past historical possibilities" in light of the insights of the "ethical" self provides a *productive* conception of identification, where the mimetic process contains *also* an element of critique, resistance, and displacement toward the community's historical tradition and particularly the community's past *possibilities*. Such a displacing and resisting toward the community's past possibilities forms the contours of a practice through which community itself is constituted outside of conventional modes of association. Such a discussion is useful both for an international political theory of coexistence and for illustrating that Heidegger's communal determination of Being-with need not be inevitably nationalistic or *völkisch*, regardless of Heidegger's own political commitments. In other words, Heidegger's text contains within it critical possibilities that belie the historical juncture of its writing, as well as Heidegger's discernible authorial intentions; as such, it can be appropriated for contemporary political thinking.

### Coexistence as "Critical Belonging": Tradition, Repetition, Destructive Retrieve

Contentiously, in paragraph 74 Heidegger discusses Dasein's relationship to the heritage and tradition of the public group in which it is historically manifested. While this has been cast as part of a conservative agenda, it is also open to alternative readings, and crucially, I propose, it can be made a central part of the theorization of the constitution of coexistence and community. Let us return to Heidegger's text, where he writes that

> [the] resoluteness in which Dasein comes back to itself discloses current factical possibilities of authentic existing, and discloses them *in terms of the heritage* which that resoluteness, as thrown, *takes over.* (*Being and Time*, 435; emphases in original)

Dasein, in other words, in resolutely grasping the finitude of its existence, is able to "take over" particular possibilities that are handed down to it by the historical tradition of the public group in which it is thrown. "Taking over" is associated with a process Heidegger calls "repetition," examined in greater detail later in this section. Let us first discuss the usage of "heritage" and "tradition."

The discussion of "tradition" is part of the overall "determination" of historical being-there, which is always embedded in a historically situated public group into which Dasein has been thrown. Stated otherwise, Dasein is radically embedded *(thrown)* in its world, and this world is manifested publicly and historically; when resolutely projecting itself onto possibilities (see the discussion in chapter 3), it must do so in terms of those possibilities that are publicly and historically available to it. However, the discussion of the historical tradition is also part of Heidegger's attempts to distinguish between history and his own claim that Dasein is *historical.* History is commonly understood as "something past," as "that belonging to an earlier time," as "context of events," and as "the transformations and vicissitudes of man, of human groupings and the 'cultures' as distinguished from Nature" (*Being and Time,* 430). Dasein, however, is itself said to be *historical;* Heidegger forthrightly asks of his own argument, "[B]y what right do we call this entity 'historical,' when it is not yet past?" (431). According to his account, since Dasein is never merely occurrent (present-at-hand), it can never be past in the sense of "now *no longer either present-at-hand or ready-to-hand*" (432; emphasis in original). Dasein's capacity-to-be-a-whole (to be self-constant) "is the movement of Dasein as it stretches itself through time and is called Dasein's happening or *Geschehen.*"[45] David Couzens Hoy argues that "Dasein becomes aware of how it *is* its past (the past of its generation, i.e., its tradition) insofar as the past is an essential part of the *constitution* of Dasein's understanding of its futural possibility."[46] Recalling the discussion of thrownness and projectiveness in chapter 3, Dasein projects itself futurally onto the possibilities available to it as such a *thrown* being. Its projection must take place within, and is shaped by, this "heritage," understood as "that in which *Dasein* is always immersed and implicated: its historical possibilities."[47]

In light of this, Hoy further suggests that the notion of "taking over" inherited possibilities has to be interpreted as "a recognition of the compelling situation of the actual historical world" but one that can lead Dasein "to an urgent commitment to what is most unique and individual about one's way of being-there."[48] This urgent commitment is what has been called "resoluteness," already discussed in chapter 4 as Dasein's readiness for anxiety in light of its finitude; in its resolute response to its finitude Dasein plunges itself toward the factical world and in recognition of its heteronomy rather than remain lost in the comfort of the "they." Although this

is paramount for Heidegger, because "[t]hrough anticipatory resoluteness, the 'there' or the situation of Dasein is made transparent
to Dasein," the actual choices or options that Dasein can resolutely
make about its possibilities are intentionally not discussed by Heidegger.[49] Neither is speculation about them entertained, because a
consideration of actual factical possibilities is not *possible* in the abstract: they can only be thought through by each individual Dasein
finding itself in a uniquely different factical situation and thrown
in a distinct public group. Therefore, Beistegui argues, "If an ethics
or a politics could indeed unfold from this fundamental existential
constitution, Heidegger refuses to consider it. Dasein's resoluteness
remains empty."[50]

But as noted earlier, the emptiness of resoluteness is but a step
away from "the abyss of steely and *völkish* rhetoric."[51] This is a step
that Heidegger apparently takes when he asserts, as already quoted
in the preceding discussion, that "our" heritage and tradition guide
our projection upon possibilities:

> Our fates have already been guided in advance, in our Being with
> one another in the same world and in our resoluteness for definite
> possibilities. Only in communicating and in struggling does the
> power of destiny become free. Dasein's fateful destiny in and with
> its "generation" goes to make up the full authentic historizing of Da-
> sein. (*Being and Time*, 436)

This can be, and has been, read as the emergence of a conservative
nationalism in Heidegger, where the struggle of the community in
its self-determination leads to a process of repetition and, hence,
identification and mimesis.[52] Such a reading would concur with
Lacoue-Labarthe's assessment of the unstated identificatory process
at play in *Being and Time* and justify his concern that "[a]n unacknowledged mimetology seems to overdetermine the thought of
Heidegger politically."[53]

Can "repetition," "fate," and "destiny" avoid a nationalist communal specification? Hoy suggests that in the discussion of historicality, "Destiny *(Geschick)* and fate *(Schicksal)* are technical terms
for Heidegger" where "fate represents the way Dasein becomes
definite and actual through its relation to events in the world" and
destiny "involves the essential connection of the individual to the
*community* or a *people*."[54] One could suggest, following this, that

it is possible to consider the determination of the "with" in terms of a community's tradition and heritage to be a technical matter, a *repercussion,* so to speak, of the primacy of relationality, which dictates that "since Dasein is essentially in the world with others . . . and since Dasein is essentially fateful or historical it follows that Dasein's fate is a co-fate and its history a co-history."[55]

But it is not until the conception of "repetition" is examined more closely that the general discussion of the historical tradition can be better located. Heidegger suggests that the relationship of Dasein toward the tradition can be understood as *repetition* and that "[r]epeating is handing down [Überlieferung] explicitly—that is to say, going back to the possibilities of the Dasein that has-been-there" (*Being and Time,* 437; emphasis in original). For Lacoue-Labarthe, as noted earlier, this discussion of Dasein repeating the tradition's possibilities as part of its "historizing" reveals the troubling presence of a nationalist or "communitarian" identification process, which nevertheless remains "unthought" by Heidegger himself. Yet, "repetition" is a particular kind of "taking over" possibilities that belies its immediate association with nationalist identification. Heidegger is explicit that "the Dasein that has-been-there is not disclosed in order to be actualized over again . . . repetition does not let itself be persuaded of something by what is 'past,' just in order that this, as something which was formerly actual, may recur" (437–38).[56] Therefore, it is wrong to assume that repetition implies the unquestioning reenactment of what has occurred in the past. Rather, this sort of repetition "is an attempt to retrieve a more original, a more positive and hence *constructive* comportment toward one's history."[57] In typical polysemic fashion,[58] the Heideggerian text makes difficult the understanding of repetition as mere replication of what had previously occurred to the community in which Dasein is thrown, or an uncritical reiteration of the community's values and ideas.

In this vein, Peg Birmingham has developed a notion of "critical mimesis" by examining specifically the *response* toward the heritage that resolute Dasein takes over (*Being and Time,* 435). She explores the possibilities of the discussion of repetition to elucidate Dasein's agonistic relationship toward the tradition. According to her analysis, Dasein's is a *critical* process of identification, and this calls into question Lacoue-Labarthe's claim that in Heidegger's discussion of historicity there is a process of nationalist or communitarian mimesis at play. She asserts that "Lacoue-Labarthe overlooks a crucial aspect of the discussion of destiny and historicity in *Being and Time,* namely, Heidegger's discussion of *Erwidert: Dasein's* response to its repeatable possibilities."[59] Birmingham notes Heidegger's opening up of the meaning of repetition beyond its casual connotations and highlights that, remarkably, "the repetition of tradition opens up our destiny."[60] Indeed, Beistegui argues that repetition affords a "'go[ing] back' to a given situation, but in such a way that this situation is thus disclosed, illuminated in a new way, revealed as a unique historical possibility."[61] Once this occurs, Dasein "takes over" this historical heritage, *responds* to it, in a specific way: it comports itself toward the past historical possibilities in the manner of *erwidern.*

What does it mean to respond by way of *Erwiderung?* Macquarrie and Robinson's translation rendered *Erwiderung* as a "reciprocative rejoinder" to correspond to the normal usage of *erwidern* in the sense of "to reply." This, however, fails to clearly indicate its full implications and those of the root *wider,* which include "strife" and which in casual discourse mean "contrary to or against."[62] To emphasize this particular aspect of repetition, Birmingham argues, "The response to repeatable historical possibilities is one which disavows any notion of continuity or identity with the past."[63] Therefore, when the factical situation is "illuminated," there is no guarantee that Dasein will accept the tradition's possibilities uncritically or allow itself to be submerged in what is "past" so that it can make it occur all over again. On the contrary, the disclosure of the tradition may well lead Dasein to attempt "to *overcome* the way the tradition conditions or limits its possibilities."[64] It can, in other words, "take over" or "repeat" its inherited possibilities by engaging in critical mimesis: a "repetition" that practices critique and retrieval with respect to the possibilities available to it within its heritage. The notion of "destructive retrieve," put to use by Heidegger with respect to the ontological tradition of philosophy, comes to describe Dasein's very response to the heritage and tradition in which it is thrown.

Beistegui concurs with such an assessment, asking in addition, "Is it not in the context of such a strifely or adverse attitude of Dasein in the face of its own historical situation that we must understand the use that Heidegger makes of the word *Kampf?* Does the 'struggle' not refer to Dasein's ability to engage with its own time in a strifely dialogue"?[65] When Heidegger states that "[o]nly in *communicating* and in *struggling* does the power of destiny become free" (*Being and Time,* 436; emphasis added),[66] "communication" *(Mitteilung)* and "struggle" must be evaluated as part of this agonistic attitude and disposition that Dasein displays toward the tradition. *Mit-teilung* communicates that which is shared, which is itself "communicated through the sharing *(Teilung)*."[67] The contentious reference to "struggling" and "communicating" thus performs two functions: first to initiate the internal contestation of community by its own members in order to counteract the account of idle talk with which the "they" drown all communication, as discussed in chapter 3; and second, to indicate the way in which Dasein's historicality unfolds as a *critically* disposed repetition or mimesis of the past repeatable possibilities of the community's tradition.[68]

This kind of agonistic "repetition" in the manner of *erwidern* "does not abandon itself to that which is past, nor does it aim at progress" (*Being and Time,* 438). In this way, it neither lends itself to "reactionism" as a political modality that "is nourished by a thinking of the return (to the origins, God, to values, to meaning, etc.)" nor does it support a teleological understanding of politics and history as "the arche-teleological unfolding of a meaningful process in a certain appropriation of the philosophy of the Enlightenment."[69] Heidegger's analytic, therefore, is as suspicious of the conservative alternative as of the liberal political understanding. The future does not unfold according to a teleology: it is perhaps best imagined (as an extrapolation from Heidegger's work) in the sense of "engender[ing] a collective field of imaginable possibilities . . . a restricted array of plausible scenarios of how the future can or cannot be changed."[70] The future is critically projected onto past possibilities, which *become* "imaginable" in a factical situation through the very process of critical mimesis.

Such a response in the manner of *erwidern* to Dasein's historical being-there is the response that the "ethical" self would make to its tradition. The "ethical" self participates in a critical engagement with the customary practices of its historical being-there in order to reveal the positive possibilities it inherits and to recover a constructive way of relating to this heritage without blindly reenacting it. This movement of a factical "destructive retrieve" enables

Birmingham to suggest that the concern regarding the nationalist identification entailed in Dasein's cohistorizing must be reinterpreted on the basis of *Erwiderung,* namely, as "displacement and disruption."[71] Employed in this disruptive mode, mimesis encourages a radical rethinking of the determination of Being-with in terms of a "people" and also of the understanding of community as such, because Heidegger's articulation of mimesis is "not based on a classical model of identification"[72] of part to whole.

If Dasein's response is understood as a critical, rather than a "reciprocative," rejoinder with respect to its tradition and more generally to the social context in which it is thrown, there ought to be more than one possibility in which to think its cohistorizing. The suggestion that Being-with becomes historical by way of a *critical* mimetic response to the historically manifested publicness of tradition and "people," a response whose manifold meanings include *struggle,* strife, or agonism, accommodates both the condition of indistinguishability (Dasein does not distinguish itself from the "they") and a struggle against the prevalent average intelligibility (and inauthenticity) of such understandings. Moreover, it leaves open the space to think about tradition or heritage not only in terms of a people and a national or local community but as a "group-in-becoming," a group that can be inclusive in its practice of critical belonging.[73] As Slavoj Žižek notes in this regard, there is a certain "transgression" constitutive of the community that points to the "way we are allowed/expected to violate its explicit rules," to the extent that "a subject which closely follows the explicit rules of a community will never be accepted by its members by 'as one of us.'"[74] In this way,

> we are "in," integrated, perceived by the other members as "one of us," only when we succeed in practicing this unfathomable DISTANCE from the symbolic rules. It is ultimately only this distance, which exhibits our identity, our belonging to the culture in question.[75]

In sum, Dasein's identification might be always already embedded in a historical tradition and thus part of a "thicker" understanding of community, but if authentic, it ought to be critical, disruptive, and at the same time productively applied to the factical situation. It is in this sense that the constitution of community can be seen as an instance of critical mimesis, and coexistence can be understood as constituted through the practice of critique against the background of repeatable historical possibilities. The notion of *critical* mimesis, therefore, provides a response to the question of political identification, an identificatory response already infused with critique, rather than the mere unquestioning repetition of the historical heritage.

The discussion of Dasein's historicality and cohistorizing, then, need not be immediately thrust aside as the premonition of a conservative agenda, tied to a racist or biological understanding of the community and the tradition; rather, it is open to alternative readings, ones that are useful for a theoretical account of a critical practice of identification or mimesis. The notion of "critical mimesis" can lead not only to the constitution of community through a response that has the disposition of critique toward its past possibilities, but also to a community in which the mode of belonging is itself critical. Such "critical belonging" makes concrete Dasein's thrownness and the primacy of relation through disavowing, displacing, and resisting the tradition. Critical belonging is the mode in which the "ethical" self makes the community out of her disposition of "liberating solicitude." In Birmingham's words, *"Dasein* determines itself authentically in a codetermination of being-with wherein the indifferent and efficient mode of solicitude becomes emancipatory."[76]

In this way, and parallel to the process of recovering the "ethical" self, the mode of "critical belonging" also allows solicitude to be "radically transformed" into a liberating kind of comportment: "no longer viewed as part of the indifferent emptiness of the crowd, the homogeneous anonymity of the anyone, the other is freed to be who he or she is in his or her potentiality-for-Being."[77] In Dasein's becoming-proper, "being-with others now has a sense of a heterogeneous space, a differentiated temporality in which each is grasped in his or her own specificity."[78] This is a critical activity that rests on the centrality of critique and agonism in social life.[79]

The critical mimetic response of the "ethical" self, understood as a form of "critical belonging," denies the reduction of coexistence to copresence by the "logic of composition" but also refutes the reading of Dasein's cohistorizing according to a nationalist essence. This allows a return to the question of Heidegger's politics and whether scholars ought to refrain from using his thought for a political thought of coexistence. This discussion of "critical mimesis" and critical belonging is *itself* a practice of disavowal, displacement, and resistance. It has disavowed Heidegger's politics and resisted the determination that he imposed on the analysis of *Being and Time* by his political engagement. This is not a case of "sorting what in his thought may be preserved free of his own Nazified orientation."[80] Discussing the possibility of a "critical mimesis" according to Birmingham's analysis and delineating an account of communal constitution through the mode of critical belonging in the community are akin to undertaking the *Abbau* of Heidegger's legacy: an act of resistance and critique toward the determination of *Being and Time* given to it by Heidegger's political involvement with the Nazis. What is given herein, in other words, is not a blind reading of *Being and Time*, but a constructive retrieval of certain unacknowledged insights within the text. This is tantamount to releasing the past possibilities of that text, as was provided through the examination of the "optics of coexistence" out of Heidegger's phenomenology of everydayness in chapter 3 and the recovery of the ethical self through a critical rereading of "authenticity" in chapters 4 and 5. The present discussion disrupts, displaces, and resists Heidegger's political determination of the thought of Being-with and disavows his politics. This, arguably, is the Heideggerian gesture par excellence, which he undertook toward the ontological tradition and which has been employed here in order to retrieve from his thought a critical account of political coexistence and communal constitution.

### CONCLUSION: POIESIS, PRAXIS, AND POLITICS

In this chapter, I addressed the question "how might one think about coexistence *politically*, if not in terms of composition?" The unworking of the modern subject, and its politics of self-sufficiency, resists the reduction of coexistence to the logic of composition and enables its conceptualization beyond copresence. I examined a number of concerns, articulated within the context of the debate on Heidegger's politics, that any conception of coexistence derived from the thought of Heidegger inevitably falls into the trap of an essentialist nationalist determination of community. Rereading the contentious paragraph 74 of *Being and Time* in light of the recovery of the "ethical" self led to a critical appropriation of the process of repetition described by Heidegger; rather than falling prey to an essentialist mimetology, as charged by Lacoue-Labarthe, I suggested that the very constitution of community occurs through a process of "critical mimesis." Peg Birmingham's analysis in this area shows how Dasein can comport itself toward the past possibilities of the historical tradition in which it is thrown with the same critical attitude described as part of the recovery of an "ethical" selfhood in chapter 5. The radically embedded self identifies with the community by critically repeating and retrieving the repeatable possibilities of its tradition. Such a relationship toward the tradition does not refute the thrownness of the self and its location in a particular public group, but it does point to a mode of critical belonging where this kind of political selfhood belongs precisely by exercising critique, resistance, and displacement toward the tradition's past possibilities. Those productive possibilities found within the tradition's past are emphasized and rearticulated within the political space opened up by the very act of critical engagement. The ones regarded as not wholly expressive of the tradition's historical potential are abandoned.

The "ethical" self's continuous practice of critical mimesis is useful for international political theory because it enables a movement toward a politics of non-self-sufficiency and away from the heteronomy-effacing practices of the modern subject. The issue of heteronomy, which had served as the impetus for challenging the logic of composition at the outset of this volume, is restated as a central issue for international political theory. The discussion of how the community is constituted, which might be called in shorthand "community through critique," not only displaces Heidegger's own determination of the phenomenology of *Being and Time,* but offers an understanding of communal constitution that is open to otherness in general and to the self's heteronomy in particular. Although any understanding of a historical public group would be exclusionary in some sense, the notion of a critical mimesis as the mode of constitution of the group is exclusionary in ways that are not arbitrary. When *critique* becomes the mode of belonging, the public group is not arbitrarily excluding others because of race, religion, color, birthplace, and so on. The questioning of ethics, out of which the "ethical" self is recovered, is paralleled in a political project of working out through practices of critique which possibilities are worth repeating from those inherited by the tradition.

Such an act of disruption and retrieval toward the tradition's past is open to otherness because, as was shown in the previous chapter, this otherness is carried internally and it is *as other* that the "ethical" self recovers itself. This recovery reveals how Dasein is other

to itself, in the sense of being indistinguishable from, and constituted by, otherness in average everydayness, but also in the process
of becoming-proper to itself through its self-recovery from habitual
practices and norms. Its propriety entails a certain becoming-strange,
also to be understood as becoming *not* subject. Furthermore, others
who might not be embedded in the specific historical public group
in question are acknowledged by the "ethical" self as having a voice,
the voice that Dasein carries within, which is the "phonic presence"
of the other in the self. Regard for the other moves away from subjectivist self-sufficiency and is disclosed beyond additive inclusion
by a self letting itself be seen, and acknowledged, as heteronomously
coexistential. Hence, Nancy argues, "That which is not a subject
opens up and *onto* a community whose conception, in turn, exceeds
the resources of a metaphysics of the subject."[81] In this sense, where
the unworking of the subject shows it to be contingent, strange, and
other to itself, "[c]ommunity is what takes place through others and
for others."[82]

The constitution of community, however, is open to otherness in
a second, more concrete way as well. Coexistence, being the proximal fact of Dasein's everyday existence, becomes actively endorsed
through the process of critical mimesis. The openness of the "ethical" self to otherness is paralleled in the mode of communal constitution. Others, who wish to critically repeat possibilities in a public
group where they might not be members under more commonplace
criteria, such as the figurations of family, nation, ethnicity, or religion,[83] may also engender critique and thus participate in the critical
mimesis of possibilities of the group in which they envision their
future projection. Critical belonging notes only the desire to engage
in a critique of the possibilities handed down to the group to which
one *wishes* to belong (as in the case of migrants, for example).[84] The
praxeological character of this critique, the critical engagement without end with the repeatable possibilities of the tradition, constitutes
membership as such. The mimetic process, in other words, does not
limit belonging to territorial or other identity-related criteria.[85]

Such a mode of critical belonging, open to heteronomy and otherness, makes two further contributions to international political
theory. First, it enables the discussion of community constitution
outside of the dichotomy of proceduralism (additive logic of compo-

sition) and essence (as determined by language, religion, ethnicity, etc.). The understanding of community constitution, as provided earlier, acknowledges "thickness" in the sense that it is based on Dasein's thrownness in a historical tradition but in no way constrains the opening up of the tradition. The tradition is historical, in the sense of the location of the ideas, projects, and practices that it comprises in a specific public group; membership, however, is not restricted to those who inherit it in a conventional sense (as might be the case with other so-called immutable characteristics). This is because membership and belonging are based on a substantially different understanding of tradition as such, where the terms are conceived not only as *open* to critique, but as *constituted* by the "ethical" self's critical engagement with the past possibilities of the tradition in which it wishes to locate itself.

Second, critical belonging is essential for international political theory in an era of globalization precisely because of its focus on otherness and heteronomy. Liberating solicitude, which was discussed in chapter 5 as a disposition of the "ethical" self for coexistence, invites others outside of the particular historical tradition to enter the critical mimetic process because it acknowledges

> the claim of others who, from beyond "our" horizon, call into question the parochialism of our tradition insofar as it does not speak for them and who demand that we include their perspectives in the effort to understand ourselves.[86]

The multiplicity of perspectives that globalization involves, referred to as the intensification of "value pluralism" in IR literature,[87] does not negate this process. On the contrary, plurality *assists* the forcefulness of critique by rearticulating and reimagining the repeatable possibilities of the tradition by bringing difference to bear on them productively. Therefore, critical belonging, open to all those who wish to disrupt and retrieve a tradition's possibilities, constructively theorizes the "friendly struggle" of the negotiations of multiple perspectives in an era of global transformations.[88] Most significant, the awareness of an internal, already present form of otherness is exemplary in that it illustrates that plurality is to be found *within* the tradition. This enables a movement from the community's conceptualization as uniform and essentialist to its diversification, both from inside and from an outside that is already within. Therefore, coexistence, while tied to the facticity and thrownness of existence, also dispels the contention that politics ought to always be considered as the "appropriation of essences"[89] and comes full circle to support the movement toward non-self-sufficiency.

# Conclusion

## THE CURIOUS STATUS OF COEXISTENCE
## IN INTERNATIONAL RELATIONS

Why is coexistence such a neglected concept in the discipline of international relations—a body of thought that claims to have *relations* at its center, and at a time when issues of coexistence remain at the forefront of international praxis? Can such institutional neglect be reversed and coexistence accorded its proper place as a question-worthy topic, as an *aporia* of world politics? These two questions provided the impetus for the exploration of coexistence undertaken in this volume. In the introduction and chapter 1, I mapped the historical evolution of this neglect through cold war and contemporary international theorizing, suggesting that the undeniable absence of specific thinking about coexistence in international relations can be traced to the ontological commitments of the discipline. As a human science located within the larger parameters of *modern* social and political thought, international relations comes to comprehend its "units of analysis" through the distorting lens of modern subjectivity. The centrality accorded to the modern subject, whose historical evolution as the ontological figure of modern philosophy and social science was examined in chapter 1, has led to the undertheorization of coexistence in international relations: the assumptions commonly held about the modern subject centered around nonrelationality, self-sufficiency, and mastery of itself and others obscure an analysis of human existence *as it shows itself.* On the basis of these presuppositions about the self, coexistence comes to be implicitly (and almost always *only* implicitly) understood as mere copresence, a condition that requires both an act of coming together and continuous efforts at staying together. Nonrelational and self-sufficient subjects, in other words, must be composed in mere cohabitation of the same physical space: Inspired by Jean-Luc Nancy, I have called this "the logic of composition."

Why is the reduction of coexistence according to the logic of composition so problematic? The analysis herein pointed to both a phenomenal and a normative reason for concern with the reduction of coexistence to copresence according to the logic of composition. Phenomenologically, the presuppositions of sovereign subjectivity pay little attention to the phenomena of human existence, what one might call the "facticity" of human life. As such, the role of the other, and indeed otherness in general, in the constitution of the self is occluded. I called this the "effacement of heteronomy": the ways in which others create "my" world, the ways in which "I" flee from anxiety and find comfort and sustenance in others, as well as the ways in which "I" am other to myself, all these fundamental indications of the primacy of relation for the constitution of the self are obscured. This phenomenal concealing of otherness and relationality also has a normative and political effect as it makes possible the effacement of heteronomy in ethical, political, and institutional contexts. Chapter 1 in particular examined how the configuration of the rational and self-interested subject in Thomas Hobbes's *Leviathan* constructs for the discipline of international relations a heterology of danger that necessitates the mechanism of the social contract to assemble the (ever so tentative) polity.

## SEEING COEXISTENCE IN EXISTENCE

Highlighting the importance of restating the question of coexistence was only the first task I set for myself. A second and even more important task was to bring about a hermeneutic shift away from the discursive parameters of the modern subject toward an understanding of existence that could allow the heteronomy of the self to show itself and that would enable the reconceptualization of coexistence beyond mere copresence. In order to facilitate such an unworking of modern subjectivity, I turned to the thought of Martin Heidegger—

a thought that has been at the center of the deconstructive enterprise of philosophy and the social sciences. Not only does Heidegger's thought offer a useful analysis of human existence in his seminal work *Being and Time,* it also exposes philosophy's unquestioned reliance on the modern subject. In chapter 2, I explored Heidegger's subsequent search for a method that would make possible a renewed ontological examination of life, which culminated in the articulation of a "hermeneutics of facticity," that is, a radical phenomenology whose purpose was to access the phenomena of existence by examining the being that philosophy had long captured under the heading of *subject.* Radical phenomenology demanded rigorous attention to specific human phenomena (a phenomenology of human praxis)[1] rather than relying on widely held assumptions about the attributes of the subject of coexistence. Moreover, the ontological examination of human existence moved this inquiry beyond the theoretic construction of merely a different theoretical account of selfhood to vie with that of the modern subject.

The turn to Heidegger's thought and method, however, is not without contention. Today, Emmanuel Levinas's well-known critique colors any reception of the ontological turn given to phenomenology by Heidegger. For Levinas, ontology grasps the self only in her relation to Being, disallowing alterity from showing itself. Moreover, Levinas argued that phenomenology and ontology privileged comprehension and knowledge as the predominant modes of relating to the other, appropriating the other in this way, and denying the ethical relationship with the other that constitutes the self. Therefore, for Levinas, phenomenology and ontology are "philosophies of violence," whose totalizing gaze subsumes the other to the same. Levinas argued that Heidegger's existential analysis, whose central concern was restating the question of Being, was the best exemplar of these dangers, despite calling for and bringing about greater attention to facticity.

In light of Levinas's critique, indeed, precisely *because* of Levinas's critique, I then turned to Heidegger in a specific way: with the concern about the other in mind, I retrieved from Heidegger's existential analysis *(Daseinanalytik)* a heterology, a discourse about the other. Specifically, in chapter 3 I outlined, under the heading of the "optics of coexistence," four related elements that illustrate how otherness and others are in fact primary for the constitution of the self (Dasein, Being-there) as a Being-in-the-world. These elements reveal Dasein to be heteronomously constituted in its average everydayness, a conception that unworks the reflective, nonrelational, and self-sufficient features of modern subjectivity.

First, Dasein initially and primarily finds itself immersed in its dealings with the world. Understanding the primary mode of Dasein to be "engaged immersion" challenges the assumption that reflection and "knowing" are the definitive modes of human relationality toward other beings and the world.

Second, Dasein's disclosive character reveals a conception of the world as a background totality of meanings and references against which existence makes sense of itself prereflectively and also as a totality of assignments and relations with available things and other beings. This totality is not solely authored or created by Dasein; rather, the practices, norms, and rules that help Dasein cope with its involvements in the world are structured by otherness and already exist in advance of Dasein's activities. Crucially, the understandings that Dasein has of "itself" and of the world are always already ontologically mediated through otherness.

Third, Dasein could then be said to be essentially Being-with. "Withness" is an attribute of the kind of being that Dasein is. For Dasein, in other words, existence is already coexistence, Being-there is always Being-with. Selfhood is fundamentally coexistential, but this is not to be understood in the sense of composition or copresence assumed of the completed and autonomous subject of modernity. Withness, furthermore, manifests itself in such a way that in its everydayness Dasein cannot be distinguished from others: the answer to the question "who is Dasein?" is not the "I," says Heidegger, but rather the "they."

Fourth, Dasein is fundamentally attuned to the world, and its understanding of itself and the surrounding world is affected by this attunement. Dasein's attunement is evident in its disposition for moods, from the structure of its understanding and its use of language or discourse. Such attunement illuminates a radical embeddedness that is best described as being-*thrown* into the world, but at the same time, Dasein's understanding of itself as "possibility" indicates that it is the kind of being that also *projects* itself onto possibilities and toward the future. Dasein's embeddedness has the structure of *thrown projection:* this means nothing other than that the world and others *matter* to Dasein. In everydayness, the world matters to such an overwhelming extent that Dasein can be said to have fallen prey to the world. Fallenness, thrownness, and projectiveness together suggest that, rather than self-presence and self-sufficiency, Dasein's Being is better understood as *care*.

The optics of coexistence did not *only* provide a substantive account of how the self is coexistentially heteronomous—permeated through and through with otherness, thrown into an other-created world—which helped us move beyond the parameters of subjectivist thinking; the optics of coexistence *also* showed how ontology itself is a *critical* activity. Normally considered a conservative, status quo–preserving mode of inquiry, I illustrated the ways in which ontological thinking disrupts the presuppositions about the subject of international relations and helps retrieve an account of selfhood that positively enables the reconsideration of coexistence beyond composition. This reconsideration of ontology is only made possible by the in-depth introduction of Heidegger's early thought to international relations.[2]

## COEXISTENCE, OTHERWISE

Following the retrieval of the optics of coexistence found in Heidegger's existential analytic, and the self's process of becoming proper explored in chapter 4, I returned to the *subject* of coexistence and pursued it as a question for world politics in the context of two related discourses, which the introduction had identified as the more productive of contemporary discourses pertaining to the subject of coexistence: those, first, of creating a global ethics by protecting the other through the extension of human rights to a universal humanity and, second, of transforming and expanding political community.

In chapter 5, I examined recent proposals toward a global ethics in which human rights are seen to inaugurate a new era of a "world society of individuals" brought about following the destabilization of the "international society of states" that globalization entails. Such proposals aim to protect the other beyond "our" borders by bestowing human rights on her and by enshrining these in cosmopolitan law. This legalist gesture toward the other is but the subsuming of the other to the same in the assumption of her universal humanity. I contested the appropriateness of constructing universal moral codes, as well as the legalization of such norms, for preventing the effacement of heteronomy and encouraging inclusiveness of the other. I called into question whether according human rights to an increasingly globalized humanity was sufficient for inaugurating a global ethics attentive to otherness and suggested, instead, that an inclusive global ethics requires a different openness to the other, an openness not necessarily brought about through the mere bestowal of legal entitlements, such as human rights, on the other. I showed that such a global ethics based on human rights merely overlays such instruments on the structure of already existing communal norms and morality, which remain closed off to the other.

Rather, in chapter 5 I suggested that any attempts to articulate a truly inclusive ethics must first question the ethical formations of the community in which the self has been thrown and whose analysis shows them to contain xenophobic elements by the very fact of their distinctiveness. Exploring the linguistic evolution of the term *ethics* showed this to be contained within an *éthos,* a community's own, and to be a stage in the codification and promulgation of habitual practices and norms. For international relations, whose initial and primary attempts at ethical theorizing have been dominated by universalizing theories, this contextualization locates such attempts within their particularist, almost exclusively Western, locations. In this sense, universal aspirations for ethics remain little more than a *plea.* Instead of assuming that the creation of ethics in the sense of moral codes is sufficiently attuned to, and protective of, the self's heteronomy and of otherness in general, the discussion used these insights to more fully understand how Dasein's constitution within (and *as*) the "they" leads it to be unaware of its heteronomy, of how the other and otherness is constitutive for it. Openness to others cannot come from universalizing ethical construction and codification; rather, it requires questioning of "our" own ethics and the cultivation of a disposition toward the other. In light of this analysis, I called for the recovery of an "ethical" selfhood, "which knows itself as opening to alterity."[3] Such an opening to otherness requires a radical confrontation of, and a turning away from, ethics, if ethics are derivative of habitual communal practice, distinctive of the "they."

Recovering the "ethical" self becomes possible through hearing and silence, in which the other's voice and suffering can be heard. This "ethical" self, however, cannot be utilized as a basis or foundation for universal ethics. It cannot serve as a deconstructed but reasserted ground for ethical construction; rather, it is a kind of selfhood that is at the heart of the ethicity of ethics. The move away from ethical construction (and its attendant codification) and toward the recovery of the "ethical" self, understood as a stance of heteronomous selfhood, forms a different path toward coexistence and ethics. This shift away from foundationalism and universalism directed the discussion to the articulation of *disposition* or *sensibility* of liberating solicitude toward the other. "Liberating solicitude" must be understood as a caring-for (in the sense of *Fürsorge*) that calls the other to her own anxious Being-in-the-world and lets her assume her fundamental mortal possibility. The recovery of the "ethical" self as best manifested in this disposition has also come full circle to think coexistence as the sensibility of a heteronomous being who is aware of its disclosive role for itself and the other.

For international relations this is significant because it points to a different possibility of preventing the effacement of heteronomy, in a move away from universal ethical construction. The recovery of the "ethical" self suggests that global ethics must be sought in an openness to the other not immediately possible for the rights-bearing subject. This recovery enables the reconceptualization of the coexistential self, the *subject* of coexistence, and consequently makes a contribution to international political theory by furnishing it with a form of selfhood amenable to nonmasterful relations; a selfhood that is instantiated as "open to the other." The "ethical" self's disposition of liberating solicitude brings into being a questioning relationship toward the éthos of the public group in which the self is thrown and responds to the plea for a global ethics by heeding the desire to hear the voice of the other and witness its suffering and by pursuing no ethical project that unwittingly obscures its very object of concern.

Chapter 6, then, continued the attempt to reinstate the status of coexistence as a question-worthy concept for international relations by exploring how coexistence is to be conceptualized *politically*, given the shift away from the subjectivist discursive domain toward a hermeneutic of non-self-sufficiency best exemplified in the recovery of the "ethical" self. The chapter, moreover, dealt with the serious and pressing issue of "Heidegger's politics"—a phrase that has come to signify both Heidegger's involvement with the National Socialists in the 1930s, when he became the rector of the University of Freiburg, and also the equally important concern of whether his thought betrays a communal or nationalist, some would say fascist, determination of authentic Being-with that would radically challenge the suitability of his thought for a critical questioning of modern subjectivity and coexistence.

Two prominent objections were outlined in this regard. The first suggested that the unworking of the modern subject leaves a gap, a *caesura*, in political thinking that is not addressed in the hermeneutics of facticity one finds in Heidegger's *Being and Time*. The second objection disputed this assessment of *Being and Time* and (re)read it in light of Heidegger's involvement with the Nazis, deeming it to be at best politically vague, and thus open to conservative revolutionism, and at worst as determining community along nationalistic and racist lines. To discuss the effects of the debate on Heidegger's politics, chapter 6 examined the fundamental question of identification in *Being and Time* and attempted to retrieve out of Heidegger's discussion an account of how community is constituted without being bound to a homogeneous totality tied to an essence, while at the same time avoiding the determination of coexistence according to the logic of composition. For this purpose, it offered a reading of the core and contentious relations of Dasein with destiny, heritage, and the historical past, and more specifically the ways in which Dasein *repeats* the historical possibilities of the tradition and the kind of *response* it makes to its heritage. Using Peg Birmingham's proposed notion of "critical mimesis," the chapter developed the concept of critical belonging to indicate a relation of questioning toward the community that parallels that of the "ethical" self's calling its self-understanding as subject into question. Critical belonging allows community to become constituted by and through the critical, questioning relation that one has to one's communal heritage and historical tradition. Thus, the "ethical" self's openness to alterity is brought into the political by destroying (in the sense of destructive retrieve discussed in chapter 2) inappropriate past possibilities and by retrieving those possibilities that are productive and that might have been marginalized and silenced by dominant collective understandings at specific historical moments. This deconstruction liberates groups and others that were silenced by the tradition, making their voices heard.

This use of "critical mimesis" and the development of critical belonging is *not* a misreading of *Being and Time*—as those claiming that there is only one (nationalist) right interpretation of this polysemic work might wish to believe; rather, such a reading must be understood as a critical appropriation of Heidegger's thought. The possibility of such a reading exists, arguably, within the analysis of *Being and Time* and can be retrieved for a political thought of coexistence. Discussing the possibility of a critical mimesis according to Birmingham's analysis, and delineating an account of communal constitution through the mode of critical belonging toward the community, is therefore an *Abbau* of Heidegger's legacy, in what may be the Heideggerian gesture par excellence: an act of disavowal of Heidegger's politics, an exercise of displacement of the nationalist determination of Being-with arguably imposed on the analysis of *Being and Time* by Heidegger's own political engagement, and a practice of resistance to suggestions that there is only one correct interpretation of the thought of Being-with. This releases the past possibilities of the text and possibly performs a constructive retrieval of certain unacknowledged insights within it. As such, it is parallel to the task, attitude, and work of this book as a whole: it mirrors the retrieval of the optics of coexistence out of Heidegger's phenomenology of everydayness in chapter 3 and the recovery of the ethical self through a critical rereading of authenticity in chapters 4 and 5.

For international political theory this reading is, in the end, an important step in that it arrests the heteronomy-effacing practices of the modern subject and moves the discussion of ethics, politics, and community away from the discursive horizon of modern subjectivity. The consideration of community as the result of critical practices toward the historical past disrupts the dichotomous determination of coexistence as mere copresence according to a nationalist and exclusionary essence, articulating coexistence as the critical praxis of a self who is thrown into the world but projects itself toward this world, critically.

# Notes

## INTRODUCTION

1. Roland Paris, "Peacebuilding and the Limits of Liberal Internationalism," *International Security* 22, no. 2 (1997): 55.

2. Robert C. Solomon has suggested that the rise of the subject to prominence has been the single most defining trend in continental thinking. See his *Continental Philosophy since 1750: The Rise and Fall of the Self* (Oxford: Oxford University Press, 1988).

3. Fred Halliday notes that IR academic work is embedded within the social science context, itself ensconced within the political and social context of developments in the world. See Fred Halliday, "Gender and IR: Progress, Backlash, and Prospect," *Millennium: Journal of International Studies* 27, no. 4 (1998): 833–39. See also M. Hakan Seckinelgin, "The Law of the Sea and the South Pacific: An Ecological Critique of the Philosophical Basis of International Relations" (Ph.D. thesis, London School of Economics and Political Science, 2000), 140–76.

4. Emmanuel Levinas, *Totality and Infinity: An Essay on Exteriority*, trans. Alphonso Lingis (The Hague: Martinus Nijhof, 1979).

5. In the sense of being phenomenologically brought forward. See Martin Heidegger, *Being and Time*, trans. John Macquarrie and Edward Robinson (Oxford, UK: Blackwell, 1962), ¶7.

6. The term is not to be understood in the way intended by Richard Wolin as the "abandonment" of the self to "the despotic rule of nameless, higher powers" and a subsequent relinquishment of responsibility, or associated with "paternalism" as suggested by Jonathan Salem-Wiseman.

See Richard Wolin, *The Politics of Being: The Political Thought of Martin Heidegger* (New York: Columbia University Press, 1990), 150; Jonathan Salem-Wiseman, "Heidegger's Dasein and the Liberal Conception of the Self," *Political Theory* 31, no. 4 (August 2003): 550.

7. Christopher Paget Mayhew, *Coexistence Plus: A Positive Approach to World Peace* (London: Bodley Head, 1962), 4.

8. Howard Caygill, *Levinas and the Political* (London: Routledge, 2002), 69.

9. Bertrand Russell, *Has Man a Future?* (Harmondsworth, UK: Penguin Books, 1961), 120.

10. Ibid., 90.

11. V. I. Lenin had indicated that in the international climate of the 1920s coexistence was possible and also preferable for the Soviet Union in order to provide the peace that the newly founded USSR needed to survive in its first years of existence. With the Bolshevik Revolution under threat after its initial success, in a seminal speech at Brest Litovsk in 1918, Lenin reminded the revolutionaries of the fact that the majority of states surrounding the newly created socialist Soviet Union were capitalist.

12. Y. P. Frantsev, *Peace, Peaceful Coexistence, and Prospects Ahead for Socialism* (Moscow: Novosti Press Agency Publishing House, 1965), 9.

13. V. I. Lenin, *Collected Works,* 33: 129, cited in Frantsev, *Peace,* 12.

14. This brief account obscures, of course, the extensive role played by proxy wars, where military confrontation between the superpowers was afforded through conventional warfare. See Tarak Barkawi and Mark Laffey, "The Imperial Peace: Democracy, Force, and Globalization," *European Journal of International Relations* 5, no. 4 (1999): 403–34.

15. Nikita S. Khrushchev, "On Peaceful Coexistence," *Foreign Affairs,* October 1959, 5.

16. Frantsev, *Peace,* 15.

17. Commission to Study the Organization of Peace, *Peaceful Coexistence: A New Challenge to the United Nations,* Twelfth Report (New York: Commission to Study the Organization of Peace, 1960), 4.

18. Ibid., 9.

19. Ibid., 5. Toward further codification of this notion, Marshal Tito of Yugoslavia succeeded in convincing the Nonaligned movement to accept eighteen principles of peaceful coexistence law as the Cairo Declaration of 1964. See John Newbold Hazard, *Coexistence Law Reconsidered* (Copenhagen: Juristforbundets Forlag, 1969), 196 n. 13. Yet, events such as the Prague Spring and its quashing by Soviet troops in 1968 led to a reconsideration of the nominal acceptance and hopes for peaceful coexistence among the superpowers. At the very least, such events led to the speculation whether a new Soviet position with respect to coexistence with capitalism was in the making (191).

20. Barkawi and Laffey, "The Imperial Peace," 403–34.

21. Mayhew, *Coexistence Plus,* 5.

22. Ibid., 22.

23. Ibid., 2.

24. Kenneth George Grubb, *Coexistence and the Conditions of Peace* (London: S. C. M. Press, 1957), 5.

25. Ibid.

26. Ibid., 3.

27. Ibid., 9.

28. Susan L. Woodward, "Violence-Prone Area or International Transition? The Role of Outsiders in Balkan Violence," in *Violence and Subjectivity,* ed. Veena Das, Arthur Kleinman, Mamphela Ramphele, and Pamela Reynolds (Berkeley: University of California Press, 2000), 19.

29. Samuel P. Huntington, *The Clash of Civilizations and the Remaking of World Order* (New York: Simon & Schuster, 1996).

30. See, for example, Stephen Chan, "Too Neat and Under-thought a World Order: Huntington and Civilisations," *Millennium: Journal of International Studies* 26, no. 1 (1997): 137–40; and Patrick Thaddeus Jackson, "'Civilization' on Trial," *Millennium* 28, no. 1 (1999): 141–53. However, efforts to rescue civilizational thinking from its realist premises appear to be increasing. See Marc Lynch, "The Dialogue of Civilisations and International Public Spheres," *Millennium* 29, no. 2 (2000): 307–30.

31. See Gianni Vattimo, "Toward an Ontology of Decline," trans. Barbara Spackman, in *Recoding Metaphysics: The New Italian Philosophy,* ed. Giovanna Borradori (Evanston, Ill.: Northwestern University Press, 1988), 63–75, although admittedly this would assume a different sense in post–cold war realist ontology.

32. Lynch, "The Dialogue of Civilisations," 311.

33. Robert W. Cox, "Thinking about Civilizations," special issue, *Review of International Studies* 26 (2000): 217–34.

34. See, as examples in an ever increasing literature, Stephen John Stedman, "UN Intervention in Civil Wars: Imperatives of Choice and Strategy," in *Beyond Traditional Peacekeeping,* ed. Donald C. F. Daniel and Bradd C. Hayes (Basingstoke, UK: Macmillan, 1995), 40–63; Eva Bertram, "Reinventing Governments: The Promise and Perils of United Nations Peace Building," *Journal of Conflict Resolution* 39, no. 3 (1995): 387–418; and Michael E. Brown, ed., *Ethnic Conflict and International Security* (Princeton, N.J.: Princeton University Press, 1993).

35. Bertram, "Reinventing Governments," 388.

36. Ibid., 389.

37. Veena Das and Arthur Kleinman, introduction to *Violence and Subjectivity,* ed. Das et al., 1.

38. Saskia Sassen has argued that the world economic system is not, as

often claimed, a spontaneous order, but rather is designed and maintained; see *Globalization and Its Discontents* (New York: New Press, 1998) and *Losing Control? Sovereignty in an Age of Globalization* (New York: Columbia University Press, 1996). Similarly, the increased engagement of the UN "as an agent of democratic transitions," as noted by Bertram, "Reinventing Governments," should illustrate, I argue, how the international system, in some respects, is likewise designed and maintained.

39. Francis Fukuyama, *The End of History and the Last Man* (London: Penguin, 1992).

40. Paris, "Peacebuilding and the Limits of Liberal Internationalism," 58.

41. In this sense, one might disagree with Slavoj Žižek, who finds the center of political ontology to be vacant since the modern (Cartesian) subject has been "chased away," so to speak, by concerted critique mounted on multiple fronts. See Slavoj Žižek, *The Ticklish Subject: The Absent Centre of Political Ontology* (London: Verso, 1999). Naturally, Žižek is referring primarily to philosophical circles; upon closer attention to the concerns of the international community, with its newly found focus on human rights, the modern subject is definitely securely holding court.

42. Molly Cochran, *Normative Theory in International Relations: A Pragmatic Approach* (Cambridge: Cambridge University Press, 1999), 14. See also Andrew Linklater, *The Transformation of Political Community: Ethical Foundations of the Post-Westphalian Era* (Cambridge, UK: Polity Press, 1998), 14–45 and 60; as well as Gerard Delanty, *Citizenship in a Global Age: Society, Culture, Politics* (Philadelphia: Open University Press, 2000), 136.

43. Swasti Mitter, "Universalism's Struggle," *Radical Philosophy*, no. 108 (July–August 2001), 42.

44. Linklater, *The Transformation of Political Community*, 16.

45. Ulrich Beck, "The Cosmopolitan Perspective: Sociology of the Second Age of Modernity," *British Journal of Sociology* 51, no. 1 (2000): 83–84. See also Jürgen Habermas, *The Inclusion of the Other: Studies in Political Theory*, ed. Ciaran Cronin and Pablo De Greiff (Cambridge, Mass.: MIT Press, 1998); and Jürgen Habermas, *The Postnational Constellation: Political Essays*, ed. Max Pensky (Cambridge, Mass.: MIT Press, 2001).

46. See Linklater, *The Transformation of Political Community*.

47. The phrase belongs to Darel E. Paul, "Sovereignty, Survival, and the Westphalian Blind Alley in International Relations," *Review of International Studies* 25, no. 2 (1999): 217–31.

48. Linklater, *The Transformation of Political Community*, 16.

49. Ibid., 2. It would appear that Linklater's work is expressive of a desire to transcend the sharp divide between cosmopolitans and communitarian thinkers, which was seen to lead to an impasse (see Cochran, *Normative Theory in International Relations*). Gerard Delanty recently suggested

that the greater majority of "communitarians can be seen as liberals disenchanted by liberal individualism" but who anchor their positions on "the liberal principle of equality" (Delanty, *Citizenship in a Global Age,* 25, 27). As to the credence given to particularist ties and sentiment, see also Alan Finlayson, "Psychology, Psychoanalysis and Theories of Nationalism," *Nations and Nationalism* 4, no. 2 (1998): 145–62, who argues that there is a reductive *psychological* account on which most theories of nationalism and nationalists sentiment rest.

50. Werner Hamacher, "Heterautonomies: Multiculturalism and the Politics of Respect," trans. Dana Hollander, *Centre for Theoretical Studies Working Papers,* no. 15 (1997), 5.

51. Ibid., 8.

52. See, for instance, Hassan Melehy, *Writing Cogito: Montaigne, Descartes, and the Institution of the Modern Subject* (Albany: State University of New York Press, 1997).

53. Diana Coole, "Thinking Politically with Merleau-Ponty," *Radical Philosophy,* no. 108 (July–August 2001): 25.

54. Jean-Luc Nancy, "Being-With," trans. Iain Macdonald, *Centre for Theoretical Studies Working Papers,* no. 11 (1996), 1.

55. See, for example, Kenneth N. Waltz, *Theory of International Politics* (Reading, Mass.: Addison-Wesley, 1979); foreign policy analysis scholars have sought to counter the notion of the state as unitary subject.

56. See the introduction to C. Fred Alford, *The Self in Social Theory: A Psychoanalytic Account of Its Construction in Plato, Hobbes, Locke, Rawls, and Rousseau* (New Haven, Conn.: Yale University Press, 1991).

57. Stephen K. White, "Weak Ontology and Political Reflection," *Political Theory* 25, no. 4 (1997): 503.

58. David Carr, "The Question of the Subject: Heidegger and the Transcendental Tradition," *Human Studies* 17, no. 4 (1995): 403.

59. White, "Weak Ontology and Political Reflection," 503.

60. Heidegger, *Being and Time,* 67.

61. White, "Weak Ontology and Political Reflection," 503. See also Žižek, *The Ticklish Subject,* 1.

62. Tracy B. Strong, "Introduction: The Self and the Political Order," in *The Self and the Political Order,* ed. Tracy B. Strong (Oxford, UK: Blackwell, 1992), 1–21.

63. Alexander Wendt, *Social Theory of International Politics* (Cambridge: Cambridge University Press, 1999), 90. For an assessment of Wendt's ontological discussion, see Michael Cox, Ken Booth, and Tim Dunne, "Editors' Introduction to the Forum on Social Theory of International Politics," *Review of International Studies* 26, no. 1 (2000): 123. See also Waltz, *Theory of International Politics.*

64. Cox, Booth, and Dunne, "Editors' Introduction," 123.

65. It is quite interesting that in response to Wendt's inquiry, some of the commentators on his project have sought to curtail ontological explorations of IR, seeking to limit the discipline's output to "analysis of international relations" and to discourage the onset of "ontological debates," achieving in this way a closure of questions about *what* it is that IR examines, that is, states, their interactions, and affiliated issues. Robert O. Keohane, "Ideas Part-way Down," *Review of International Studies* 26, no. 1 (2000): 126.

66. Influenced and inspired by Jean-Luc Nancy's analysis in writings such as "Being-With," 5; "Of Being-in-Common," trans. James Creech, in *Community at Loose Ends,* ed. Miami Theory Collective (Minneapolis: University of Minnesota Press, 1991), 1–12; "La Comparution/The Compearance," trans. Tracy B. Strong, *Political Theory* 20, no. 3 (1992): 371–98; and also Jean-Luc Nancy, trans. Robert D. Richardson and Anne E. O'Byrne, *Being Singular Plural* (Stanford, Calif.: Stanford University Press, 2000), 41–43.

67. Jean-Luc Nancy, *The Inoperative Community,* trans. Peter Connor, Lisa Garbus, Michael Holland, and Simona Sawhney (Minneapolis: University of Minnesota Press, 1991), 3.

68. Nancy, *Inoperative Community,* 3.

69. For what this *as* might itself reveal, see Giorgio Agamben, *The Coming Community,* trans. Michael Hardt (Minneapolis: University of Minnesota Press, 1993), 98–99.

70. Nancy, "Being-With," 17; emphasis added.

71. Heidegger, *Being and Time,* 191.

72. Martin Heidegger, "The Age of the World Picture," in *The Question concerning Technology and Other Essays,* trans. William Lovitt (New York: Harper and Row, 1977), 132–33.

73. Nancy, *The Inoperative Community,* 4.

74. Ibid.

75. In the sense discussed by Joseph J. Kockelmans, "Destructive Retrieve and Hermeneutic Phenomenology in *Being and Time,*" in *Radical Phenomenology: Essays in Honor of Martin Heidegger,* ed. John Sallis (Atlantic Highlands, N.J.: Humanities Press, 1978).

76. Charles E. Scott, *The Question of Ethics: Nietzsche, Foucault, Heidegger* (Bloomington: Indiana University Press, 1990), 138.

77. Ibid.

78. Ibid., 138–39.

79. Ibid., 139.

80. Thomas Trezise, foreword to Philippe Lacoue-Labarthe, *The Subject of Philosophy,* ed. Trezise, trans. Trezise et al. (Minneapolis: University of Minnesota Press, 1993), xv.

81. Julia Kristeva, *Crisis of the European Subject*, trans. Susan Fairfield (New York: Other Press, 2000), 119.

82. Paul Standish, *Beyond the Self: Wittgenstein, Heidegger, and the Limits of Language* (Aldershot, UK: Avebury, 1992), 170, 210.

83. Ute Guzzoni, "Do We Still Want to Be Subjects?" in *Deconstructive Subjectivities,* ed. Simon Critchley and Peter Dews (Albany: State University of New York, 1996), 201–16, 203. See also David Campbell, "Why Fight: Humanitarianism, Principles, and Poststructuralism," *Millennium: Journal of International Studies* 27, no. 3 (1998), 505.

84. See Theodore Kisiel, *The Genesis of Heidegger's "Being and Time"* (Berkeley: University of California Press, 1993), 49.

85. See Agnes Heller, *A Theory of Modernity* (Malden, Mass.: Blackwell, 1999), 227.

86. Michel Foucault, *The Order of Things: Archaeology of the Human Sciences* (London: Tavistock Publications, 1974), 324.

87. Lacoue-Labarthe, *The Subject of Philosophy,* 79–80.

88. Ibid., 82.

89. Nancy, *The Inoperative Community,* 6.

90. Ibid., 6–7.

91. Chris Brown, Terry Nardin, and Nicholas J. Rengger, eds., *International Relations in Political Thought* (Cambridge: Cambridge University Press, 2003).

92. See Levinas, *Totality and Infinity,* as well as key essays such as "Ethics as First Philosophy," in *The Levinas Reader,* ed. Sean Hand (Oxford: Oxford University Press, 1989), 75–87; "Is Ontology Fundamental?" (1951) and "Peace and Proximity" (1984), trans. Peter Atterton, Simon Critchley, and Graham Norton, in *Emmanuel Levinas: Basic Philosophical Writings,* ed. Adriaan T. Peperzak, Simon Critchley, and Robert Bernasconi (Bloomington: Indiana University Press, 1996), 1–10 and 161–69. Also, David Campbell, "The Deterritorialization of Responsibility: Levinas, Derrida, and Ethics after the End of Philosophy," *Alternatives* 19 (1994): 455–84; David Campbell, "The Politics of Radical Interdependence: A Rejoinder to Daniel Warner," *Millennium: Journal of International Studies* 25, no. 1 (1996): 129–41; Simon Critchley, *Ethics—Politics—Subjectivity: Essays on Derrida, Levinas, and Contemporary French Thought* (London: Verso, 1999); and Simon Critchley, *The Ethics of Deconstruction: Derrida and Levinas,* 2nd ed. (Edinburgh: Edinburgh University Press, 1999).

93. See both Martin Heidegger, *Ontology: The Hermeneutics of Facticity,* trans. John van Buren (Bloomington: Indiana University Press, 1999), 5; and Heidegger, *Being and Time,* 67.

94. See Robert Bernasconi, *Heidegger in Question: The Art of Existing* (Atlantic Highlands, N.J.: Humanities Press, 1993), 150–69; and also

Martin Heidegger, *Nietzsche,* trans. David Farrell, vol. 4, *Nihilism* (New York: Harper and Row, 1991), 86–120, for a discussion of the evolution of Heidegger's attempts to go beyond the domination of modern subjectivity in philosophy and *in his own thought.* Bernasconi highlights the transition from destroying the history of ontology and providing a phenomenological account of the structures of Dasein to a history of Being *(Seynsgeschichte),* which attempts not to provide ontologically informed alternatives to modern subjectivity but to account for how Being makes possible "the sending of that which brings the completion of Western metaphysics: representation, subjectivity, certainty, and *Historie* itself." This became known as "Die Kehre" or "the turn" in Heidegger's thinking. See Heidegger, "The Turning," in *The Question concerning Technology,* 36–49. For the present discussion, however, engagements with the early work are still productive, as David Wood suggests, because Heidegger's turn to the history of Being "is surely too much of a *reaction* to a predominantly subject-centered tradition, and as a *reaction,* flawed" (David Wood, "Reiterating the Temporal: Toward a Rethinking of Heidegger on Time," in *Reading Heidegger: Commemorations,* ed. John Sallis (Bloomington: Indiana University Press, 1993), 153; emphasis in original.

95. Gianni Vattimo, *The Adventure of Difference: Philosophy after Nietzche and Heidegger,* trans. Cyprian Blamires and Thomas Harrison (Cambridge, UK: Polity Press, 1993), 47.

## 1. MANIFESTATIONS OF COMPOSITION

1. I delineate "the modern age" not necessarily as a historical spectrum but as an era where certain philosophic concerns become prevalent. See Jürgen Habermas, *Theory and Practice,* trans. John Viertel (Cambridge, UK: Polity Press, 1988); and William E. Connolly, *Political Theory and Modernity* (Oxford, UK: Blackwell, 1988).

2. Martin Wight, *International Theory: The Three Traditions* (London: Leicester University Press, 1991).

3. Karl Ameriks and Dieter Sturma, introduction to *The Modern Subject: Conceptions of the Self in Classical German Philosophy,* ed. Karl Ameriks and Dieter Sturma (Albany: State University of New York Press, 1995), 1–2.

4. A certain *éthos* of survival has been acutely influential for the perspective of political realism in international relations and more generally for discourses that invoke the notion of anarchy. See Louiza Odysseos, "Dangerous Ontologies: The Ethos of Survival and Ethical Theorising in International Relations," *Review of International Studies* 28, no. 2 (2002): 403–18.

5. Andrew Linklater, *Beyond Realism and Marxism: Critical Theory and International Relations* (London: Macmillan Press, 1990), and *The Transformation of Political Community: Ethical Foundations of the Post-Westphalian Era* (Cambridge, UK: Polity Press, 1998); see also Alexander Wendt, *Social Theory of International Politics* (Cambridge: Cambridge University Press, 1999).

6. Simon Critchley and Peter Dews, introduction to *Deconstructive Subjectivities,* ed. Simon Critchley and Peter Dews (Albany: State University of New York Press, 1996), 1.

7. David Carr, *The Paradox of Subjectivity: The Self in the Transcendental Tradition* (New York: Oxford University Press, 1999), 30.

8. See Simon Critchley, "What Is Continental Philosophy?" *International Journal of Philosophical Studies* 5, no. 3 (1997): 347–65; Andrew Bowie, "Rethinking the History of the Subject: Jacobi, Schelling, and Heidegger," in *Deconstructive Subjectivities,* ed. Critchley and Dews, 105–26; Etienne Balibar, "Citizen Subject," in *Who Comes after the Subject?* ed. Eduardo Cadava, Peter Connor, and Jean-Luc Nancy (New York: Routledge, 1991), 33–57; Etienne Balibar, "Subjection and Subjectivation," in *Supposing the Subject,* ed. Joan Copjec (London: Verso, 1994), 1–15; and, finally, Agnes Heller, "Death of the Subject?" in *Constructions of the Self,* ed. George Levine (New Brunswick, N.J.: Rutgers University Press, 1992), 269–84. All contest a narrow reading of the term.

9. Jane Flax, *Disputed Subjects: Essays on Psychoanalysis, Politics, and Philosophy* (London: Routledge, 1993), 95–96. See also Paul Standish, *Beyond the Self: Wittgenstein, Heidegger, and the Limits of Language* (Aldershot, UK: Avebury, 1992), 132, on the preoccupation of analytical philosophy with the subject of the utterance.

10. Hassan Melehy, *Writing Cogito: Montaigne, Descartes, and the Institution of the Modern Subject* (Albany: State University of New York Press, 1997) denies the possibility of writing about "one beginning of the subject in modernity" (3) while suggesting that the story of the reassertions of the Cartesian subject points to a certain institutionalization of the subject through the modern academy (27–35).

11. David Carr, "The Question of the Subject: Heidegger and the Transcendental Tradition," *Human Studies* 17, no. 4 (1995): 404.

12. Ibid.

13. Simon Critchley, "Prolegomena to Any Post-Deconstructive Subjectivity," in *Deconstructive Subjectivities,* ed. Critchley and Dews, 13.

14. Ibid.

15. Martin Heidegger, "The Age of the World Picture," in *The Question concerning Technology and Other Essays,* trans. William Lovitt (New York: Harper and Row, 1977), 128.

16. Ibid.

17. Martin Heidegger, *Nietzsche*, trans. David Farrell Krell, vol. 4, *Nihilism* (New York: Harper and Row, 1991), 91–95.

18. See Martin Heidegger, *What Is a Thing?*, trans. W. B. Barton Jr. and Vera Deutsch (Chicago: Henry Regnery, 1967), 98–108; Dalia Judovitz, *Subjectivity and Representation in Descartes: The Origins of Modernity* (Cambridge: Cambridge University Press, 1988); Walter Soffer, *From Science to Subjectivity: An Interpretation of Descartes' Meditations* (Westport, Conn.: Greenwood Press, 1987); Richard A. Watson, *The Breakdown of Cartesian Metaphysics* (Indianapolis: Hackett, 1987); Bernard Flynn, "Descartes and the Ontology of Subjectivity," *Man and World* 16 (1983): 3–23; and Joseph Claude Evans, *The Metaphysics of Transcendental Subjectivity: Descartes, Kant, and W. Sellars* (Amsterdam: Verlag B. R. Grüner, 1984).

19. Carr, "The Question of the Subject," 404. See also the discussion in Martin Heidegger, *The End of Philosophy*, trans. Joan Stambaugh (New York: Harper and Row, 1972), 46–49.

20. Paul Barry Clarke, *Autonomy Unbound* (Aldershot, UK: Ashgate, 1999), 15.

21. Heidegger, "The Age of the World Picture," 148–49.

22. Ibid., 142.

23. Ernesto Laclau and Chantal Mouffe, *Hegemony and Socialist Strategy: Towards a Radical Democratic Politics* (London: Verso, 1985), 94.

24. See Heidegger, *What Is a Thing?* 94–106, especially 104–6; and also Heidegger, "The Age of the World Picture." Melehy suggests that Montaigne's thought had unsettled "much of the old philosophy" that had served to "clear the way for Descartes" who then "assumes his skepticism in order to subordinate it, in order to find the ground of certainty required by the notion of modernity." See Melehy, *Writing Cogito*, 94. Jacques Derrida rejects this Cartesian image, arguing, "Descartes never elaborated a philosophical concept of the subject." See *Rogues: Two Essays on Reason* (Stanford, Calif.: Stanford University Press, 2005), 43.

25. Robert C. Solomon and Kathleen M. Higgins, *A Short History of Philosophy* (New York: Oxford University Press, 1996), 179.

26. Carr, *The Paradox of Subjectivity*, 18.

27. Heidegger, *Nietzsche*, 4: 86.

28. Ibid., 4: 99.

29. Ibid., 4: 100; emphasis in original.

30. Heidegger, "The Age of the World Picture," 148.

31. Critchley, "Prolegomena to Any Post-Deconstructive Subjectivity," 15.

32. Martin Heidegger, *Being and Time*, trans. John Macquarrie and Edward Robinson (Oxford, UK: Blackwell, 1962), 123–29.

33. John McCumber, *Metaphysics and Oppression: Heidegger's Challenge to Western Philosophy* (Bloomington: Indiana University Press, 1999), 219.

34. Heidegger, *Being and Time*, 131. See also Werner Marx, *Heidegger and the Tradition*, trans. Theodore Kisiel and Murray Greene (Evanston, Ill.: Northwestern University Press, 1971), 85.

35. Heidegger, *Nietzsche*, 4: 89.

36. Michel Foucault, *The Order of Things: Archaeology of the Human Sciences* (London: Tavistock Publications, 1974), 324.

37. Friedrich Nietzsche, *La Volonte de Puissance*, trans. G. Bianquis (Paris: Gallimard, 1948), 1: 255; cited in Michel Haar, *Nietzsche and Metaphysics*, trans. Michael Gendre (Albany: State University of New York Press, 1996), 89.

38. Melehy, *Writing Cogito*, 3.

39. Judovitz, *Subjectivity and Representation in Descartes*, 181. This mastery over the world is also "its major failure," she argues further.

40. See Philippe Lacoue-Labarthe, "The Echo of the Subject," trans. Christopher Fynsk, in *Typography* (Stanford, Calif.: Stanford University Press, 1998), 141.

41. Carr, "The Question of the Subject," 404–5.

42. Richard Polt, "Metaphysical Liberalism in Heidegger's *Beiträge zur Philosophie*," *Political Theory* 25, no. 5 (1997): 657.

43. Flynn, "Descartes and the Ontology of Subjectivity," 14.

44. Polt, "Metaphysical Liberalism," 657.

45. Ibid. See also Judovitz, *Subjectivity and Representation in Descartes*, 126.

46. Ibid.

47. Critchley, "Prolegomena to Any Post-Deconstructive Subjectivity," 15.

48. Carr, "The Question of the Subject," 405.

49. Thomas Trezise, "Foreword: Persistence," in Philippe Lacoue-Labarthe, *The Subject of Philosophy* (Minneapolis: University of Minnesota Press, 1993), xiv.

50. Polt, "Metaphysical Liberalism," 657.

51. Trezise, "Foreword: Persistence," xiii–xiv.

52. Richard N. Williams and Edwin E. Gantt, "Intimacy and Heteronomy: On Grounding Psychology in the Ethical," *Theory and Psychology* 8, no. 2 (1998): 253; emphasis added.

53. Carr, "The Question of the Subject," 405.

54. The German word is *Bestand*. See Heidegger, "The Turning," in *The Question concerning Technology and Other Essays*, 36–49; and Heidegger, "The Age of the World Picture."

55. Foucault, *The Order of Things*, 345.

56. Habermas, *Theory and Practice*, 43.

57. Ibid.

58. Ibid.

59. Polt, "Metaphysical Liberalism," 667.

60. Heidegger, "The Age of the World Picture," 133.

61. Foucault, *The Order of Things*, 340. In this way, "the end of man, for its part, is the return of the beginning of philosophy," 342.

62. Robert B. Pippin, "Heideggerean Postmodernism and Metaphysical Politics," *European Journal of Philosophy* 4, no. 1 (1996): 23.

63. Solomon and Higgins, *A Short History of Philosophy*, 178.

64. Ibid.

65. Ibid.

66. Heidegger, Nietzsche, 4: 86.

67. For objections to this account of the modern subject see Bowie, "Rethinking the History of the Subject"; and Etienne Balibar, "Subjection and Subjectivation." On the notion of critique as embodied in the ethos of the enlightenment see Michel Foucault, "What Is Enlightenment?" trans. Catherine Porter, in *The Foucault Reader*, ed. Paul Rabinow (London: Penguin, 1984), 32–50.

68. C. Fred Alford, *The Self in Social Theory: A Psychoanalytic Account of Its Construction in Plato, Hobbes, Locke, Rawls, and Rousseau* (New Haven, Conn.: Yale University Press, 1991), vii.

69. Ibid.

70. Stephen K. White, "Weak Ontology and Political Reflection," *Political Theory* 25, no. 4 (1997): 502–23, documents increased interest in ontology; and in IR, Wendt, *Social Theory of International Politics*, has conducted an ontological examination of the state system.

71. Alford, *The Self in Social Theory*, 3.

72. IR scholars interested in ethics have questioned subjectivity; see Vivienne Jabri, "Restyling the Subject of Responsibility in International Relations," *Millennium: Journal of International Studies* 27, no. 3 (1998): 591–611. Also, critical international relations names subjectivity as a neglected area in IR; see R. B. J. Walker, *Inside/Outside: International Relations as Political Theory* (Cambridge: Cambridge University Press, 1993).

73. Wight, *International Theory*, 15 and 7–24.

74. For Immanuel Kant, see Evans, *The Metaphysics of Transcendental Subjectivity;* David Carr, "Kant: Subjectivity and Apperception," in *The Paradox of Subjectivity;* and the essays in Ameriks and Sturma, *The Modern Subject.* Kant has also received treatment in international relations scholarship; see Kimberly Hutchings, *Kant, Critique, and Politics* (New York: Routledge, 1996); Andrew Hurrell, "Kant and the Kantian Paradigm in International Relations," *Review of International Studies* 16, no. 3 (1990):183–205; Hakan Seckinelgin, *International Relations and*

*the Environment: International Fisheries, Heidegger, and Social Method* (London: Routledge, 2006); and Andrew Linklater, *The Transformation of Political Community: Ethical Foundations of the Post-Westphalian Era* (Cambridge, UK: Polity Press, 1998).

75. McCumber, *Metaphysics and Oppression,* 155.

76. See Robert H. Jackson, "The Political Theory of International Society," in *International Relations Theory Today,* ed. Ken Booth and Steve Smith (Cambridge, UK: Polity Press, 1995).

77. Heidegger, cited in Karsten Harries, "Heidegger as a Political Thinker," in *Heidegger and Modern Philosophy: Critical Essays,* ed. Michael Murray (New Haven, Conn.: Yale University Press, 1978), 304.

78. John W. Burton, most notably, had been at the forefront of emphasizing the need to focus on individuals. See John W. Burton, *Conflict: Human Needs Theory* (Basingstoke, UK: Macmillan, 1990).

79. Kenneth N. Waltz, *Theory of International Politics* (Reading, Penn.: Addison-Wesley, 1979).

80. Mark W. Zacher and Richard A. Matthew, "Liberal International Theory: Common Trends, Divergent Strands," in *Controversies in International Relations Theory: Realism and the Neo-Liberal Challenge,* ed. Charles W. Kegley (New York: St. Martin's Press, 1995), 118.

81. Ole Waever, "The Rise and Fall of the Inter-Paradigm Debate," in *International Theory: Positivism and Beyond,* ed. Steve Smith, Ken Booth, and Marysia Zalewski (Cambridge: Cambridge University Press, 1996), 163. On this synthesis see Robert O. Keohane, "International Institutions: Two Approaches," *International Studies Quarterly* 32, no. 4 (December 1988): 379–96; and also Chris Brown, *Understanding International Relations* (London: Macmillan Press, 1997), 49.

82. Wendt, *Social Theory of International Politics,* 10.

83. Ibid., 194.

84. Ibid., 165–84.

85. Wendt distinguishes between individuality and what he calls "the social terms of individuality." Ibid., 181.

86. Williams and Gantt, "Intimacy and Heteronomy," 253.

87. Habermas, *Theory and Practice,* 51.

88. Ibid.

89. Odysseos, "Dangerous Ontologies." See also Noël O'Sullivan, "Postmodernism, Difference, and the Concept of the Political," unpublished paper, 27; and Vilho Harle, *The Enemy with a Thousand Faces: The Tradition of the Other in Western Political Thought and History* (Westport, Conn.: Praeger, 2000).

90. Thomas Hobbes, *Leviathan* (Cambridge: Cambridge University Press, 1991), 89.

91. Ibid., 88–89.

92. Ibid., 86–87.

93. Ibid., 87.

94. McCumber, *Metaphysics and Oppression*, 138.

95. Hobbes, *Leviathan*, 70.

96. McCumber, *Metaphysics and Oppression*, 138.

97. Leo Strauss, "Notes to 'The Concept of the Political,'" trans. George Schwab, in *The Concept of the Political*, by Carl Schmitt (Chicago: University of Chicago Press, 1996), 99.

98. Hobbes, *Leviathan*, 201.

99. Connolly, *Political Theory and Modernity*, 27.

100. Hobbes, *Leviathan*, 93.

101. Leo Strauss, *The Political Philosophy of Hobbes: Its Basis and Its Genesis*, trans. Elsa M. Sinclair (Oxford, UK: Clarendon Press, 1936), 23.

102. Connolly, *Political Theory and Modernity*, 28. See also Christine Di Stefano, *Configurations of Masculinity: A Feminist Perspective on Modern Political Theory* (Ithaca, N.Y.: Cornell University Press, 1991), 69.

103. Connolly, *Political Theory and Modernity*, 29.

104. Ibid.

105. Ibid.

106. John Dunn, *The History of Political Theory and Other Essays* (Cambridge: Cambridge University Press, 1996), 52.

107. Connolly, *Political Theory and Modernity*, 29.

108. Ibid., 27.

109. Strauss, *The Political Philosophy of Hobbes*, 22.

110. Connolly, *Political Theory and Modernity*, 29.

111. Strauss, *The Political Philosophy of Hobbes*, 25.

112. Stuart Umphrey, "Why Politike Philosophia?" in *Phenomenology and the Human Sciences*, ed. J. N. Mohanty (The Hague: Martinus Nijhoff Publishers, 1985), 193.

113. Mary G. Dietz, introduction to *Thomas Hobbes and Political Theory*, ed. Mary G. Dietz (Lawrence: University Press of Kansas, 1990), 4.

114. Wight, *International Theory*; and R. John Vincent, "The Hobbesian Tradition in Twentieth Century International Thought," *Millennium: Journal of International Studies* 10, no. 2 (1981): 91–101. Habermas argues that "[t]he rationale for Hobbes's absolutist state, constructed according to Natural Law, is a liberal one" (*Theory and Practice*, 67). But he continues, "The liberal contents of Natural Law are sacrificed to the absolutist form of its sanctions" (69).

115. Brian C. Schmidt, *The Political Discourse of Anarchy: A Disciplinary History of International Relations* (Albany: State University of New York Press, 1998), 231.

116. Leo Strauss, "Notes to 'The Concept of the Political,'" 90.

117. James Der Derian, "The Value of Security: Hobbes, Marx, Nietzsche, Baudrillard," in *The Political Subject of Violence,* ed. David Campbell and Michael Dillon (Manchester, UK: Manchester University Press, 1993), 99.

118. Ibid.

119. Walker, *Inside/Outside.*

120. Beate Jahn, "IR and the State of Nature: The Cultural Origins of a Ruling Ideology," *Review of International Studies* 25, no. 3 (1999): 411.

121. Habermas, *Theory and Practice,* 72.

122. Georges Van den Abbeele, introduction to *Community at Loose Ends,* ed. Miami Theory Collective (Minneapolis: University of Minnesota Press, 1991), xi; emphasis in original.

123. Odysseos, "Dangerous Ontologies."

## 2. TOWARD A "HERMENEUTICS OF FACTICITY"

1. C. Fred Alford, *The Self in Social Theory: A Psychoanalytic Account of Its Construction in Plato, Hobbes, Locke, Rawls, and Rousseau* (New Haven, Conn.: Yale University Press, 1991).

2. Martin Heidegger, *Nietzsche,* trans. David Farrell Krell, vol. 4, *Nihilism* (New York: Harper and Row, 1991), 96.

3. Heidegger's concern with "Being," however, cannot be associated with "any of its traditional philosophical meanings"; see Thomas Sheehan, "*Kehre* and *Ereignis:* A Prolegomenon to *Introduction to Metaphysics,*" in *A Companion to Heidegger's Introduction to Metaphysics,* ed. Richard Polt and Gregory Fried (New Haven, Conn.: Yale University Press, 2001), 5. See also the very instructive and interesting account of the spectrum of positions within Heidegger scholarship, as well as the oscillations of interpretational paradigms as regards "Heidegger's focal topic" in Thomas Sheehan, "A Paradigm Shift in Heidegger Research," *Continental Philosophy Review* 34 (2001): 183–202.

4. The term "entities" is interchangeable with "beings," but is here used to avoid confusion between "Being" and "beings."

5. Charles Guignon, introduction to *The Cambridge Companion to Heidegger,* ed. Charles Guignon (Cambridge: Cambridge University Press, 1993), 5.

6. John van Buren, *The Young Heidegger: Rumor of the Hidden King* (Bloomington: Indiana University Press, 1994), 38.

7. Guignon, "Introduction," 7, citing Martin Heidegger, *Being and Time,* trans. John Macquarrie and Edward Robinson (Oxford, UK: Blackwell, 1962), 25, subsequently cited in text as *Being and Time,* followed by the page number to this English edition.

8. Martin Heidegger, "Phenomenological Interpretations with Respect to Aristotle: Indication of the Hermeneutical Situation," *Man and World* 25 (1992): 355–93.

9. See also Samuel Ijsseling, "Heidegger and the Destruction of Ontology," *Man and World* 15 (1982): 3–16; and William McNeill, "Metaphysics, Fundamental Ontology, Metontology, 1925–1935," *Heidegger Studies* 8 (1992): 63–79.

10. Dorothea Frede, "The Question of Being: Heidegger's Project," in *The Cambridge Companion to Heidegger,* ed. Charles Guignon (Cambridge: Cambridge University Press, 1993), 44.

11. Ibid.

12. Plato, "The Republic," trans. W. H. D. Rouse, *The Great Dialogues of Plato* (New York: Mentor Books, 1956), 306–7.

13. van Buren, *The Young Heidegger,* 31.

14. Ibid., 30.

15. Ibid., 31.

16. Ibid., 31, 33.

17. Ibid., 33.

18. Ibid., 31.

19. Plato, *The Sophist,* trans. Nicholas P. White (Cambridge, UK: Hackett, 1993).

20. Frede, "The Question of Being," 44.

21. Ibid., 45; emphasis added.

22. Ibid.

23. Guignon, "Introduction," 4.

24. Frede, "The Question of Being," 45.

25. Ibid.

26. Ibid., 44.

27. All quotes in Guignon, "Introduction," 4.

28. Frede, "The Question of Being," 46; emphasis in original. For Husserl's turn away from psychologism, also see Robert C. Solomon, *From Rationalism to Existentialism: The Existentialists and Their Nineteenth-Century Backgrounds* (Lanham, Md.: Littlefield Adams Books, 1972), 147–50.

29. Frede, "The Question of Being," 47; second emphasis added.

30. Ibid.

31. Ibid., 48.

32. Ibid.; emphasis in original.

33. Ibid.

34. Ibid.; emphasis in original.

35. Ibid.; emphasis in original.

36. Ibid., 49, citing Martin Heidegger, *Gesamtausgabe,* vol. 1, *Frühe Schriften,* ed. Friedrich-Wilhelm von Hermann (Frankfurt am Main: Klostermann, 1978), 400; emphasis in original.

37. See Theodore Kisiel, *The Genesis of Heidegger's "Being and Time"* (Berkeley: University of California Press, 1993), 25–32; Roderick M. Stewart, "Signification and Radical Subjectivity in Heidegger's *Habilitationsschrift*," *Man and World* 12 (1979): 360–86; and John D. Caputo, "Phenomenology, Mysticism, and the 'Grammatica Speculativa': Heidegger's *Habilitationsschrift*," *Journal of the British Society for Phenomenology* 5 (1974): 101–17. See also the separate conclusion to the *Habilitationsschrift* written for publication by Martin Heidegger, "The Problem of the Categories," *Man and World* 12 (1979): 278–86, an appendix to Stewart, "Signification and Radical Subjectivity in Heidegger's *Habilitationsschrift*."

38. Guignon, "Introduction," 5.

39. Ibid.

40. Kisiel, *The Genesis of Heidegger's "Being and Time*," 21–56; and Hubert L. Dreyfus, *Being-in-the-World: A Commentary on Heidegger's "Being and Time," Division I* (Cambridge: MIT Press, 1991), 1.

41. Dreyfus, *Being-in-the-World*, 3. P. Keller and D. Weberman, "Heidegger and the Source(s) of Intelligibility (Dasein, Care, Temporality)," *Continental Philosophy Review* 31, no. 4 (1998): 369–86, contest Dreyfus's understanding of mindless ongoing coping as the ground of intelligibility and rightly suggest that "care" is this ground.

42. Frede, "The Question of Being," 43.

43. Ibid., 50–51.

44. Joseph J. Kockelmans, "Phenomenology," in *The Cambridge Dictionary of Philosophy*, ed. Roberto Audi (Cambridge: Cambridge University Press, 1995), 578–79.

45. John Sallis, "The Origins of Heidegger's Thought," in *Radical Phenomenology: Essays in Honor of Martin Heidegger*, ed. John Sallis (Atlantic Highlands, N.J.: Humanities Press, 1978), 46.

46. Ibid., 47; emphasis added.

47. Solokowski, "Edmund Husserl," in *The Cambridge Dictionary of Philosophy*, ed. Audi, 349.

48. Richard Kearney, *Modern Movements in European Philosophy* (Manchester, UK: Manchester University Press, 1994), 16.

49. All in ibid., 16.

50. Solokowski, "Edmund Husserl," 349.

51. Mary Warnock, *Existentialism* (Oxford: Oxford University Press, 1970), 28; emphasis added.

52. John D. Caputo, "The Question of Being and Transcendental Phenomenology: Reflections on Heidegger's Relationship to Husserl," in *Radical Phenomenology: Essays in Honor of Martin Heidegger*, ed. John Sallis (Atlantic Highlands, N.J.: Humanities Press, 1978), 86.

53. All in Warnock, *Existentialism*, 35. See also Solomon, *From Rationalism to Existentialism*, 166.

54. Kearney, *Modern Movements in European Philosophy*, 19.

55. Ibid., 13.

56. Ibid.

57. Ibid., 16.

58. Theodore Kisiel, "Why the First Draft of *Being and Time* Was Never Published," *Journal of the British Society for Phenomenology* 20, no. 1 (1989): 13; emphasis added.

59. Tom Nenon, "Martin Heidegger," in *The Pimlico History of Western Philosophy*, ed. Richard H. Popkin (London: Pimlico, 1999), 682.

60. Kisiel, *The Genesis of Heidegger's "Being and Time,"* 116.

61. Simon Critchley claims that Heidegger revealed through his changes the true potential of Husserlian phenomenology. See Simon Critchley, "Heidegger for Beginners," in *Appropriating Heidegger*, ed. James E. Faulconer and Mark A. Wrathall (Cambridge: Cambridge University Press, 2000), 101–18.

62. Caputo, "The Question of Being and Transcendental Phenomenology," 84–105; and Jacques Taminiaux, "Heidegger and Husserl's Logical Investigations," in *Radical Phenomenology: Essays in Honor of Martin Heidegger*, ed. John Sallis (Atlantic Highlands, N.J.: Humanities Press, 1978), 58–83.

63. George Kovacs, "Philosophy as Primordial Science *(Urwissenschaft)* in the Early Heidegger," *Journal of the British Society for Phenomenology* 21, no. 2 (1990): 125.

64. Both in ibid., 124–25.

65. Kisiel, *The Genesis of Heidegger's "Being and Time,"* 47.

66. Kovacs, "Philosophy as Primordial Science *(Urwissenschaft)* in the Early Heidegger," 125.

67. Kisiel, *The Genesis of Heidegger's "Being and Time,"* 117; emphasis added. This is not, however, entirely unproblematic. Kisiel argues, "The most basic problem of phenomenology is itself, understood as a science of origin," 117.

68. Ibid., 47.

69. Ibid.

70. Kovacs, "Philosophy as Primordial Science *(Urwissenschaft)* in the Early Heidegger," 129, citing Martin Heidegger, *Zur Bestimmung der Philosophie, Gesamtausgabe*, vol. 56/57, ed. Bernd Heimbuchel (Frankfurt am Main: V. Klostermann, 1987), 101.

71. Both in Kisiel, *The Genesis of Heidegger's "Being and Time,"* 48; emphasis added.

72. Ibid. See also Heidegger, *Zur Bestimmung der Philosophie*, 101–11.

73. Kovacs, "Philosophy as Primordial Science *(Urwissenschaft)* in the Early Heidegger," 129.

74. Ibid.

75. Ibid., citing Martin Heidegger, *Zur Bestimmung der Philosophie,* 107 and 108.

76. For Schleiermacher and Dilthey, see Kisiel, *The Genesis of Heidegger's "Being and Time,"* 89–93, 100–105.

77. Ibid., 48; emphasis added.

78. Ibid. See also Martin Heidegger, *Zur Bestimmung der Philosophie,* 99–102.

79. Kisiel, *The Genesis of Heidegger's "Being and Time,"* 48.

80. Both in ibid., 48–49; emphasis added.

81. Ibid., 49; emphasis added.

82. Ibid., 121; emphasis in original.

83. Ibid., 49.

84. Ibid., 55, citing Martin Heidegger, *Zur Bestimmung der Philosophie,* 117, and from student transcripts of the lecture and the comment on the immanent historicity of life that did not make it into the *Gesamtausgabe,* vol. 56/57.

85. Kisiel, *The Genesis of Heidegger's "Being and Time,"* 55–56.

86. Heidegger, "Phenomenological Interpretations with Respect to Aristotle," 359.

87. Kisiel, *The Genesis of Heidegger's "Being and Time,"* 49; see also *Being and Time,* ¶31 and ¶32.

88. Kisiel, *The Genesis of Heidegger's "Being and Time,"* 23.

89. Michael Gelven, *A Commentary on Heidegger's "Being and Time"* (New York: Harper and Row, 1970), 35.

90. Warnock, *Existentialism,* 49.

91. Sallis, "The Origins of Heidegger's Thought," 49.

92. Ibid., 48, citing Martin Heidegger, *Zur Sache des Denkens* (Tübingen, Germany: Max Niemeyer Verlag, 1969), 71.

93. Giorgio Agamben, *The Coming Community,* trans. Michael Hardt (Minneapolis: University of Minnesotta Press, 1993), 97–99; and *Being and Time,* 49–67.

94. Stephen K. White, "Weak Ontology and Political Reflection," *Political Theory* 25, no. 4 (1997): 503. See also the discussion about the emergence of "subjectism," in William J. Richardson, *Heidegger: Through Phenomenology to Thought* (The Hague: Martinus Nijhoff, 1963), 321–30.

95. See also John McCumber, *Metaphysics and Oppression: Heidegger's Challenge to Western Philosophy* (Bloomington: Indiana University Press, 1999), 219.

96. Ibid., 206.

97. Even Husserl's phenomenology appeared confined to subjectivity. See J. Quentin Lauer, *The Triumph of Subjectivity: An Introduction to*

*Transcendental Phenomenology* (New York: Fordham University Press, 1958).

98. Nenon, "Martin Heidegger," 682.

99. All quotes in Kisiel, *The Genesis of Heidegger's "Being and Time,"* 117.

100. Jean-Luc Nancy, *The Sense of the World,* trans. Jeffrey S. Librett (Minneapolis: University of Minnesota Press, 1997), 56; emphasis in original.

101. Robert C. Solomon, *Continental Philosophy since 1750: The Rise and Fall of the Self* (Oxford: Oxford University Press, 1988), 154.

102. Martin Heidegger, *Ontology: The Hermeneutics of Facticity,* trans. John van Buren (Bloomington: Indiana University Press, 1999), 13.

103. Joseph J. Kockelmans, "Destructive Retrieve and Hermeneutic Phenomenology in *Being and Time,*" in *Radical Phenomenology: Essays in Honor of Martin Heidegger,* ed. John Sallis (Atlantic Highlands: Humanities Press, 1978), 107.

104. Sallis, "The Origins of Heidegger's Thought," 49.

105. Yet, what remains *unthought* is "the ground of the possibility of such showings as those to which phenomenology demands we attend," where the "grounds must themselves be such as can be brought to show themselves," ibid.

106. Kisiel, *The Genesis of Heidegger's "Being and Time,"* 21; emphasis in original.

107. van Buren, *The Young Heidegger,* 94.

108. James Risser, "Philosophical Hermeneutics and the Question of Community," in *Interrogating the Tradition: Hermeneutics and the History of Philosophy,* ed. Charles E. Scott and John Sallis (Albany: State University of New York Press, 2000), 22.

109. Caputo, "The Question of Being and Transcendental Phenomenology," 103.

110. Ibid.; emphasis added.

111. Jacques Derrida, *Positions,* trans. A. Bass, 2nd English ed. (London: Continuum, 2002), 8.

112. Kockelmans, "Destructive Retrieve and Hermeneutic Phenomenology in *Being and Time,*" 118. This has become known as deconstruction (*Destruktion* or destruction, meaning de-construction, critique), in particular associated with the thought of Jacques Derrida.

113. Derrida, *Positions,* 8.

114. Kisiel, *The Genesis of Heidegger's "Being and Time,"* 117.

115. Kockelmans, "Destructive Retrieve and Hermeneutic Phenomenology in *Being and Time,*" 108.

116. "Ontic" refers to features that have to do with beings as opposed to Being. See *Being and Time,* 34; emphasis added.

117. Jacques Taminiaux, "Heidegger on Values," in *Heidegger toward the Turn: Essays on the Work of the 1930s,* ed. James Risser (Albany: State University of New York Press, 1999), 235.

118. Rudolf Bernet, "Husserl and Heidegger on Intentionality and Being," *Journal of the British Society for Phenomenology* 21, no. 2 (1990): 146.

119. Einar Øverenget, *Seeing the Self: Heidegger on Subjectivity* (Dordrecht, The Netherlands: Kluwer Academic Publishers, 1998), 1.

120. Robert B. Pippin, "On Being Anti-Cartesian: Hegel, Heidegger, Subjectivity, and Sociality," in *Idealism as Modernism: Hegelian Variations* (Cambridge: Cambridge University Press, 1997), 379.

121. See, for instance, Emmanuel Levinas, "Martin Heidegger and Ontology," *diacritics* 26, no. 1 (1996): 11–32.

122. Jacques Derrida, "Violence and Metaphysics," in *Writing and Difference,* trans. Alan Bass (London: Routledge, 1978), 91.

123. Emmanuel Levinas, "Peace and Proximity (1984)," in *Emmanuel Levinas: Basic Philosophical Writings,* ed. Adriaan T. Peperzak, Simon Critchley, and Robert Bernasconi (Bloomington: Indiana University Press, 1996), 162–65.

124. See Adriaan T. Peperzak, *Beyond: The Philosophy of Emmanuel Levinas* (Evanston, Ill.: Northwestern University Press, 1997).

125. Iver B. Neumann, "Self and Other in International Relations," *European Journal of International Relations* 2, no. 2 (1996): 150.

126. Committee of Public Safety, "'My Place in the Sun': Reflections on the Thought of Emmanuel Levinas," *diacritics* 26, no. 1 (Spring 1996): 3–4. Howard Caygill argues that Levinas's texts must be read "within the horizon of political horror" of National Socialism and the Holocaust, and that this actually requires us to reverse many of our preconceptions about Levinas's work. Rather than conceiving of his work as taking "the ethical" into "the political," or that *"ethics is ethical for the sake of politics"* as Simon Critchley suggests (Simon Critchley, *The Ethics of Deconstruction: Derrida and Levinas,* 2nd ed. [Edinburgh: Edinburgh University Press, 1999], 223; emphasis in original), Caygill asserts that "the ethical emerges as a fragile response to political horror." See Howard Caygill, *Levinas and the Political* (London: Routledge, 2002), 2. In part, then, and Levinas is quite explicit about this, his critique of ontology is tied to Heidegger's own involvement with National Socialism and subsequent silence after the war. See his essays, "As If Consenting to Horror," *Critical Inquiry* 15, no. 2 (Winter 1989): 485–88, and "Reflections on the Philosophy of Hitlerism," *Critical Inquiry* 17 (Autumn 1990): 63–71.

127. David Wood, *Thinking after Heidegger* (Cambridge, UK: Polity Press, 2002), 81.

128. Emmanuel Levinas, *Totality and Infinity: An Essay on Exteriority,* trans. A. Lingis (Pittsburgh: Dusquesne University Press, 1969), 21–22.

129. Wood, *Thinking after Heidegger*, 81–82.

130. Ibid., 82.

131. Emmanuel Levinas, *Ethics and Infinity: Conversations with Philippe Nemo*, trans. Richard A. Cohen (Pittsburgh: Duquesne University Press, 1985), 57; emphasis in original.

132. Emmanuel Levinas, "Ethics as First Philosophy," in *The Levinas Reader*, ed. Sean Hand (Oxford: Oxford University Press, 1989), 76–77.

133. Levinas, *Ethics and Infinity*, 60.

134. Levinas uses Heidegger to criticize Husserl and then turns to a critique of Heidegger. Emmanuel Levinas, *Totality and Infinity*, 45; emphasis in original.

135. Tina Chanter, "The Temporality of Saying: Politics beyond the Ontological Difference," *Graduate Faculty Philosophy Journal* 20/21, no. 2/1 (1998): 508.

136. Ibid., 515.

137. Robert J. S. Manning, "Derrida, Levinas, and the Lives of Philosophy at the Death of Philosophy: A Reading of Derrida's Misreading of Levinas in 'Violence and Metaphysics,'" *Graduate Faculty Philosophy Journal* 20/21, no. 2/1 (1998): 394, 395. A certain amount of contention follows what Levinas means by "absolutely other." According to Jacques Derrida's influential essay "Violence and Metaphysics," in which he engages with the thought of Levinas and contests certain of its objectives and claims, "absolutely other" is understood as "pure otherness"; Manning suggests that this is a misreading, and that rather Levinas means that "the other's alterity is inexhaustible," that "[a]s much as I try to relate to and comprehend the other, I will never know the other completely, which for Levinas means that I will never exhaust the otherness of the other" (397).

138. Manning, "Derrida, Levinas," 400.

139. Levinas, *Totality and Infinity*, 67.

140. Emmanuel Levinas, *Otherwise Than Being, or Beyond Essence*, trans. Alphonso Lingis (The Hague: Martinus Nijhoff, 1981), 25.

141. See, for example, Richardson, *Heidegger*, 34 n. 15.

142. See Krzysztof Ziarek, *Inflected Language: Toward a Hermeneutics of Nearness* (Albany: State University of New York Press, 1994).

143. Derrida, "Violence and Metaphysics," 118; see also 118–33. Also see Jacques Derrida, "At This Very Moment in This Work Here I Am," trans. R. Berezdivin, in *Re-reading Levinas*, ed. Robert Bernasconi and Simon Critchley (Bloomington: Indiana University Press, 1991), 11–48.

144. Derrida, "Violence and Metaphysics," 133.

145. Manning, "Derrida, Levinas," 392.

146. See Levinas, "Martin Heidegger and Ontology."

147. "Levinas simultaneously proposes to us a humanism and a meta-

physics," that is, Derrida reminds us precisely what Heidegger "has in mind when he speaks of the unity of metaphysics, humanism and onto-theology." See Derrida, "Violence and Metaphysics," 142.

148. See Caygill, *Levinas and the Political,* as well as Chanter, "The Temporality of Saying," 526–27.

149. Levinas refers to "the third party," that is, to the others beyond the face-to-face relationship. More accurately, it accounts for the multiplicity of others in a secondary, derivative way by claiming that the third party is reflected in the face of the other. In so doing, Levinas's framework has trouble moving from the particularism of the other's face to the wider social sphere made up of multiple others. Therefore, the theorization of the social, which can be thought of as a transition from the face-to-face relation to a relation encompassing the third party (or multiplicity of third parties), is problematic in Levinasian thought. See, for example, Levinas, "Peace and Proximity" (1984).

150. Critchley, *The Ethics of Deconstruction,* 223.

## 3. AN OPTICS OF COEXISTENCE

1. Martin Heidegger, *Being and Time,* trans. John Macquarrie and Edward Robinson (Oxford, UK: Blackwell, 1962), thereafter cited in text with the page number of this English translation.

2. See Stephen K. White, "Weak Ontology and Political Reflection," *Political Theory* 25, no. 4 (1997): 503.

3. On the Cartesian formulation of "subjectity" into "subjectivity," see Martin Heidegger, *Nietzsche,* trans. David Farrell Krell, vol. 4, *Nihilism* (New York: Harper and Row, 1991), 85–122; on the subject as I-saying being, see Christoph Menke, "Modernity and Subjectivity: From an Aesthetic Point of View," *Graduate Faculty Philosophy Journal* 21, no. 2 (1999): 217–32.

4. Ontological inquiry, as used by Heidegger, is distinguished from ontic inquiry in a distinction known as the "ontological difference." *Ontic* inquiry has to do with beings and entities, as the type of research undertaken by the natural and human sciences, while *ontological* inquiry has to do with Being. See Martin Heidegger, *The Basic Problems of Phenomenology,* trans. Albert Hofstadter (Bloomington: Indiana University Press, 1982), 318–30. In an ontic sense, it can be argued that Dasein regards itself as subject, and its human sciences are predicated on such an understanding.

5. "Its" world, but also the world it shares with others.

6. See, in particular, Emmanuel Levinas, "Ethics as First Philosophy," in *The Levinas Reader,* ed. Sean Hand (Oxford: Oxford University Press,

1989), 76–77; and Emmanuel Levinas, *Totality and Infinity: An Essay on Exteriority,* trans. A. Lingis (Pittsburgh: Dusquesne University Press, 1969), 45.

7. "Copresence" has two senses, the first referring to being-present as substance *(ousia),* and the second to being-present in time, that is, "now-ness" *(parousia).* For an exposition, see Jacques Derrida, *"Ousia* and *Gramme:* Note on a Note from *Being and Time,"* trans. Alan Bass, in *Margins of Philosophy* (New York: Harvester Wheatsheaf, 1982), 29–68.

8. Martin Heidegger, *What Is a Thing?* trans. W. B. Barton Jr. and Vera Deutsch (Chicago: Henry Regnery, 1967), 11–12.

9. Ibid., 12.

10. Robert B. Pippin, "On Being Anti-Cartesian: Hegel, Heidegger, Subjectivity, and Sociality," in *Idealism as Modernism: Hegelian Variations* (Cambridge: Cambridge University Press, 1997), 376.

11. See the account of the rise of the subject in Robert C. Solomon, *Continental Philosophy since 1750: The Rise and Fall of the Self* (Oxford: Oxford University Press, 1988).

12. Hubert L. Dreyfus, *Being-in-the-World: A Commentary on Heidegger's "Being and Time," Division I* (Cambridge, Mass.: MIT Press, 1991), 58.

13. For a discussion of the various understandings of "primacy" and "priority," see Joseph P. Fell, "The Familiar and the Strange: On the Limits of Praxis in the Early Heidegger," *Southern Journal of Philosophy* 28, Spindel Supplement (1989): 23–49.

14. Slavoj Žižek, *The Ticklish Subject: The Absent Centre of Political Ontology* (London: Verso, 1999), chapter 1.

15. David Carr, *The Paradox of Subjectivity: The Self in the Transcendental Tradition* (New York: Oxford University Press, 1999), 19. "It is in this sense," Carr suggests, "that ontology or metaphysics is always prior to epistemology."

16. Moreover, the focus on immersion rids intentionality of its mentalistic connotations and allows Dasein to show itself as "directed-toward" the world and other entities; see Heidegger, *The Basic Problems of Phenomenology,* 58.

17. Dreyfus, *Being-in-the-World,* 52.

18. Stephen Mulhall, *Heidegger and "Being and Time"* (London: Routledge, 1996), 43.

19. In order to understand the practical activity through which Heidegger wants to access "world," we must remember that "[t]here are two basic ways of being. Being-human, which Heidegger calls Dasein, and non-human being. The latter divides into two categories: *Zuhandenheit* and *Vorhandenheit."* These are normally translated respectively as "readiness-

to-hand" and "presence-at-hand," but the meaning of these terms can be best rendered by "availableness" and "occurrentness." Dreyfus, *Being-in-the-World*, xi.

20. Jean-Luc Nancy, *Être Singulier Pluriel* (Paris: Galilee, 1996), 27, cited in Simon Critchley, *Ethics—Politics—Subjectivity: Essays on Derrida, Levinas, and Contemporary French Thought* (London: Verso, 1999), 240.

21. John Haugeland, "Dasein's Disclosedness," *Southern Journal of Philosophy* 28, Spindel Supplement (1989): 57.

22. Ibid., 56.

23. Mulhall, *Heidegger and "Being and Time,"* 48; emphasis in original.

24. Heidegger, *The Basic Problems of Phenomenology*, 164. See also the discussions in Heidegger, *What Is a Thing?*

25. Dreyfus, *Being-in-the-World*, 94.

26. Heidegger, *The Basic Problems of Phenomenology*, 170; emphasis in original.

27. Dreyfus, *Being-in-the-World*, 95.

28. Mulhall, *Heidegger and "Being and Time,"* 75.

29. Dreyfus, *Being-in-the-World*, 49.

30. Ibid., 54; emphasis in original.

31. According to Heidegger there are "three modes of disturbance—conspicuousness, obstinacy, and obtrusiveness." Conspicuousness reveals that equipment is no longer available and in being so "it shows itself as an equipmental Thing which looks so and so, and which, in its readiness-to-hand as looking that way, has constantly been present-at-hand too" (*Being and Time*, 103). However, usual and ordinary breakdowns perhaps do not necessarily lead the user to deliberate reflection. Based on habit and experience, the user might switch to another immersed mode of repairing the equipment or asking for help. In a situation where things are missing, rather than broken, the unavailability of equipment renders it obtrusive. In other words, its momentary unavailability, its ureadiness-to-hand, clarifies its very usual availability. So much so, Heidegger argues, that it seems to lose its readiness-to-hand in the very urgency with which it is needed and therefore reveals itself as present-at-hand. In the case of equipment being neither unusable nor missing, something may "stand in the way of our concern" when it does not, for example, belong in this context or has not been taken care of. "Anything which is unready-to-hand in this way is disturbing to us, and enables us to see the *obstinacy* of that which we must concern ourselves in the first instance before we do anything else" (103).

32. Žižek, *The Ticklish Subject*, 15.

33. See Jacques Derrida, "Geschlecht II: Heidegger's Hand," trans. John P. Leavey Jr., in *Deconstruction and Philosophy: The Texts of Jacques Derrida*, ed. John Sallis (Chicago: University of Chicago Press, 1987), 161–96.

34. Charles E. Scott, *The Question of Ethics: Nietzsche, Foucault, Heidegger* (Bloomington: Indiana University Press, 1990), 108.

35. Martin Heidegger, *The Concept of Time*, trans. William McNeill (Oxford: Blackwell, 1992), 7E.

36. In addition to the cases of the accidental disturbance of Dasein's engaged immersion, the "world" as a referential totality is also brought into perspective by entities "whose function it is to show their practical context." Dreyfus, *Being-in-the-World*, 100. Such entities are "signs" that help Dasein achieve orientation in its own environment by "explicitly rais[ing] an equipmental whole into our circumspection" (*Being and Time*, 110–14).

37. Werner Marx, *Heidegger and the Tradition*, trans. Theodore Kisiel and Murray Greene (Evanston, Ill.: Northwestern University Press, 1971), 88-89.

38. Mulhall, *Heidegger and "Being and Time,"* 51.

39. Ibid., 50; emphasis added.

40. As observed in note 4, Heidegger distinguishes between the terms "ontological," having to do with Being, and "ontic" (or "ontical"), having to do with beings or entities and Dasein's constant involvement with them. See *Being and Time*, 31; Michael Inwood, *A Heidegger Dictionary* (Oxford, UK: Blackwell, 1999), 147; and William J. Richardson, *Heidegger: Through Phenomenology to Thought* (The Hague: Martinus Nijhoff, 1963), 49–50.

41. Dreyfus, *Being-in-the-World*, 106.

42. Ibid., 104; emphasis in original.

43. Haugeland, "Dasein's Disclosedness," 61.

44. Dreyfus, *Being-in-the-World*, 142; second emphasis added.

45. Mulhall, *Heidegger and "Being and Time,"* 50.

46. Haugeland, "Dasein's Disclosedness," 58.

47. Dreyfus, *Being-in-the-World*, 146.

48. Pippin, "On Being Anti-Cartesian," 383.

49. Dreyfus, *Being-in-the-World*, 144.

50. Haugeland, "Dasein's Disclosedness," 61.

51. See René Descartes, *Discourse on Method, and Other Writings*, trans. F. E. Sutcliffe (Harmondsworth, UK: Penguin, 1968), 150–69.

52. Haugeland, "Dasein's Disclosedness," 61–62. Also see John Haugeland, "Heidegger on Being a Person," *Nous* 16, no. 1 (1982): 15–26.

53. Pippin, "On Being Anti-Cartesian," 377; emphasis added. Despite the potential that exists in the *Mitsein* analytic, it was itself underdeveloped by Heidegger as is claimed by Frederick A. Olafson, *Heidegger and the Ground of Ethics: A Study of Mitsein* (Cambridge: Cambridge University

Press, 1998), and Michael Theunissen, *The Other: Studies in the Social Ontology of Husserl, Heidegger, Sartre, and Buber,* trans. Christopher Macann (Cambridge, Mass.: MIT Press, 1984).

54. Recall Levinas's concerns about the violence of objectification and comprehension of the other in the Western philosophical tradition, in which he includes phenomenology and ontology.

55. Mulhall, *Heidegger and "Being and Time,"* 67.

56. Ibid., 66. The use of language in the work world also constitutes "not just a human world, but a common world." James Risser, "Philosophical Hermeneutics and the Question of Community," in *Interrogating the Tradition: Hermeneutics and the History of Philosophy,* ed. Charles E. Scott and John Sallis (Albany: State University of New York Press, 2000), 19.

57. Theunissen, *The Other,* 182.

58. Ibid., 176.

59. N. Georgopoulos, *The Structures of Existence: A Reading of Heidegger's "Being and Time"* (University Park, Pa.: Dialogue Press of Man and World, 1994), 91.

60. Michael Gelven, *A Commentary on Heidegger's "Being and Time"* (New York: Harper and Row, 1970), 67–68.

61. Georgopoulos, *The Structures of Existence,* 93.

62. Lawrence Vogel, *The Fragile "We": Ethical Implications of Heidegger's "Being and Time"* (Evanston, Ill.: Northwestern University Press, 1994), 14.

63. Theunissen, *The Other,* 175. See also *Being and Time,* 160.

64. Both in Walter A. Davis, *Inwardness and Existence: Subjectivity in/and Hegel, Heidegger, Marx, and Freud* (Madison: University of Wisconsin Press, 1989), 115–16. See also the discussion in Fred Dallmayr, *Twilight of Subjectivity: Contributions to a Post-Individualist Theory of Politics* (Amherst: University of Massachusetts Press, 1981), 56–58.

65. Davis, *Inwardness and Existence,* 118.

66. Ibid., 115.

67. Dreyfus, *Being-in-the-World,* 154. Dreyfus claims that this "constitutive conformity" is not fully developed by Heidegger who obscures the constitutive role of the with-world by not distinguishing between it, on the one hand, and the impropriety of conformism for Dasein's Being, on the other.

68. Herman Philipse, "Heidegger and Ethics," *Inquiry* 42 (1999): 451.

69. Howard N. Tuttle, *The Crowd Is Untruth: The Existential Critique of Mass Society in the Thought of Kierkegaard, Nietzsche, Heidegger, and Ortega y Gasset* (New York: Peter Lang, 1996), 67.

70. Dreyfus, *Being-in-the-World,* 144.

71. Philipse, "Heidegger and Ethics," 451.

72. For a contrary view on distantiality, see Johannes Fritsche, "Competition and Conformity: Heidegger on Distantiality and the 'They' in *Being and Time*," *Graduate Faculty Philosophy Journal* 24, no. 2 (2003): 75–107.

73. Tuttle, *The Crowd Is Untruth*, 67–68.

74. However, self-dispersal does not mean that Dasein does not have its world: "The lack of reflexivity, the complete self-identification as well as the total identification with the environment, in other words, narcissism and conformity, do not prevent any Joh from conjuring up a world 'according to Joh,'" writes Agnes Heller. See her "Death of the Subject?" in *Constructions of the Self*, ed. George Levine (New Brunswick, N.J.: Rutgers University Press, 1992), 280.

75. Davis, *Inwardness and Existence*, 116.

76. Pierre Bourdieu, *The Political Ontology of Martin Heidegger*, trans. Peter Collier (Oxford, UK: Polity Press, 1991), 57.

77. Michael E. Zimmerman, *Heidegger's Confrontation with Modernity: Technology, Politics, Art* (Bloomington: Indiana University Press, 1990), 38; emphasis in original.

78. Davis, *Inwardness and Existence*, 5.

79. Michel Haar, "Attunement and Thinking," in *Heidegger: A Critical Reader*, ed. Hubert L. Dreyfus and Harrison Hall (Oxford, UK: Blackwell, 1992), 159–72. This term is far more appropriate than "state of mind" used in the Macquarrie and Robinson translation of *Befindlichkeit*; see *Being and Time*, 172–82). Haugeland, on the other hand, prefers "so-foundness," which also has its merits; see Haugeland, "Dasein's Disclosedness," 63 and 73.

80. Mulhall, *Heidegger and "Being and Time,"* 76.

81. Ibid.

82. Ibid., 79.

83. Ibid.

84. Tuttle, *The Crowd Is Untruth*, 59.

85. Mulhall, *Heidegger and "Being and Time,"* 83.

86. Ibid., 81.

87. Tuttle, *The Crowd Is Untruth*, 58.

88. Mulhall, *Heidegger and "Being and Time,"* 81.

89. Ibid., 82. How Dasein decides on these definite possibilities, as well as their success, depends on its "authenticity."

90. Ibid., 84.

91. Ibid., 111.

92. Tuttle, *The Crowd Is Untruth*, 72.

93. Mulhall, *Heidegger and "Being and Time,"* 106.

94. Tuttle, *The Crowd Is Untruth*, 72.

95. Ibid., 72–73.

96. Martin Heidegger, *Being and Time: A Translation of Sein und Zeit*, trans. Joan Stambaugh (Albany: State University of New York Press, 1996), 164.

97. Mulhall, *Heidegger and "Being and Time,"* 61–62.

98. Ibid., 110.

99. Ibid., 133.

100. Ibid., 110–11.

101. Ibid., 110.

102. Georgopoulos, *The Structures of Existence*, 148.

103. Mulhall, *Heidegger and "Being and Time,"* 111.

104. J. Glenn Gray, "Martin Heidegger: On Anticipating My Own Death," *Personalist* 46 (1965): 439.

105. John McCumber, *Metaphysics and Oppression: Heidegger's Challenge to Western Philosophy* (Bloomington: Indiana University Press, 1999), 208.

106. Mulhall, *Heidegger and "Being and Time,"* 112.

107. See Jean-Luc Nancy, *The Inoperative Community*, trans. Peter Connor, Lisa Garbus, Michael Holland, and Simona Sawhney (Minneapolis: University of Minnesota Press, 1991), 3.

108. Jürgen Habermas, *Theory and Practice*, trans. John Viertel (Cambridge, UK: Polity Press, 1988), 72.

## 4. BECOMING-PROPER

1. Martin Heidegger, *Being and Time*, trans. John Macquarrie and Edward Robinson (Oxford, UK: Blackwell, 1962), hereafter cited in text with the page number of this English translation.

2. John D. Caputo, "Heidegger's *Kampf*," *Graduate Faculty Philosophy Journal*, 14/15, no. 2/1 (1991): 67.

3. As was noted in chapter 3, there is a distinction between "others" and the "they." In the "they" the others have already "lost" their distinctiveness, just as Dasein has.

4. Stephen Mulhall, *Heidegger and "Being and Time"* (London: Routledge, 1996), 133.

5. Ibid., 114.

6. Jacques Derrida, *Aporias*, trans. Thomas Dutoit (Stanford, Calif.: Stanford University Press, 1993), 22.

7. Mulhall, *Heidegger and "Being and Time,"* 117.

8. Ibid., 119.

9. In German: "So enthüllt sich der *Tod* als die *eigenste, unbezügliche, unüberholbare Möglichkeit.*" Martin Heidegger, *Sein und Zeit* (Tübingen,

Germany: Max Niemeyer Verlag, 1993), 251. In Joan Stambaugh's more recent translation, "outstripped" is more appropriately rendered as "by-passed." See Martin Heidegger, *Being and Time: A Translation of Sein und Zeit,* trans. Joan Stambaugh (Albany: State University of New York Press, 1996), 232.

10. Mulhall, *Heidegger and "Being and Time,"* 119.

11. Ibid., 120.

12. Ibid., 127.

13. François Raffoul, *Heidegger and the Subject,* trans. David Pettigrew and Gregory Recco (Atlantic Highlands, N.J.: Humanities Press, 1998), 234.

14. Mulhall, *Heidegger and "Being and Time,"* 129.

15. Raffoul, *Heidegger and the Subject,* 234.

16. Jean-Luc Nancy, *The Inoperative Community,* trans. Peter Connor, Lisa Garbus, Michael Holland, and Simona Sawhney (Minneapolis: University of Minnesota Press, 1991), 14.

17. Simon Critchley and Peter Dews, introduction to *Deconstructive Subjectivities,* ed. Simon Critchley and Peter Dews (Albany: State University of New York Press, 1996), 5.

18. Emmanuel Levinas, *Time and the Other,* trans. Richard A. Cohen (Pittsburgh: Duquesne University Press, 1987), 70.

19. Emmanuel Levinas, *God, Death, and Time,* trans. Bettina Bergo (Stanford, Calif.: Stanford University Press, 2000), 34.

20. Ibid., 33.

21. Ibid., 26.

22. Ibid., 25. See chapter 2 in this volume for this priority of Dasein as the being who can ask the question of Being.

23. Ibid., 34.

24. Ibid., 62.

25. David Wood, *Thinking after Heidegger* (Cambridge, UK: Polity Press, 2002), 18. Levinas suggests that the relation to the other becomes less primary than the relationship to one's own finite being and, by extension, less important than the question of ontology that Heidegger wishes to privilege through Being-towards-death. Ontology, then, does become first philosophy in lieu of ethics as understood by Levinas in the sense of the face-to-face relation with the other. Levinas wishes to "place ontology in question in its pretense to be the encompassing adventure of humanity." We have highlighted this in chapter 2. See also Levinas, *God, Death, and Time,* 59.

26. Levinas, *God, Death, and Time,* 45.

27. Ibid., 39, 47.

28. Levinas, *Time and the Other,* 70.

29. Wood, *Thinking after Heidegger,* 18.

30. Tina Chanter, *Time, Death, and the Feminine: Levinas with Heidegger* (Stanford, Calif.: Stanford University Press, 2001), 157.

31. Ibid., 162; emphasis added.

32. Ibid.

33. See Levinas, *God, Death, and Time,* 34.

34. Wood, *Thinking after Heidegger,* 19.

35. See Richard Wolin, *The Politics of Being: The Political Thought of Martin Heidegger* (New York: Columbia University Press, 1990), 35–40; Richard Wolin, ed., *The Heidegger Controversy: A Critical Reader* (Cambridge, Mass.: MIT Press, 1991); Jürgen Habermas, "The Undermining of Western Rationalism through the Critique of Metaphysics: Martin Heidegger," trans. Frederick G. Lawrence, in *The Philosophical Discourse of Modernity: Twelve Lectures* (Cambridge, UK: Polity Press, 1987), 141; Fred Dallmayr, "Ontology of Freedom: Heidegger and Political Philosophy," *Political Theory* 12, no. 2 (1984): 208, 213–15; and Charles Guignon, "History and Commitment in the Early Heidegger," in *Heidegger: A Critical Reader,* ed. Hubert L. Dreyfus and Harrison Hall (Oxford, UK: Blackwell, 1992), 130.

36. See Carl Schmitt, *The Concept of the Political,* trans. George Schwab (Chicago: University of Chicago Press, 1996). Such a charge might be considered justified by Heidegger's 1933 political involvement with National Socialism and also based on a letter exchanged between Schmitt and Heidegger and translated into English as Martin Heidegger, "Heidegger and Schmitt: The Bottom Line," *Telos,* no. 72 (1987): 132.

37. Karl Löwith, *Martin Heidegger and European Nihilism,* trans. Gary Steiner (New York: Columbia University Press, 1995), 146.

38. Ibid., 160–61; emphasis in original.

39. In addition to avoiding subjectivist readings of the resoluteness of authentic Dasein, there is still another way to illustrate that the charge of decisionism cannot be sustained. The examination of a linguistic form known as "the middle voice" promotes an understanding of Dasein's becoming-proper beyond the self-appropriation of a hyperindividualist and decisionist subjectivity. The middle voice is the form that is linguistically situated between the active and passive voices but is no longer prevalent in modern Western languages. Charles Scott suggests, "In the active voice the verb is for another. In the passive voice the verb acts on the subject. The middle voice is used when the subject is in some way specifically *implicated* in the result of the action but is neither active subject nor the passive object of the action." Charles E. Scott, *The Question of Ethics: Nietzsche, Foucault, Heidegger* (Bloomington: Indiana University Press, 1990), 19; emphasis added. Heidegger employs the middle voice when writing on authenticity and the call of conscience, and this usage dissuades charges of

decisionism. Such unfolding resoluteness enables the unique appropriation of everydayness in terms of mineness understood as an enactment that enacts itself in each case without the assumption of the willing and sovereign modern subject.

40. Richard Polt, "Metaphysical Liberalism in Heidegger's *Beiträge zur Philosophie*," *Political Theory* 25, no. 5 (1997): 675 n. 6.

41. Joanna Hodge, *Heidegger and Ethics* (London: Routledge, 1995), 172.

42. Paul Standish, *Beyond the Self: Wittgenstein, Heidegger, and the Limits of Language* (Aldershot, UK: Avebury, 1992), 218.

43. Miguel de Beistegui, *Heidegger and the Political: Dystopias* (London: Routledge, 1997), 15.

44. Ibid.

45. Standish, *Beyond the Self,* 218. See also Heidegger's later reformulation of "letting-be" or "releasement" in Martin Heidegger, *Discourse on Thinking: A Translation of Gelassenheit,* trans. John M. Anderson and E. Hans Freund (New York: Harper and Row, 1966).

46. Standish, *Beyond the Self,* 210.

47. Paul Barry Clarke, *Autonomy Unbound* (Aldershot, UK: Ashgate, 1999), 112.

48. Beistegui, *Heidegger and the Political,* 15.

49. Howard N. Tuttle, *The Crowd Is Untruth: The Existential Critique of Mass Society in the Thought of Kierkegaard, Nietzsche, Heidegger, and Ortega y Gasset* (New York: Peter Lang, 1996), 73.

50. Martin Heidegger, "On the Essence of Ground (1929)," trans. William McNeill, in *Pathmarks,* Martin Heidegger, ed. William McNeill (Cambridge: Cambridge University Press, 1998), 121; emphasis in original.

51. Ibid.

52. Ibid., 111.

53. Ibid., 109.

54. Walter A. Davis, *Inwardness and Existence: Subjectivity in/and Hegel, Heidegger, Marx, and Freud* (Madison: University of Wisconsin Press, 1989), 142.

55. Hodge, *Heidegger and Ethics,* 182. Such a distinction, however, is unstable and can never become concrete; it is heuristically used to create a space for thinking.

56. Ibid.

57. Davis, *Inwardness and Existence,* 141–42.

58. Michael Gelven, *A Commentary on Heidegger's "Being and Time"* (New York: Harper and Row, 1970), 69.

59. Charles E. Scott, "Nonbelonging/Authenticity," in *Reading Heidegger: Commemorations,* ed. John Sallis (Bloomington: Indiana University Press, 1993), 70; emphasis in original.

60. Scott, *The Question of Ethics,* 97.

61. Raffoul, *Heidegger and the Subject,* 251.

62. Scott, *The Question of Ethics,* 99–100.

63. Ibid., 99.

64. Ibid., 99–100.

65. See Levinas, *God, Death, and Time,* 34–35.

66. Martin Heidegger, *The Basic Problems of Phenomenology,* trans. Albert Hofstadter (Bloomington: Indiana University Press, 1982), 171.

67. Raffoul, *Heidegger and the Subject,* 235.

68. Scott, "Nonbelonging/Authenticity," 67.

69. Raffoul, *Heidegger and the Subject,* 235.

70. Jean-Luc Nancy, *The Experience of Freedom,* trans. Bridget McDonald (Stanford, Calif.: Stanford University Press, 1993), 67.

71. Ibid.; emphases in original.

72. See Jean-Luc Nancy, *Être Singulier Pluriel* (Paris: Galilee, 1996), cited in Simon Critchley, *Ethics—Politics—Subjectivity: Essays on Derrida, Levinas, and Contemporary French Thought* (London: Verso, 1999).

73. Lawrence Vogel, *The Fragile "We": Ethical Implications of Heidegger's "Being and Time"* (Evanston, Ill.: Northwestern University Press, 1994), 12.

74. Raffoul, *Heidegger and the Subject,* 251; emphasis in original.

75. Joan Stambaugh, "An Inquiry into Authenticity and Inauthenticity in *Being and Time,*" in *Radical Phenomenology: Essays in Honor of Martin Heidegger,* ed. John Sallis (Atlantic Highlands, N.J.: Humanities Press, 1978), 158.

76. Raffoul, *Heidegger and the Subject,* 250.

77. Christopher Fynsk, "Foreword: Experiences of Finitude," in *The Inoperative Community,* Jean-Luc Nancy, trans. Peter Connor, Lisa Garbus, Michael Holland, and Simona Sawhney (Minneapolis: University of Minnesota Press, 1991), xiii.

78. Jean-Luc Nancy, "Being-With," trans. Iain Macdonald, *Centre for Theoretical Studies Working Papers,* no. 11 (1996), 14.

79. William McNeill, *The Glance of the Eye: Heidegger, Aristotle, and the Ends of Theory* (Albany: State University of New York Press, 1999), 103, n. 15.

80. Polt, "Metaphysical Liberalism," 661. For an interpretation of authenticity in terms of an improved intelligibility see Hubert L. Dreyfus, "Could Anything Be More Intelligible Than Everyday Intelligibility? Reinterpreting Division I of *Being and Time* in Light of Division II," in *Appropriating Heidegger,* ed. James E. Faulconer and Mark A. Wrathall (Cambridge: Cambridge University Press, 2000), 155–74.

81. Michael Roth, *The Poetics of Resistance: Heidegger's Line* (Evanston, Ill.: Northwestern University Press, 1996), 181.

82. Though such an exercise might appear as a grounding one, i.e., one that provides ultimate foundations, it is important to note that it can only occur on the basis of a groundless entity, a Being-toward-Death. In this regard, the "transcendental 'condition of possibility' of our experience . . . is revealed as also the historical finite 'condition' of *Dasein*," who is a thrown project and as such cannot constitute an ultimate ground as did God, Spirit, and human subjectivity. Gianni Vattimo, "Toward an Ontology of Decline," trans. Barbara Spackman, in *Recoding Metaphysics: The New Italian Philosophy*, ed. Giovanna Borradori (Evanston, Ill.: Northwestern University Press, 1988), 69.

83. See, for example, Stanley Hoffmann, *Duties beyond Borders: On the Limits and Possibilities of Ethical International Politics*, 1st ed. (Syracuse, N.Y.: Syracuse University Press, 1981); Ulrich Beck, "The Cosmopolitan Perspective: Sociology of the Second Age of Modernity," *British Journal of Sociology* 51, no. 1 (2000): 79–105; Molly Cochran, *Normative Theory in International Relations: A Pragmatic Approach* (Cambridge: Cambridge University Press, 1999); and Andrew Linklater, *The Transformation of Political Community: Ethical Foundations of the Post-Westphalian Era* (Cambridge, UK: Polity Press, 1998).

84. Such discussions further respond to those critiques that question the validity of Heidegger's thought for ethics and the other, voiced most prominently by Levinas who suggests that the other is "cut off" by the "abyssal thought" of Being-towards-death and the primacy granted to the question of Being in Heidegger; that, in other words, coexistential heteronomy is only ever accidentally discovered by Heidegger. Levinas argued that even the rich phenomenological descriptions of Being-with and "world" in Division I of *Being and Time* only led to an account of the other as "side by side" with Dasein, and that such descriptions, although richly steeped in Dasein's facticity, could not account for the ethical relation to the other and reduced the other to the same. See Emmanuel Levinas, "Martin Heidegger and Ontology," *diacritics* 26, no. 1 (1996): 11–32; and Emmanuel Levinas, *Totality and Infinity: An Essay on Exteriority*, trans. A. Lingis (Pittsburgh: Dusquesne University Press, 1969).

## 5. RECOVERING THE "ETHICAL" SELF

1. A global era is understood as requiring different approaches to the state and the individual than is assumed in traditional accounts of the international system. See Ulrich Beck, "The Cosmopolitan Perspective: Sociology of the Second Age of Modernity," *British Journal of Sociology* 51, no. 1 (2000): 79–105; and the majority of the essays in Tim Dunne and

Nicholas J. Wheeler, eds., *Human Rights in Global Politics* (Cambridge: Cambridge University Press, 1999).

2. See Andrew Linklater, *The Transformation of Political Community: Ethical Foundations of the Post-Westphalian Era* (Cambridge, UK: Polity Press, 1998); and John D. Clark, *Worlds Apart: Civil Society and the Battle for Ethical Globalization* (Bloomfield, Conn.: Kumarian Press, 2003).

3. Though the term "coexistence," as noted in the introduction, is hardly ever used as such. See Chris Brown, *Sovereignty, Rights, and Justice: International Political Theory Today* (Cambridge, UK: Polity, 2002), 115–24; Mary Kaldor, "Towards a Cosmopolitan Approach," in *New and Old Wars: Organized Violence in a Global Era* (Cambridge, UK: Polity Press, 2001), 112–37; and Mary Kaldor, *Global Civil Society: An Answer to War* (Cambridge, UK: Polity Press, 2003).

4. See, most prominently, Beck, "The Cosmopolitan Perspective," 83–84. Beck grounds cosmopolitan law on an order that ensures that "human rights precedes international law," an order that reverses the premises of the modern international statist order where "international law (and the state) precedes human rights."

5. Charles Champetier, "Reflections on Human Rights," *Telos*, no. 118 (Winter 2000): 77–87; Upendra Baxi, *The Future of Human Rights* (New Delhi: Oxford University Press, 2002); Costas Douzinas, "Law's Subjects: Rights and Legal Humanism," in *The End of Human Rights: Critical Legal Thought at the Turn of the Century* (Oxford, UK: Hart, 2000), 229–61; Chris Brown, "Universal Human Rights: A Critique," in *Human Rights in Global Politics,* ed. Tim Dunne and Nicholas J. Wheeler (Cambridge: Cambridge University Press, 1999); and Fred Dallmayr, "'Asian Values' and Global Human Rights," *Philosophy East & West* 52, no. 2 (2002): 173–89.

6. Jack Donnelly, "Human Rights: A New Standard of Civilization," *International Affairs* 74, no. 1 (1998): 1–24; Tony Evans, *US Hegemony and the Project of Universal Human Rights* (Basingstoke, UK: Macmillan Press, 1996); Tony Evans, *The Politics of Human Rights: A Global Perspective* (London: Pluto Press, 2001); Nikhil Aziz, "The Human Rights Debate in an Era of Globalization: Hegemony of Discourse," *Bulletin of Concerned Asian Scholars* 27, no. 4 (1995): 9–23.

7. On protecting others in terms of a solidarist perspective, see Nicholas J. Wheeler, *Saving Strangers: Humanitarian Intervention in International Society* (Oxford: Oxford University Press, 2000); on codification and criminalization, see Michael Dillon, "Criminalising Social and Political Violence Internationally," *Millennium: Journal of International Studies* 27, no. 3 (1998): 543–67.

8. Christopher Fynsk, "Foreword: Experiences of Finitude," in *The*

*Inoperative Community,* Jean-Luc Nancy, trans. Peter Connor, Lisa Garbus, Michael Holland, and Simona Sawhney (Minneapolis: University of Minnesota Press, 1991), xiii.

9. Or a "disposition" but without the subjectivist connotations of this term. See John Haugeland, "Dasein's Disclosedness," *Southern Journal of Philosophy* 28, Spindel Supplement (1989): 72 n. 37.

10. Albert Borgmann, "Heidegger and Ethics beyond the Call of Duty," in *Appropriating Heidegger,* ed. James E. Faulconer and Mark A. Wrathall (Cambridge: Cambridge University Press, 2000), 68.

11. Charles E. Scott, *The Question of Ethics: Nietzsche, Foucault, Heidegger* (Bloomington: Indiana University Press, 1990), 4. This citation might be taken to resonate with the cultural relativist position. It is moderated, however, by the clarification made by Kai Nielsen as early as 1966 that, anthropologically, similar types of obligations or prohibitions are evident in all cultures signifying a cross-cultural overlap. However, the content of the rules "varies considerably from culture to culture." See Kai Nielsen, "Ethical Relativism and the Facts of Cultural Relativity," *Social Research* 33 (1966): 531–51.

12. See James P. Sterba, ed., *Ethics: The Big Questions* (Oxford, UK: Blackwell, 1998); Mervyn Frost, *Ethics in International Relations: A Constitutive Theory* (Cambridge: Cambridge University Press, 1996).

13. Molly Cochran, *Normative Theory in International Relations: A Pragmatic Approach* (Cambridge: Cambridge University Press, 1999), 206, 249.

14. See specifically Chris Brown, "'Turtles All the Way Down': Anti-Foundationalism, Critical Theory and International Relations," *Millennium: Journal of International Studies* 23, no. 2 (1994): 227–30; David Campbell and Michael Dillon, "The Political and the Ethical," in *The Political Subject of Violence,* ed. David Campbell and Michael Dillon (Manchester, UK: Manchester University Press, 1993); Louiza Odysseos, "Dangerous Ontologies: The Ethos of Survival and Ethical Theorising in International Relations," *Review of International Studies* 28, no. 2 (2002): 403–18; and Vivienne Jabri, "Restyling the Subject of Responsibility in International Relations," *Millennium: Journal of International Studies* 27, no. 3 (1998): 591–611.

15. Scott, *The Question of Ethics.*

16. Joanna Hodge, *Heidegger and Ethics* (London: Routledge, 1995), 2.

17. Such neglect is, of course, partly attributable to Heidegger's own comments about his work not being related to ethics and to the widely held perception that there is a profound absence of normative concerns in phenomenology. See Martin Heidegger, "Letter on Humanism (1946)," trans.

Frank A. Capuzzi, in *Pathmarks,* Martin Heidegger, ed. William McNeill (Cambridge: Cambridge University Press, 1998), 239–76.

18. See, for example, Emmanuel Levinas, *God, Death, and Time,* trans. Bettina Bergo (Stanford, Calif.: Stanford University Press, 2000); and Emmanuel Levinas, *Time and the Other,* trans. Richard A. Cohen (Pittsburgh: Duquesne University Press, 1987).

19. Scott, *The Question of Ethics,* 2; Hodge, *Heidegger and Ethics,* 1. This new type of work has succeeded earlier writings that had, in part, assumed that Heidegger's contribution to ethics lay primarily in questioning the fact-value dichotomy, a distinction that had largely contributed to the academic "neglect of human conduct." Fred R. Dallmayr, *The Other Heidegger* (Ithaca, N.Y.: Cornell University Press, 1993), 109. Surpassed is also the assumed equivalence between ontological concepts, such as "authenticity," "resoluteness," or "solicitude," and ethics. See, for example, Charles M. Sherover, "Founding an Existential Ethic," *Human Studies* 4 (1981): 223–36; and Marjorie Grene, "Authenticity: An Existential Virtue," *Ethics* 62, no. 4 (1952): 266–74.

20. Martin Heidegger, *Being and Time,* trans. John Macquarrie and Edward Robinson (Oxford, UK: Blackwell, 1962), 167; hereafter cited in text with the page number of this English translation.

21. Slavoj Žižek, *The Ticklish Subject: The Absent Centre of Political Ontology* (London: Verso, 1999), 48; emphases in original.

22. Scott, *The Question of Ethics,* 106.

23. Additionally, in a Foucauldian argument, the process of habituation can be supplemented with the exercise of power beyond its traditional understanding as coercion, since "[i]n modern societies, power operates in a much more complex manner: through normalisation rather than prohibition." Andrew Schaap, "Power and Responsibility: Should We Spare the King's Head?" *Politics: Surveys and Debates for Students of Politics* 20, no. 3 (2000): 129.

24. See John Haugeland, "Heidegger on Being a Person," *Nous* 16, no. 1 (1982): 15–26.

25. This statement brings together conceptions of mores and morals.

26. Charles Chamberlain, "From 'Haunts' to 'Character': The Meaning of *Ethos* and Its Relation to Ethics," *Helios* 11, no. 2 (1984): 97.

27. Ibid., 99.

28. Scott, *The Question of Ethics,* 144–45.

29. Chamberlain, "From 'Haunts' to 'Character,'" 100.

30. Ibid., 101.

31. Scott, *The Question of Ethics,* 143.

32. Ibid., 144.

33. Ibid., 145.

34. See Hubert L. Dreyfus, *Being-in-the-World: A Commentary on Heidegger's "Being and Time," Division I* (Cambridge, Mass.: MIT Press, 1991), 157; and Haugeland, "Dasein's Disclosedness," 51–73, for an account of the "they" as shared historical practices.

35. For a discussion of average intelligibility, see Richard Polt, "Metaphysical Liberalism in Heidegger's *Beiträge zur Philosophie*," *Political Theory* 25, no. 5 (1997): 655–79.

36. The assignment of value is but a sign of nihilism. See Martin Heidegger, *Nietzsche*, trans. David Farrell Krell, vol. 4 (New York: Harper and Row, 1991), 44; and also Martin Heidegger, "The Age of the World Picture," trans. William Lovitt, in *The Question concerning Technology and Other Essays* (New York: Harper and Row, 1977), 115–54.

37. David Wood, "Ethos beyond Ethics: Remarks on Charles Scott," *Research in Phenomenology* 30 (2000): 217.

38. This is of course traceable not only to Heidegger; it is part of a longer heritage of the "hermeneutics of suspicion" that refutes the possibility of "an ethical system able to give laws to reality by imposing norms and prohibitions to be respected." See Silvia Benso, "On the Way to an Ontological Ethics: Ethical Suggestions in Reading Heidegger," *Research in Phenomenology* 24 (1994): 176.

39. See also Robert W. Cox, "Social Forces, States, and World Orders: Beyond International Relations Theory," *Millennium: Journal of International Studies* 10, no. 2 (1981): 129. Mark Neufeld directs Cox's approach to international ethics in Mark Neufeld, "Thinking Ethically—Thinking Critically: International Ethics as Critique," in *Value Pluralism, Normative Theory, and International Relations*, ed. Maria Lensu and Jan-Stefan Fritz (Basingstoke, UK: Macmillan Press, 1999), 41–58.

40. Even Andrew Linklater's universalist approach acknowledges this: "A new universality may yet bring an end to the West's use of universalist moral concepts to celebrate the achievements of Western modernity and to enlarge its control of other peoples." Linklater, *The Transformation of Political Community*, 24.

41. "Mores" in the sense of local habitual practices; *das Moralische* in Hegel's distinction. See Benso, "On the Way to an Ontological Ethics," 160. For another account of the customary and the ethical, see Gernot Böhme, "Ethical Life or 'The Customary,'" trans. John Farrell, *Thesis Eleven* 60 (2000): 1–10.

42. Of course, as Ken Booth writes, "To say that human rights comes from somewhere—and the West is not the only geographical expression claiming to be a parent—should never be allowed to be the end of the story: it is only a discussion of how we should live, as humans, on a global scale."

Ken Booth, "Three Tyrannies," in *Human Rights in Global Politics,* ed. Timothy Dunne and Nicholas J. Wheeler (Cambridge: Cambridge University Press, 1999), 53.

43. Scott, *The Question of Ethics,* 106.

44. Ibid., 142.

45. Ibid., 106.

46. Ibid., 107.

47. See Dreyfus, *Being-in-the-World,* 144, 155, and 157–62; and Martin Heidegger, "On the Essence of Ground (1929)," trans. William McNeill, in *Pathmarks,* Martin Heidegger, ed. William McNeill (Cambridge: Cambridge University Press, 1998), 97–135, for a discussion of the "generation of ground."

48. On suffering, see Philip Allott, "Globalization from Above: Actualising the Ideal through Law," *Review of International Studies* 26 (December 2000): 76–77. The focus on suffering necessarily refers to a Western conception of ethics and morality because the unworking of modern subjectivity is aimed at the Western modern conception of the subject, though to call the modern subject "Western" might be redundant. See Etienne Balibar, "Subjection and Subjectivation," in *Supposing the Subject,* ed. Joan Copjec (London: Verso, 1994), 14 n. 12; and also his "Citizen Subject," in *Who Comes after the Subject?* ed. Eduardo Cadava, Peter Connor, and Jean-Luc Nancy (New York: Routledge, 1991), 33–57.

49. Scott, *The Question of Ethics,* 178.

50. Of course, this is a rhetorical question; such isolation is ontologically impossible given that the self is shared practices in its everydayness. See Dreyfus, *Being-in-the-World.*

51. Henry G. Golz, *Plato and Heidegger: In Search of Selfhood* (Lewisburg, Pa.: Bucknell University Press, 1981), 301. Is authenticity, in other words, predicated on a notion of "grace"?

52. "If that capacity [to become-proper] is genuinely repressed, how can it possibly speak out? If it can, its repression must have already been lifted; but it is just that lifting, that transition from inauthenticity to authenticity, which the call of conscience is supposedly invoked to explain"; for Mulhall, therefore, the external source of the call is a requirement of coherence for the account provided by Heidegger. See Stephen Mulhall, *Heidegger and "Being and Time"* (London: Routledge, 1996), 130.

53. Ibid., 133.

54. Ibid. The notion of mimesis involved in Mulhal's modification is attuned to the "problematic of attestation" required by Heidegger in which "a proper *existential* possibility of Dasein is shown in an *existentiell* manner" (*Being and Time,* 34).

55. Does this "catching-up" comply with the need for the call to be

perceived by Dasein "not in some external and superficial way" but as the means of revealing that becoming-proper is a necessity grounded in Dasein's existence? See François Raffoul, *Heidegger and the Subject*, trans. David Pettigrew and Gregory Recco (Atlantic Highlands, N.J.: Humanities Press, 1998), 226.

56. Mulhall, *Heidegger and "Being and Time,"* 133. "Uncanniness" translates *Unheimlichkeit*, which might be better understood as "homelessness." See *Being and Time*, 233 n. 3.

57. Mulhall, *Heidegger and "Being and Time,"* 133.

58. Rudi Visker, *Truth and Singularity: Taking Foucault into Phenomenology* (Dordrecht, The Netherlands: Kluwer Academic Publishers, 1999), 31. See also his "Dropping: The 'Subject' of Authenticity: Being and Time on Disappearing Existentials and True Friendship with Being," *Research in Phenomenology* 24 (1994): 141.

59. See also the discussion in Louiza Odysseos, "On the Way to Global Ethics? Cosmopolitanism, 'Ethical' Selfhood and Otherness," *European Journal of Political Theory* 2, no. 2 (April 2003): 183–207; and Stuart Elden, *Speaking against Number: Heidegger, Language, and the Politics of Calculation* (Edinburgh: Edinburgh University Press, 2006), 40–42.

60. Martin Heidegger, *Being and Time: A Translation of Sein und Zeit*, trans. Joan Stambaugh (Albany: State University of New York Press, 1996), 153.

61. Miguel de Beistegui, *Heidegger and the Political: Dystopias* (London: Routledge, 1997), 149; emphasis in original.

62. Ibid., 148.

63. Ibid.

64. Ibid., 148–49.

65. Ibid., 149.

66. Ibid.

67. Jacques Derrida, "Heidegger's Ear: Philopolemology (*Geschlecht* IV)," in *Reading Heidegger: Commemorations*, ed. John Sallis (Bloomington: Indiana University Press, 1993), 175. This voice is "something that could make the 'they' 'collapse.' Such is the power of the 'voice of the friend whom each Dasein carries with it.'" See Visker, "Dropping," 143, citing *Being and Time*, 206.

68. Derrida, "Heidegger's Ear," 164.

69. Ibid., 174.

70. Ibid., 164.

71. Beistegui, *Heidegger and the Political*, 149.

72. Derrida, "Heidegger's Ear," 164.

73. Beistegui, *Heidegger and the Political*, 150.

74. Derrida, "Heidegger's Ear," 174.

75. Ibid., 176.

76. Ibid.; emphasis in original.

77. There are still objections to this by scholars influenced by Emmanuel Levinas's critique of Heidegger who claim that, despite the potentials of the analysis of the existential structures of Dasein, the ontological nature of this work prevents it from being useful to a discussion on ethics. In other words, the discussion remains about Dasein and not really about the other; the other is still too removed from this consideration. See, for example, Simon Critchley, *The Ethics of Deconstruction: Derrida and Levinas*, 2nd ed. (Edinburgh: Edinburgh University Press, 1999); Simon Critchley, *Ethics—Politics—Subjectivity: Essays on Derrida, Levinas, and Contemporary French Thought* (London: Verso, 1999). Critchley's discussion of Jean-Luc Nancy's *Being Singular Plural*, trans. Robert D. Richardson and Anne E. O'Byrne (Stanford, Calif.: Stanford University Press, 2000) in *Ethics—Politics—Subjectivity* is especially interesting as it contests Nancy's reliance on Dasein's otherness. However, I argue here that inasmuch as this ontological discussion has anything to say to ethics, it is through the move of unworking modern autonomous subjectivity. At the point of deconstruction, the ethical and the ontological come together and enable a consideration of concrete otherness as well as heteronomous selfhood. This is further addressed in the following section, "Toward a Recovery of the 'Ethical Self.'"

78. Beistegui, *Heidegger and the Political*, 151. It can be argued that the connection between silence, hearing the other in Dasein, and ethics is not sustained in the later thought of Heidegger, where the emphasis on Dasein is relinquished and substituted with an emphasis on epochality (history of Being). This neo-Hegelian insight asserts that "each historical epoch is based upon a fundamental metaphysical stance that determines how things show up for human beings in that epoch," writes Herman Philipse, "Heidegger and Ethics," *Inquiry* 42 (1999): 440. See also Robert Bernasconi, *Heidegger in Question: The Art of Existing* (Atlantic Highlands, N.J.: Humanities Press, 1993), chapter 9. The withdrawal and oblivion of Being, which the later Heidegger thought described the present epoch, "is deaf to the appeal of suffering" because "nowhere in the call of Being is the cry of the *victim* to be heard, nowhere the plea for mercy, the summons for help," writes John D. Caputo, "Heidegger's Scandal: Thinking and the Essence of the Victim," in *The Heidegger Case: On Philosophy and Politics*, ed. Tom Rockmore and Joseph Margolis (Philadelphia: Temple University Press, 1992), 277. Heidegger's abandonment of worldly Dasein and its projective thrown resoluteness found in his early work is partly responsible for Heidegger's own silence about the Holocaust. Within the later approach of the history of being, "there is no call of conscience, no response that

says 'guilty,' and so there are no victims. There is/it gives *(es gibt)* only the epochal shifts which have fallen into an escalating history of oblivion from *eidos to Technik*" (Caputo, "Heidegger's Scandal," 278). So, for the early Heidegger, silence is a positive possibility, the only way Dasein can be-with others in a proper way, while years later silence is an escape for Heidegger from the Holocaust and the "greatest blunder," as he called his rectorship of the University of Freiburg. Beistegui writes in this regard, "One might wish, then, to hear the silent voice of Heidegger sympathetically, as if echoing the almost imperceptible moan of his victims. One would like to understand this silence as memory and mourning, as if language, wounded and bruised, had found refuge only in the inner ear of thinking. Yet the meaning of Heidegger's silence lies elsewhere: not in memory, not in mourning, but in a lack and failure of thinking itself." Beistegui, *Heidegger and the Political*, 152–53. See also David Farrell Krell, *Daimon Life: Heidegger and Life-Philosophy* (Bloomington: Indiana University Press, 1992), 138–42.

79. Scott, *The Question of Ethics*, 111.

80. Ibid., 110; emphasis added.

81. Ibid., 217 n. 4.

82. Ibid., 100.

83. Ibid.; emphasis in original.

84. For a Freudian account, see Julia Kristeva, *Strangers to Ourselves*, trans. Leon S. Roudiez, (New York: Columbia University Press, 1991), 191–92; and in international relations, see Vivienne Jabri, "Restyling the Subject of Responsibility in International Relations," 607–9.

85. "Factical" refers to the possibilities within Dasein's concrete situation. The phrase "repeatable possibilities" is suggested by Peg Birmingham, "The Time of the Political," *Graduate Faculty Philosophy Journal* 14/15, no. 2/1 (1991): 25–45.

86. Scott, *The Question of Ethics*, 106.

87. There is no choice to hear otherness once Dasein embarks on this process of self-estrangement. "Choice is at the heart of ethics, but our choices are never entirely free." Ken Booth, Tim Dunne, and Michael Cox, "How Might We Live? Global Ethics in a New Century," special issue, *Review of International Studies* 26 (December 2000): 1. The difference with the presupposition that choice always informs ethical decisions is that the recovery of the "ethical" self is not about *this* or *that* choice because these issues would be determined within the specific factical context. The recovery of the "ethical" self involves a "turn away from ethics" in which customary moral practices are deconstructed: recovering ethicity is about opening up and remaining within the question of ethics, aware that any factical momentary choice is contingent.

88. See Walter A. Davis, *Inwardness and Existence: Subjectivity in/and Hegel, Heidegger, Marx, and Freud* (Madison: University of Wisconsin Press, 1989), 142.

89. Ibid., 113.

90. Ibid.

91. See Heidegger, "Letter on Humanism (1946)," 269; and Scott, *The Question of Ethics*, 143–47.

92. It can be noted that the later Heidegger no longer speaks of authenticity as a process to be achieved by Dasein but speaks of regions of Being. See Michael E. Zimmerman, *Eclipse of the Self: The Development of Heidegger's Concept of Authenticity*, rev. ed. (Athens: Ohio University Press, 1986); and Charles B. Guignon, "Heidegger's 'Authenticity' Revisited," *Review of Metaphysics* 38 (1984): 321–39.

93. Heidegger, "Letter on Humanism (1946)," 269.

94. Thus, "ethicity" refers to "the essence of ethics." See Robert Bernasconi, "Justice without Ethics?" *PLI: Warwick Journal of Philosophy* 6 (1997): 58–69; see also Jacques Derrida, "Passions: An Oblique Offering," trans. David Wood, in *On the Name*, Jacques Derrida (Stanford, Calif.: Stanford University Press, 1995), 3–31.

95. See Michel Foucault, "Ethics and Politics: An Interview," trans. Catherine Porter, in *The Foucault Reader*, ed. Paul Rabinow (London: Penguin Books, 1991), 377.

96. Michel Foucault, "On the Genealogy of Ethics: Overview of Work in Progress," in *The Foucault Reader*, ed. Paul Rabinow (London: Penguin Books, 1991), 343.

97. This is also the view of Scott, that "Dasein's temporal and mortal movement, its *Vorlauf*, would then be the basis for the way we design our lives." See Scott, *The Question of Ethics*, 98.

98. Although the most prominent cosmopolitan discourses within the debate of global ethics are liberal (some would say neoliberal; see Peter Gowan, "The New Liberal Cosmopolitanism," in *Debating Cosmopolitics*, ed. Daniele Archibugi [London: Verso, 2003]) in origin and attitude, there are other discourses that aspire to a different cosmopolitanism away from the limitations of liberal commitments to the modern subject. See Fred Dallmayr, "Cosmopolitanism: Moral and Political," *Political Theory* 31, no. 3 (June 2003): 421–42; Peter G. Mandaville, "Conversing beyond the Cosmopolitan," paper presented at the British International Studies Association Annual Conference, 16–18 December 2002, London.

99. "Ground means: possibility, basis, account," writes Heidegger, adding that ground is inseparable from transcendence. See Heidegger, "On the Essence of Ground (1929)," 131.

100. Jean-Luc Nancy, "Being-With," trans. Iain Macdonald, *Centre for Theoretical Studies Working Papers*, no. 11 (1996): 1.

101. Scott, *The Question of Ethics*, 145.

102. Philipse, "Heidegger and Ethics," 456.

103. Ibid. See also Brown, "'Turtles All the Way Down.'"

104. Philipse, "Heidegger and Ethics," 468.

105. Linklater, *The Transformation of Political Community*, 48.

106. Cochran asks the same question with respect to international ethics in Cochran, *Normative Theory in International Relations*, 204.

107. Jacques Derrida, *Spurs: Nietzsche's Styles/Éperons: Les Styles de Nietzsche*, trans. Barbara Harlow, English-French ed. (Chicago: University of Chicago Press, 1979), 117.

108. Derrida, "Passions," 11; emphasis added. Of course, the refusal of foundationalism involves its own universal claim about the "universal questionability of philosophical grounds." Horace L. Fairlamb, *Critical Conditions: Postmodernity and the Question of Foundations* (Melbourne: Cambridge University Press, 1994), 7.

109. John van Buren, "The Young Heidegger, Aristotle, Ethics," in *Ethics and Danger: Essays on Heidegger and Continental Thought*, ed. Arleen B. Dallery, Charles E. Scott, and P. Holley Robert (Albany: State University of New York Press, 1992), 178.

110. van Buren, "The Young Heidegger, Aristotle, Ethics," 178, citing Martin Heidegger, "Comments on Karl Jasper's *Psychology of Worldviews* (1919/21)," trans. John van Buren, in *Pathmarks*, Martin Heidegger, ed. William McNeill (Cambridge: Cambridge University Press, 1998), 1–38.

111. Hans-Georg Gadamer, "The Political Incompetence of Philosophy," in *The Heidegger Case: On Philosophy and Politics*, ed. Tom Rockmore and Joseph Margolis (Philadelphia: Temple University Press, 1992), 366. See also Heidegger, "Letter on Humanism (1946)."

112. Gadamer, "The Political Incompetence of Philosophy," 366.

113. Ibid.

114. Nielsen, "Ethical Relativism and the Facts of Cultural Relativity," 544.

115. Tzvetan Todorov, *On Human Diversity: Nationalism, Racism, and Exoticism in French Thought* (Cambridge, Mass.: Harvard University Press, 1989), 32.

116. Philippe Lacoue-Labarthe, *Heidegger, Art, and Politics: The Fiction of the Political*, trans. Chris Turner (Oxford, UK: Blackwell, 1990), 31. See also Brown, "'Turtles All the Way Down,'" 215–18.

117. Lacoue-Labarthe, *Heidegger, Art, and Politics*, 31.

118. Jacques Derrida notes that Levinas's own call for a renewed human-

ism of the other, that ethics escapes "the end of philosophy" and ought to be "first philosophy," may suffer from this exhaustion. See his seminal essay on the thought of Emmanuel Levinas, "Violence and Metaphysics: An Essay on the Thought of Emmanuel Levinas," trans. Alan Bass, in *Writing and Difference* (London: Routledge and Kegan Paul, 1978), 79–153.

119. Martin Heidegger, *The End of Philosophy*, trans. Joan Stambaugh (New York: Harper and Row, 1972), especially the essay "Overcoming Metaphysics," 84–110.

120. See David Campbell and Michael Dillon, "The End of Philosophy and the End of International Relations," in *The Political Subject of Violence*, ed. David Campbell and Michael Dillon (Manchester, UK: Manchester University Press, 1993), 5.

121. Nielsen, "Ethical Relativism and the Facts of Cultural Relativity," 545; emphasis in original. This notion of a plea is slowly also being heeded in international ethical theorizing. See Ken Booth, for example, who articulates, it seems, a similar plea for universality "not because we are human, but to make us human." Booth, "Three Tyrannies," 52; and also Molly Cochran, who writes in a similar vein, "There may be a hope for a principle to have a range of applicability, a degree of universality beyond the context of the situation from which it arises." Cochran, *Normative Theory in International Relations*, 206.

122. Linklater notes that the conversation that IR ethical theories sustain with their critics opens up the very possibility of "a radically improved universalism." See Linklater, *The Transformation of Political Community*, 48.

123. See the essays in Maria Lensu and Jan-Stefan Fritz, eds., *Value Pluralism, Normative Theory, and International Relations* (Basingstoke, UK: Macmillan Press, 1999).

124. Christopher Fynsk, "Foreword: Experiences of Finitude," xiii.

125. Jean-Luc Nancy, *The Experience of Freedom*, trans. Bridget McDonald (Stanford, Calif.: Stanford University Press, 1993), 68. This singularity is different from individuality that "equated identity with sameness." Noël O'Sullivan, "Postmodernism and the Politics of Identity," in *Politics and the End of Identity*, ed. Kathryn Dean (Aldershot, UK: Ashgate, 1997), 234. Being singular only occurs in its concrete relation to others.

126. John D. Caputo, *Demythologizing Heidegger* (Bloomington: Indiana University Press, 1993), 127.

127. Fred Dallmayr renders "liberating solicitude" as "anticipating-emancipatory solicitude." See the discussion in his "Rethinking the Political: Some Heideggerian Contributions," *Review of Politics* 52 (1990): 537. Also, the earlier translation of *Being and Time* by Macquarrie and

Robinson uses the word "solicitude" for *Fürsorge*, while the more recent 1996 translation by Joan Stambaugh employs the term "concern." See Heidegger, *Being and Time: A Translation of Sein und Zeit,* 114.

128. Lawrence Vogel, *The Fragile "We": Ethical Implications of Heidegger's "Being and Time"* (Evanston, Ill.: Northwestern University Press, 1994), 75.

129. Ibid., 82.

130. John D. Caputo, *Radical Hermeneutics: Repetition, Deconstruction, and the Hermeneutic Project* (Bloomington: Indiana University Press, 1987), 258–59.

131. Vogel, *The Fragile "We,"* 70. Vogel's account places this disposition in a deconstructed notion of the moral conscience that transforms the ontological insight into a moral mechanism. This, however, should be treated with caution. I retained only the useful examination of solicitude as a disposition, which can be employed without Vogel's account of the moral conscience.

132. Ibid.; emphasis in original.

133. Ibid., 71. See also Campbell and Dillon, "The Political and the Ethical," 167–68.

134. Vogel, *The Fragile "We,"* 71.

135. Polt, "Metaphysical Liberalism," 657.

136. Fynsk, "Foreword: Experiences of Finitude," xiii.


**6. COEXISTENCE, COMMUNITY, AND CRITICAL BELONGING**

1. Jean Greisch, "Ethics and Lifeworlds," trans. Eileen Brennan, in *Questioning Ethics: Contemporary Debates in Philosophy,* ed. Richard Kearney and Mark Dooley (London: Routledge, 1999), 44–61.

2. Stanley Rosen, "Political Philosophy and Ontology," *Philosophy and Phenomenological Research* 18, no. 4 (1958): 537. Of course, the persistence with delineating a politics entails a danger that these insights are appropriated by dominant subjectivist conceptions of politics. See Slavoj Žižek, *Did Somebody Say Totalitarianism? Five Interventions in the (Mis)Use of a Notion* (London: Verso, 2001).

3. Rosen, of course, means this in a rather disparaging way. See Stanley Rosen, *Hermeneutics as Politics* (New York: Oxford University Press, 1987), 141.

4. This occurs at both the level of Dasein's personal self-relationship and also at the level of community (in the sense of the questioning relationship one develops toward the "they"). Naturally, articulating this distinction is a subjectivist remnant: Dasein is, initially and primarily, the "they,"

i.e., a specific manifestation of shared practices; in other words, coexistence as a questioning relationship has to begin from this starting point and, therefore, refer univocally to Dasein's self-relationship and relationships to others. See also Edgar C. Boedeker Jr., "Individual and Community in Early Heidegger: Situating das Man, the Man-self, and Self-ownership in Dasein's Ontological Structure," *Inquiry* 44, no. 1 (2001): 63–99.

5. Jean-Luc Nancy, "Being-With," trans. Iain Macdonald, *Centre for Theoretical Studies Working Papers*, no. 11 (1996): 5. See also Jean-Luc Nancy, *Being Singular Plural*, trans. Robert D. Richardson and Anne O'Byrne (Stanford, Calif.: Stanford University Press, 2000).

6. See, most prominently, Hugo Ott, *Martin Heidegger: A Political Life*, trans. Allen Blunden (New York: Basic Books, 1993); and Victor Farias, *Heidegger and Nazism*, trans. Paul Burrell and Gabriel R. Ricci (Philadelphia: Temple University Press, 1987). Also see Heidegger's address during his rectorship, "The Self-Assertion of the German University," trans. Karsten Harries, *Review of Metaphysics* 38 (1985): 470–80.

7. Molly Cochran, *Normative Theory in International Relations: A Pragmatic Approach* (Cambridge: Cambridge University Press, 1999); Chris Brown, *International Relations Theory: New Normative Approaches* (London: Harvester Wheatsheaf, 1992); and Michael Walzer, *Thick and Thin: Moral Argument at Home and Abroad* (Notre Dame, Ind.: University of Notre Dame Press, 1994).

8. See Miguel de Beistegui, *Heidegger and the Political: Dystopias* (London: Routledge, 1997); Pierre Bourdieu, *The Political Ontology of Martin Heidegger*, trans. Peter Collier (Oxford, UK: Polity Press, 1991); John D. Caputo, "Heidegger's Kampf," *Graduate Faculty Philosophy Journal* 14/15, no. 2/1 (1991): 61–83; Jacques Derrida, *Of Spirit: Heidegger and the Question*, trans. Geoffrey Bennington and Rachel Bowlby (Chicago: University of Chicago Press, 1989); Johannes Fritsche, *Historical Destiny and National Socialism in Heidegger's "Being and Time"* (Berkeley: University of California Press, 1999); Jürgen Habermas, "Work and *Weltanschauung*: The Heidegger Controversy from a German Perspective," trans. John McCumber, *Critical Inquiry* 15 (1989): 431–56; Samuel Ijsseling, "Heidegger and Politics," in *Ethics and Danger: Essays on Heidegger and Continental Thought*, ed. Arleen B. Dallery, Charles E. Scott, and P. Holley Roberts (Albany: State University of New York Press, 1992); Dominique Janicaud, *The Shadow of That Thought: Heidegger and the Question of Politics*, trans. Michael Gendre (Evanston, Ill.: Northwestern University Press, 1996); Philippe Lacoue-Labarthe, *Heidegger, Art, and Politics: The Fiction of the Political*, trans. Chris Turner (Oxford, UK: Blackwell, 1990); Emmanuel Levinas, "Reflections on the Philosophy of Hitlerism," trans. Sean Hand, *Critical Inquiry* 17, no. 1 (1990): 63–71; Tom Rockmore and

Joseph Margolis, eds., *The Heidegger Case: On Philosophy and Politics* (Philadelphia: Temple University Press, 1992); Hans Sluga, *Heidegger's Crisis: Philosophy and Politics in Nazi Germany* (Cambridge, Mass.: Harvard University Press, 1993); Richard Wolin, *The Politics of Being: The Political Thought of Martin Heidegger* (New York: Columbia University Press, 1990); and Richard Wolin, ed., *The Heidegger Controversy: A Critical Reader* (New York: Columbia University Press, 1991).

9. The term *critique* is placed in quotation marks because, although this is a widely held interpretation, for Heidegger the "they" forms part of an ontological discussion of an existential structure; see Martin Heidegger, *Being and Time*, trans. John Macquarrie and Edward Robinson (Oxford, UK: Blackwell, 1962), 167; subsequently cited in text as *Being and Time*, followed by the page number to this English translation. The everyday comportment of Dasein with others in public takes the form of the "they," as was discussed in chapter 3.

10. Janicaud, *The Shadow of That Thought*, 39.

11. Ibid., 39–40. Robert B. Pippin avoids a directly political specification of this same issue, which he refers to as the problem of intersubjectivity. Robert B. Pippin, "On Being Anti-Cartesian: Hegel, Heidegger, Subjectivity, and Sociality," in *Idealism as Modernism: Hegelian Variations* (Cambridge: Cambridge University Press, 1997), 375–94.

12. Gail Soffer, "Heidegger, Humanism, and the Destruction of History," *Review of Metaphysics* 49 (1996): 548.

13. See in chapter 3 the section "Being-there Is Being-with" for a fuller discussion.

14. Jürgen Habermas, "Work and *Weltanschauung*," 439. The initial critique regarding intersubjectivity can be found in Michael Theunissen, *The Other: Studies in the Social Ontology of Husserl, Heidegger, Sartre, and Buber*, trans. Christopher Macann (Cambridge, Mass.: MIT Press, 1984), chapter 4.

15. Theunissen, *The Other*, 189.

16. Michel Haar, "The Ambivalent Unthought of the Overman and the Duality of Heidegger's Political Thinking," *Graduate Faculty Philosophy Journal* 14/15, no. 2/1 (1991): 110.

17. Ibid., 111. Haar's charge, therefore, is that Heidegger's political involvement with the Nazis is a sort of "authorial misuse" of the deconstructive enterprise of *Being and Time*, an argument discussed in the following subsection.

18. See Ian Angus, "Walking on Two Legs: On the Very Possibility of a Heideggerian Marxism," *Human Studies* 28 (2005): 335–52.

19. Beistegui, *Heidegger and the Political*, 11; emphasis added.

20. James F. Ward, *Heidegger's Political Thinking* (Amherst: University of Massachusetts Press, 1995), xviii; emphasis added.

21. Beistegui, *Heidegger and the Political*, 11.

22. First brackets are mine; the second pair is in the original Macquarrie and Robinson translation. In German, the first sentence reads: "Wenn aber das schicksalhafte Dasein als In-der-Welt-sein wesenhaft im Mitsein mit Anderen existiert, ist sein Geschehen ein Mitgeschehen und bestimmt als *Geschick*. Damit bezeichnen wir das Geschehen der Gemeinschaft, des Volkes." Martin Heidegger, *Sein und Zeit* (Tübingen, Germany: Max Niemeyer Verlag, 1993), 384.

23. "Der Fall Heidegger," the German term *Fall* meaning both the "case" of and the "fall" of Heidegger. See Rockmore and Margolis, eds., *The Heidegger Case*.

24. See Wolin, *The Politics of Being;* and Wolin, *The Heidegger Controversy*.

25. Fritsche, *Historical Destiny and National Socialism*, xv.

26. Thomas Sheehan calls them "self-hating Heideggerians." See Thomas Sheehan, "A Paradigm Shift in Heidegger Research," *Continental Philosophy Review* 34 (2001): 183–202.

27. Fritsche, *Historical Destiny and National Socialism*, xiii.

28. Ibid.

29. Ibid., xv. On the basis of this, Fritsche regards the usage of Heidegger's thought to be itself reactionary and right wing.

30. Elliott Neaman, "Review of *Historical Destiny and National Socialism in Heidegger's 'Being and Time'* by Johannes Fritsche," *Constellations* 8, no. 1 (2001): 148–49.

31. Philippe Lacoue-Labarthe, "Transcendence Ends in Politics," in *Typography* (Stanford, Calif.: Stanford University Press, 1998), 286.

32. Beistegui, *Heidegger and the Political*, 19.

33. Jürgen Habermas, "The Undermining of Western Rationalism through the Critique of Metaphysics: Martin Heidegger," trans. Frederick G. Lawrence, in *The Philosophical Discourse of Modernity: Twelve Lectures* (Cambridge, UK: Polity Press, 1987), 132.

34. Habermas, "Work and *Weltanschauung*," 439, 441.

35. Simon Critchley, *Ethics—Politics—Subjectivity: Essays on Derrida, Levinas, and Contemporary French Thought* (London: Verso, 1999), 240.

36. R. N. Newell, "Heidegger on Freedom and Community: Some Political Implications of His Early Thought," *American Political Science Review* 78, no. 3 (1984): 783.

37. Martin Heidegger cited in Karsten Harries, "Heidegger as a Political Thinker," in *Heidegger and Modern Philosophy: Critical Essays*, ed. Michael Murray (New Haven, Conn.: Yale University Press, 1978), 304.

38. Beistegui, *Heidegger and the Political*, 22; emphasis added.

39. David Wood, "Reiterating the Temporal: Toward a Rethinking of Heidegger on Time," in *Reading Heidegger: Commemorations*, ed. John Sallis (Bloomington: Indiana University Press, 1993), 151.

40. Beistegui, *Heidegger and the Political*, 20.

41. Lacoue-Labarthe, "Transcendence Ends in Politics," 297.

42. Ibid., 299. With regard to the manifestation of this problem in the 1930s in the form of National Socialism, Lacoue-Labarthe and Nancy argue that there is a complicity or responsibility of "German thought" in the continued mythic response to this problem of identification: "There incontestably has been and there still is perhaps a German problem; Nazi ideology was a specifically political response to this problem; and there is no doubt whatsoever that the German tradition, and in particular the tradition of German thought, is not at all foreign to this ideology." Philippe Lacoue-Labarthe and Jean-Luc Nancy, "The Nazi Myth," trans. Brian Holmes, *Critical Inquiry* 16, no. 2 (1990): 295. Also, "it is because the German problem is fundamentally a problem of *identity* that the German figure of totalitarianism is racism. . . . It is because myth can be defined as an *identificatory mechanism* that racist ideology became bound up in the *construction* of a myth," 296; emphasis in original. See also the discussion of Nazism's revival and production of mythic identification, 296–312.

43. Karl Löwith, *My Life in Germany before and after 1933: A Report*, trans. Elizabeth King (Urbana: University of Illinois Press, 1994), 38.

44. Lacoue-Labarthe, "Transcendence Ends in Politics," 300.

45. David Couzens Hoy, "History, Historicity, and Historiography in *Being and Time*," in *Heidegger and Modern Philosophy: Critical Essays*, ed. Michael Murray (New Haven, Conn.: Yale University Press, 1978), 338.

46. Ibid., 336. See also the discussion of understanding and projection in chapter 3.

47. Peg Birmingham, "The Time of the Political," *Graduate Faculty Philosophy Journal* 14/15, no. 2/1 (1991): 29.

48. Hoy, "History, Historicity, and Historiography in *Being and Time*," 340.

49. Beistegui, *Heidegger and the Political*, 15.

50. Ibid. Because of the emptiness of anticipatory resoluteness, Beistegui refuses to identify it "with the heroism and decisionism with which it has been often charged" by authors such as Karl Löwith and Richard Wolin. See the discussion in chapter 4.

51. Ibid., 16.

52. Moreover, is there not the danger, as has been argued by Karl Löwith, that the reference to the struggle of the collective entity (especially in the context of Being-toward-death) entails the very constitution of the

NOTES TO CHAPTER 6 · 237

"we" through the assumed or posited threat to its continued existence by an "enemy"—much like in Carl Schmitt's *Concept of the Political?* Dasein's cohistorizing might manifest itself as the collective confrontation with an enemy. Indeed, Löwith suggests that there is a correspondence between Heidegger's Being-towards-death and "[Carl] Schmitt's 'sacrifice of life' in the politically paramount case of war." Löwith, *My Life in Germany before and after 1933,* 32; and Löwith, *Martin Heidegger and European Nihilism,* trans. Gary Steiner (New York: Columbia University Press, 1995), 160–61. See also Carl Schmitt, *The Concept of the Political,* trans. George Schwab (Chicago: University of Chicago Press, 1996), 33.

53. Lacoue-Labarthe, "Transcendence Ends in Politics," 300.

54. Hoy, "History, Historicity, and Historiography in *Being and Time*," 340–41.

55. Beistegui, *Heidegger and the Political,* 17. The reference to community may not be, in this understanding, a theoretical commitment to a (necessarily right-wing) understanding of community *(Gemeinschaft)* but might be, rather, a reminder of the *historical manifestation* of the worldliness of being-there. As Fritsche rightly reminds us, in Heidegger's case the historical situation would have been the post–World War I Weimar Republic, with its economic uncertainty and the emergent political rise of both communism and fascism. See Fritsche, *Historical Destiny and National Socialism.*

56. In Joan Stambaugh's translation: "The handing down of a possibility that has been in retrieving it, however, does not disclose the Da-sein that has been there in order to actualize it again." Martin Heidegger, *Being and Time: A Translation of Sein und Zeit,* trans. Joan Stambaugh (Albany: State University of New York Press, 1996), 352.

57. Beistegui, *Heidegger and the Political,* 25; emphasis in original.

58. See Pierre Bourdieu, *The Political Ontology of Martin Heidegger,* trans. Peter Collier (Oxford, UK: Polity Press, 1991), 57.

59. Birmingham, "The Time of the Political," 25.

60. Wood, "Reiterating the Temporal," 150.

61. Beistegui, *Heidegger and the Political,* 25.

62. Birmingham, "The Time of the Political," 31. See also Beistegui, *Heidegger and the Political,* 25–27.

63. Birmingham, "The Time of the Political," 31.

64. Hoy, "History, Historicity, and Historiography in *Being and Time*," 336–37.

65. Beistegui, *Heidegger and the Political,* 25. Beistegui rightly points out that the best example of this *Erwiderung* is none other than Heidegger's method of Destruktion or "destructive retrieve" through which he engages with traditional ontology in order to be able to restate anew the question of

Being. Naturally, this point is rejected by those who suggest that only one reading of paragraph 74 is possible; see, for instance, Fritsche, *Historical Destiny and National Socialism,* 1–28, and his refutation of such critical readings of "repetition" and "critical rejoinder," 7–28 and 251–53.

66. The sentence reads in German: "In der Mitteilung und im Kampf wird die Macht des Geschickes erst frei." Heidegger, *Sein und Zeit,* 384.

67. Beistegui, *Heidegger and the Political,* 23. See also the discussion of the interweaving of struggle, *agon,* and communication in Jacques Derrida, "Heidegger's Ear: Philopolemology *(Geschlecht IV),*" in *Reading Heidegger: Commemorations,* ed. John Sallis (Bloomington: Indiana University Press, 1993), 163–218.

68. Beistegui, *Heidegger and the Political,* 168 n. 32. The reference to the "they" and idle talk could be understood, moreover, as an explicit stance against a subjectivist conception of *Gesellschaft,* where community is invoked to contest and problematize the "absolutization of subjectivity."

69. Ibid., 29.

70. Consuelo Cruz, "Identity and Persuasion: How Nations Remember their Pasts and Make their Futures," *World Politics* 52 (2000): 277.

71. Birmingham, "The Time of the Political," 25.

72. Ibid. Regarding Heidegger's involvement with the National Socialists, she argues that at the time of the "turn" Heidegger "begins to think that the Dasein's destiny can be given a *topos,*" 44. See also the discussion of "ontopology" in David Campbell, *National Deconstruction: Violence, Identity, and Justice in Bosnia* (Minneapolis: University of Minnesota Press, 1998), 33–81.

73. See also William E. Connolly, "Suffering, Justice, and the Politics of Becoming," *Culture, Medicine, and Psychiatry* 20, no. 3 (1996): 251–77.

74. Slavoj Žižek, "The Feminine Excess: Can Women Who Hear Divine Voices Find a New Social Link?" *Millennium: Journal of International Studies* 30, no. 1 (2001): 93.

75. Ibid.

76. Birmingham, "The Time of the Political," 27.

77. Ibid.

78. Ibid.

79. See also the "ethos of political criticism" in Campbell, *National Deconstruction.*

80. Rockmore and Margolis, introduction to *The Heidegger Case,* 1.

81. Jean-Luc Nancy, *The Inoperative Community,* trans. Peter Connor, Lisa Garbus, Michael Holland, and Simona Sawhney (Minneapolis: University of Minnesota Press, 1991), 14; emphasis added.

82. Ibid., 15.

83. Jean-Luc Nancy, "Of Being-in-Common," trans. James Creech, in

*Community at Loose Ends,* ed. Miami Theory Collective (Minneapolis: University of Minnesota Press, 1991), 1–12.

84. Again see Žižek, "The Feminine Excess," 93.

85. See Noël O'Sullivan, "Postmodernism and the Politics of Identity," in *Politics and the End of Identity,* ed. Kathryn Dean (Aldershot, UK: Ashgate, 1997), 234–64.

86. Lawrence Vogel, *The Fragile "We": Ethical Implications of Heidegger's "Being and Time"* (Evanston, Ill.: Northwestern University Press, 1994), 70.

87. Maria Lensu and Jan-Stefan Fritz, eds., *Value Pluralism, Normative Theory, and International Relations* (Basingstoke, UK: Macmillan Press, 1999).

88. A "friendly struggle" in the sense of "philopolemology," as discussed in Derrida, "Heidegger's Ear." See also Diana Coole, "Thinking Politically with Merleau-Ponty," *Radical Philosophy,* no. 108 (July/August 2001): 25.

89. Wilhelm S. Wurzer, "Nancy and the Political Imaginary after Nature," in *On Jean-Luc Nancy: The Sense of Philosophy,* ed. Darren Sheppard, Simon Sparks, and Colin Thomas (London: Routledge, 1997), 98.

## CONCLUSION

1. Ian Angus, "Walking on Two Legs: On the Very Possibility of a Heideggerian Marxism," *Human Studies* 28 (2005): 335–52.

2. See also Michael Dillon, *Politics of Security: Towards a Political Philosophy of Continental Thought* (London: Routledge, 1996); David Campbell and Michael Dillon, eds., *The Political Subject of Violence* (Manchester, UK: Manchester University Press, 1993); Costas M. Constatinou, *On the Way to Diplomacy* (Minneapolis: University of Minnesota Press, 1996); and Hakan Seckinelgin, *International Relations and the Environment: International Fisheries, Heidegger, and Social Method* (London: Routledge, 2006).

3. Christopher Fynsk, "Foreword: Experiences of Finitude," in *The Inoperative Community,* Jean-Luc Nancy, trans. Peter Connor, Lisa Garbus, Michael Holland, and Simona Sawhney (Minneapolis: University of Minnesota Press, 1991), xiii.

# Index

abandoning itself to the world, 87
*Abbau,* 172, 185. *See also* deconstruction; destruction; destructive retrieve
ability, Dasein's, 79, 100, 116, 169
absolutization of subjectivity, 13
absorption, Dasein's, 69, 134
accessing life, method for, 40
activity: Dasein's, 69, 83, 180; directed, 62–65; practical, 65, 66,
  157; world of, 60, 61, 72, 83
agonistic attitude, Dasein's, 163
alterity, 8, 21, 142, 148, 151;
  constitution of self by, 8; and
  Levinas, 50–52, 179; openness
  to, 106, 115, 122, 142, 143,
  146, 147, 151, 182, 184; and
  suffering, 124, 132. *See also*
  otherness
ambiguity, 54, 86–89, 96, 105, 160
analytic of Dasein. *See* Dasein:
  existential analytic of
anarchy, 14, 16, 22, 23, 25
anticipation, 99
anxiety, 89, 92, 97, 100, 105, 131,

132, 142, 178; Dasein's readiness for, 110, 165; ready for,
  99, 102, 108, 144
anxious existence, 110, 143
appropriation, 51, 79, 106, 107,
  113, 115, 141, 169, 172;
  Dasein's, 113; of Heidegger,
  163, 185
Aristotle, 31, 33, 35, 60, 156
artifice, 19, 20
assignments, 6, 63, 64, 67, 68, 70,
  71, 83, 90, 95, 114, 130, 138,
  180
attitude: Dasein's, 163; natural,
  37; phenomenological, 37
attunement, 50, 59, 82–86, 91, 92,
  96, 148, 180; Dasein's, 83, 89,
  91, 180; worldly, 82
audibility, conditions of, 134, 135,
  137, 139
authentic: Being-with, 159, 160,
  163, 184; Dasein, 102, 103,
  141, 143, 160; friend, 133; self,
  77, 103, 107, 157
authenticity, 3, 78, 96, 103–7,

109, 110, 116, 130, 140, 161, 172, 185; relationship with inauthenticity, 80, 92, 97, 98, 112–115. *See also* becoming-proper; propriety

autonomous: Dasein as, 79, 91, 96, 104, 119, 128, 138, 156; "I" as, 53; self as, 70, 104, 128; subject or subjectivity as, 58, 59, 77, 79, 81, 91, 96, 104, 111, 115, 119, 131, 156

autonomy, xiii, xxiv, xxx, xxxi

average everydayness, 27, 61, 69, 71, 74–78, 86, 112, 131, 157, 174, 180; Dasein's, 86, 157

averageness, 69, 70, 76, 78, 92, 106, 114, 125, 129, 142

becoming-proper, 79, 93, 102, 137, 147, 171, 174; conception or understanding of, 97, 100; Dasein's, 106, 109, 111, 139; and ethics, 129, 130, 139, 147; as finite transcendence, 110; and heteronomy, 112, 115, 130; and inauthenticity, 112, 113, 115; Levina's reading of, 104, 106; process of, 92, 96, 97, 103–105, 109, 111, 113, 174; struggle of, 133. *See also* authenticity; propriety

*Being and Time*: misreading of, 163, 185; phenomenology of, 163, 173

Being-guilty, 101, 111, 113

being-in, 61, 64, 73, 82, 84, 87, 88, 96

being-in-common, xxviii, 158, 161

being-in-the-world, 36, 63, 65, 68, 75, 110, 134, 157; anxious, 151, 183

being-lost, 79, 88

being-radically-in-relation, xxxi

being-there, 59, 75, 90, 92, 97, 102, 115, 128, 165, 179, 180; historical, 164, 169

being-towards-death, 97–99, 103–7, 111, 116, 143

being-with, 59, 71–75, 79–82, 90, 92, 95, 104, 133–136, 148–150, 156, 157, 159, 161, 162, 170–172, 180, 185; authentic, 159, 160, 163, 184; communal determination of, 117, 161, 162, 164, and the "they," 75–79, 156, 169, 170

Being-with-one-another, 77, 157, 159, 162

Beistegui, Miguel de, 108, 109, 137, 157, 158, 160, 161, 166, 168

Birmingham, Peg, 168

capitalism, xv, xviii

Caputo, John D., 37

Cartesian subject or subjectivity, 15, 48

case of Heidegger. *See* Heidegger, Martin: case of

categories: Aristotle's, 32–35; of *Being and Time*, 157; and conceptual violence, 52; of politics, 153; of rational animal, 89; of reality, 35; of relation, 38; Duns Scotus's, 34–36

character: of the call of conscience, 101, 133; coexistential and heteronomous, 64, 110, 135; Dasein's, 48, 58, 62, 64, 66, 67, 73, 77, 90, 109, 180; of Dasein's world, 69; of death, 99, 105; and éthos, 126, 127; of existence, 47, 58, 103, 135; of Heidegger's thought, 80,

157, 160; of modern subject, 8, 73; of ongoing coping, 60, 62; other-determined or other-constituted, 31, 103, 105
civilizations, xix
civil society, 18, 19
codification, 117, 120, 121, 127, 145, 150, 182
coexistence, 1, 2, 22–27, 29, 30, 49, 50, 57–93, 95, 96, 103–5, 107, 108, 115–17, 119–22, 141, 149–51, 153–78, 180, 181, 183–85; determination of, 15, 25, 81, 154, 155, 161, 163, 184; multicultural, xii; optics of, xxxiv, 27, 30, 31, 49, 50, 55, 58–93, 95, 96, 103–5, 107, 108, 112, 115, 116, 119, 120, 124, 172, 179, 181; peaceful, xv–xviii; political, xv, xxxv, 1, 27, 153, 154, 159, 172; political thought of, 2, 26, 117, 154, 155, 158, 163, 171, 185; primacy of, 27, 49; reconceptualization or rethinking of, 12, 95, 123, 146, 148, 178, 181; reduction of, 25, 92, 155, 171, 172, 178; the subject of, 154, 179, 181, 183; theorization of, xix
coexistential: being, xxxiv; character of Dasein, 91, 106, 110, 115, 119; character of world, 64, 70; disposition, 151; embeddedness, 116; existence, xxiii, 30, 49, 55, 91, 106, 135; heteronomy, 57–59, 80, 81, 92, 95, 97, 104, 112, 116, 128, 130; lived experience, 31; reading of Heidegger, 103; self, 57, 59, 90, 153, 154, 174, 180, 181, 183; understanding 96

cohistorizing of Dasein, the. See Dasein: cohistoricizing, Dasein's
Cold War, xiii, xiv, xviii, xx; thinking, xix, xx
collectivities, xxvii, xxviii
communal: constitution, 1, 172–74, 185; determination of Being-with, 80, 117, 160–62, 164; éthos, 128, 132, 138, 142
communicative situation, xxiii
communism, xviii
community: constitution of, 27, 151, 155, 163, 164, 170–75, 184; critical belonging to, 171, 172, 174, 184, 185; éthos or ethical formations of, 150, 182; expansion of, 116, 181; Heidegger's determination of, 80, 117, 155, 156, 159, 164, 167, 170, 172, 184; and historicality or historical tradition, 161–64, 167, 169–171; and identification, 162, 166, 173; proper analysis or conceptualization of, 81, 151, 175, 185; self's constitution, embeddedness, or immersion in, 121, 134, 138, 146; and social contract, 24; in social theory, 13; subjectivist understanding of, 60
comportment: Dasein's, 59, 67–71, 74, 89; the ethical self's, 146, 171; everyday or average, 66, 91, 101, 128, 129, 131, 133, 135, 138; prereflective, 60, 61; proper to Dasein, 112, 147, 148, 167; as solicitude, 74
composition, xiii, xvii, xxi, xxiii, xxviii, xxxii, 26, 59, 90–93, 155, 172, 173, 178, 180, 181; beyond or otherwise than, xxx,

xxxiii, xxxv, 25, 73, 151, 154, 172, 181; fragile, 24, 25, 29; logic of, xiii, xxiii, xxv–xxix, xxxii, xxxiii, xxxv, 1–4, 15, 23–25, 27, 29, 73, 80, 81, 93, 116, 117, 120, 147, 148, 150, 154, 155, 171–73, 178; manifestations of, xxxiii, 2; reduction of coexistence to, 92; subject of, xxvi ; of units, xvii, xxi; of unrelated or nonrelational subjects, xiii, 1, 90, 149, 178

comprehension, 51–53, 58, 64

conditions: of audibility, 134, 135, 137, 139; of subjectivity, 35

configuration of subjectivity, 19, 20

conflict, xii, xiv, xviii, xxviii; ethnic, xix; nuclear, xiv, xvii; prevention, xx; resolution scholarship, xix

conformity, 76, 125, 150, 156; constitutive, 76, 78. See also Dreyfus, Hubert L.

confrontation: global ideological, xix; nuclear, xiv, xv;

conscience: call of, 100–103, 109, 132, 133; voice of, 100, 101, 133

consciousness, 6, 8, 37, 38, 41, 44, 52, 53

constitutive conformity. See conformity: constitutive

contract, social, xxxiii, 2, 13, 20, 22–25, 29, 178

copresence, xx, xxv, 24, 29, 71, 73, 91, 116, 119, 132, 178, 180, 185; of already constituted units, xxi; beyond, xxxiv, 30, 122, 172; determinations of coexistence as, xi, xiii, xvii,

xxii, xxx; of divergent political systems or ideologies, xiv, xv, xviii; reduction of coexistence to, xxvi, xxvii, xxix, xxxii, 25, 155, 171, 178

copresent subject, 71

cosmopolitan ethics, 129; proposals of, 120, 121

Critchley, Simon, 3, 103, 104, 161

critical: belonging, 117, 153, 170–175, 184, 185; mimesis, 167, 168, 170–74, 184, 185

critique of Heidegger, 31, 54, 105

curiosity, 86–89, 96, 101, 131

danger, 2, 16–23, 25, 42, 178, 179

dangerous ontology, 20, 21

Dasein: authentic, 102, 103, 141, 143, 160; cohistorizing, Dasein's, 159, 162, 163, 170, 171; concrete, 171; constitution of, 136, 165; disclosure of, 89, 92; dispersed, 78; examination of, 61, 76; existential analytic of, 30, 45, 47, 49, 58, 92, 103, 155, 161, 181 (see also Daseinanalytik); existential structures of, 47, 57, 74, 75, 95, 134; primary mode of, 67, 90, 180; radical attunement of, 83

Daseinanalytik, 45, 49, 105, 155, 179; Heidegger's, 30, 58, 92, 103, 169, 181. See also Dasein: existential analytic of

Dasein's: absorption, 69, 134; agonistic attitude, 163; average everydayness, 86, 157 (see also average everydayness); coexistential heteronomy, 101, 104, 130; everyday existence, 174; everyday self, 77, 96; heteronomy, 91, 95, 136, 139; moods,

83; ownmost possibility, 99,
102, 104, 111; possibilities, 78,
128; potentiality-for-Being,
85; prereflective relations, 61;
resoluteness, 108, 166; self-
relationship, 143; thrownness,
101, 175; transcendence 109,
110; withness, 84, 136; world,
70, 136
Dasein-with, 72–74. *See also*
being-with
death, 17, 19, 20, 98–100, 102–5,
107, 111; Dasein's, 105
decisionism, political, 103, 107,
108
deconstruction, 47, 102, 115
Derrida, Jacques, 46, 53, 54, 98,
136, 137, 141, 143, 144
Descartes, Rene, 6, 7, 9, 37, 48,
60
destiny, 159, 161, 162, 166, 168,
184
destruction, 31, 46, 47, 124
destructive retrieve, 46, 47, 124,
140, 150, 168, 169, 184
dichotomy, subject-object, 38
directed activity. *See* activity:
directed
disclosive character, Dasein's, 64,
66, 90, 180
disclosure of Dasein, 89, 92
discourse, subjectivist, xxxiv
disengaged self, 43, 57
dispersed self, 78, 100
disposition, 16, 17, 19, 22, 83, 91,
122, 126, 144, 146–49, 151,
153, 169, 171, 175, 182, 183
distantiality, 77
disturbance, 65, 66
domesticated subjects, 18
Dreyfus, Hubert L., 76, 80
Duns Scotus, John, 34, 35

effacement: of the constitutive
function of otherness, 25; of
heteronomy, 15, 25, 50, 54,
120–22, 178, 181, 183
embeddedness: Dasein's, 91, 180;
radical, 57, 67, 82, 85, 86, 91,
104, 105, 119, 180; worldly,
108
enemy, 2, 16, 17, 20, 21, 23, 25,
107
engaged immersion, 58–67, 70–72,
89, 95, 104, 157
enmity, 16, 20, 21, 25
entities: coexistential, 49; facticity
of, xxvii, xxxiii; heteronomous,
92, 97; preconstituted, xxvii;
worldly, 73, 96
*epoche,* phenomenological, 37, 38
equipment, 61–66, 69, 71–73, 128
equipmental totality, 63, 65, 72
*erwidern,* 168, 169
*Erwiderung,* 168, 170
ethical, the, 140; attitude, 27, 141;
construction, 121–25, 127, 130,
132, 142–44, 146, 150, 151,
183; face-to-face relation, 54;
foundationalism, 143; minimalist construction, 141, 143;
norms, 130, 142, 144; recovery
of self, xxix, xxxv, 106, 117,
122–24, 140–44, 150, 152–55,
158, 163, 172, 173, 182, 183,
185; regardedness, 121; relation or relationality, 51, 52,
105, 106, 124, 179; rules, 131,
141, 142, 144; self, 106, 117,
122, 124, 132, 140–48, 150,
153–55, 158, 163, 164, 169,
171–75, 182–85; selfhood, 117,
122–24, 150, 153, 163, 173,
182; universal construction,
120, 145, 146, 150, 182, 183

ethicity: of ethics, 141, 146, 151, 183; of propriety, 141
ethics: antifoundationalist, 123, 143; of community, 150; critique or calling into question of, 117, 122, 124, 125, 130–32, 173, 182; cosmopolitan or global, 116, 120, 121, 124, 129, 141, 146, 149, 150, 181–83; definitions of, 123; and éthos, 124, 126, 127, 129, 150, 182; and Heidegger, 124, 125, 129, 139, 144; inclusive, 121, 148, 182; and international political thought, 122, 185; Levinas's, 51, 54; and normalcy or socialization, 125–27, 132, 150, 182; and the other, 106, 128, 182; of otherness, 148; ontological, 140; subversion of, 122; in the "they" and average intelligibility, 129, 130, 139; universal, 126, 145, 150, 151, 182
ethnic conflict, xix
éthos: communal, group or public, 128, 129, 130, 132, 138, 142, 145–147, 183; and ethics, 124, 126, 127, 129, 141, 145, 150, 182; and habituation or socialization, 131, 132, 140, 144, 148; and otherness, 142; and suffering, 134; of survival, 2, 16, 21, 25
everyday: comportment, Dasein's, 66, 91, 101, 135; self, Dasein's, 77, 79, 96; world, 81, 89, 110
everydayness: average, 27, 61, 69, 71, 74–78, 86, 112, 128, 131, 157, 174, 180; and becoming-proper, 97, 110; Being of, 76, 86, 88, 96; Dasein's, 66, 69, 79, 82, 84, 87, 89, 91, 95, 98, 180;

Heidegger's phenomenology of, 59, 172, 185; inauthentic, 112; perspective or discussion of, 60, 86, 124; and self-dispersal, 108; and the "they," 88, 91, 95, 96, 180
evil, 15, 17
existence: Dasein's, 92, 95, 99, 100, 112, 131; facticity of, 30–32, 50, 115, 119, 146, 151; heteronomous, 107, 141; worldly, 125
existential: analysis, 27, 45, 46, 49, 50, 58, 66, 71, 106, 179; analytic of Dasein. See Dasein: existential analytic of; Dasein: existential structures of
existentiell possibility, 85, 100
existents, 52
expression, problem of, 36, 40, 42, 43, 74, 128

face-to-face ethical relation, 51, 53, 54
factical: life, 43, 46, 96; situation, 85, 111, 144–46, 148, 160, 163, 166, 168–70; world, 113, 165
facticity: Dasein's, 85, 88, 109, 112; of entities, 26, 45; of existence, 30–32, 50, 58, 81, 115, 119, 145, 146, 151, 176; and Heidegger, 44, 52–55, 107, 179; hermeneutics of, 43, 46, 156, 179, 184; of life, 7, 34, 40, 44, 178; and otherness, 92, 147; and primacy of relation, 59; of self or subject, 30, 50
fallenness, 86, 88–91, 96, 105, 181
familiarity: Dasein's, 68, 69, 110; life has of itself, 41; and mortal temporality, 113; rendered strange, 137

fate, 21, 159–62, 166, 167
features of modern subjectivity. *See* modern subjectivity: features of
finitude: and becoming-proper, 102; characteristics of, 99; as Dasein's ownmost possibility, 99, 111, 113; of existence, 100, 164; Heidegger's analysis of, 103, 107; and resoluteness, 165
flight, Dasein's, 139
Foucault, Michel, 7, 10, 141
freedom, xxx, xxxi, 5, 6, 8, 52, 105–8, 148
friend, 107, 133–40; other as, 136, 137
Fritsche, Johannes, 160–62
fundamental ontology, 31, 47, 50, 161; project of, 38, 158, 159

gear, 61–63
*Gesellschaft,* 161, 162
global ethics, 116, 120, 121, 124, 129, 141, 146, 149, 150, 181–83
globalization, xii, xxi, xxii, xxix, 175, 181
Greek philosophy, 4, 5, 7
Greeks, the, 4, 32, 33, 54, 126
ground: Being as, 7, 32, 33; of certainty, 7; as *hypokeimenon,* 4; of modern subjectivity, xiii, xxv, xxvi, xxvii, xxx, 1, 6, 71, 102; subjectivist, xxv, xxxi
groundless self, 149
groundlessness, 102, 144, 147–49; Dasein's, 143
group conflict, xix

Habermas, Jürgen, 15, 90, 157, 160, 161
habitual: behavior, 125, 132, 150; obedience to norms, 130; prac-tices, 125, 132, 140, 174, 182; self or selves, 77
habituation, 125, 127, 130, 131
hearing, 113, 134–38, 147, 151, 153, 182
Heidegger, Martin: appropriation of, 163, 185; case of, 159; controversy, 160
Heidegger's: *Daseinanalytik,* 49, 155; existential analysis, 27, 58, 71, 81, 179; existential analytic, 30, 58, 92, 103, 169, 181; nazism, 159, 161; philosophy, 52, 54, 105; politics, xxxv, 80, 107, 117, 155, 156, 171, 172, 183–85; project, 30, 31, 45, 52; thought, 27, 49, 54, 57, 80, 103, 135, 155, 158, 159, 161, 163, 179, 185
heritage, 164–70, 184
hermeneutic phenomenology, 43, 44, 47, 57; Heidegger's, 44, 57
hermeneutics of facticity, 29–41, 43–47, 49, 51, 53–55, 156, 179, 184
heteronomous: being, xxiii, xxxii, 151, 183; character of world, 64, 70; constitution of Dasein or existence, xiii, xxix, xxxii, 31, 78, 90, 91, 122, 135; Dasein, 79, 89, 91, 92, 97, 110, 115, 119, 180; existence, 30, 49, 55, 91, 107, 141, 145; facticity, xxxiii; lived experience, 31; self or selfhood, xxxiv, 26, 29, 57, 79, 123, 138, 151, 153, 154, 174, 181, 183; self-understanding, 138; understanding, 96, 104, 106, 138
heteronomy: and coexistence, 120, 122; coexistential, 57–59, 80, 81, 92, 95, 97, 104, 112, 116,

128, 130; and critical belonging, 174, 175; Dasein's, 91,
95, 96, 115, 128, 135, 136,
138, 139, 141; effacement of,
xxvi, xxxiii, 15, 25, 50, 54,
116, 120–22, 173, 178, 181,
183, 185; existential, xxxiv; in
Heidegger's analysis, 27; the
other's, 122, 151, 148, 149; as
primacy of relation, 92, 95; of
self or selfhood, 27, 57, 79,
81, 121, 122, 124, 149, 173,
178, 182; understanding of,
79, 165
historical being-there, 164, 169
Hobbes, Thomas, xxxiii, 1–3, 13,
15–25, 29, 30, 49, 178
Hobbesian subject or subjectivity,
17–19, 21, 23, 24, 29
human: existence, 27, 29, 31, 36,
44, 45, 49, 64, 75, 81, 85, 88,
91, 96, 120, 178, 179; rights,
xxi, xxii, xxiv, 120, 121, 127,
149, 150, 181, 182; sciences,
10, 11, 77, 92, 177; subject or
subjectivity, xxvii, xxviii, 6, 7,
9, 30
humanity, xxviii, 44, 143; universal, 121, 149, 181
Husserl, Edmund, 30, 34, 37–39,
41–43, 48, 50, 53, 54, 60
Husserlian phenomenology, 34,
35, 39, 40, 42, 43
hypokeimenon, 4, 5

identification, 162–64, 166, 167,
170, 171; Dasein's, 170; nationalist, 167, 168, 170
identity, 4, 12, 75, 101, 113, 122,
168, 170
ideological struggle, xxiv–xix

ideology, xv, xviii
idle talk, 86–89, 96, 98, 100, 101,
131, 134, 138, 139, 169
immanent historicity of life, 41,
42
immersion: Dasein's, 76, 134;
worldly, 109
inauthenticity: constitutive for
Dasein, 91, 112; Dasein's, 92,
97, 109, 113; of everydayness,
131, 170; as heteronomous
existence, 107; interpretations
of, 79, 113, 116; modification
of, 97, 106, 112, 146; relationship with authenticity, 80, 92,
97, 98, 112–115
inauthentic self, 110
inclusion, xxi–xxiii; moral, xxi
indistinguishability, Dasein's, 76
individuality, xxxi, xxxii, 51, 138
intelligibility: average or inauthentic, 86, 115, 128, 129, 130,
142, 150, 170; basis of, 36; of
Being, 60; Dasein's, 38, 48,
97, 104; other-determined, 48;
proper, 96, 115; and representation, 9
international: community, xix;
discipline of international relations, xi, xix, xx, 123, 129,
149, 177, 178; political theory,
59, 154, 164, 173–75, 183, 185;
politics, 12, 14, 15, 120; praxis, xi, xii, xx; relations, xi–xiii,
xviii, xx–xxiii, xv, xvii, xxxiii,
xxxv, 1, 3, 22, 25, 29, 43, 71,
90, 95, 103, 120, 150, 154,
155, 177, 181–83 (see also IR);
state system, xvii, xxii; theory,
14, 49 (see also IR: theory)
interstate warfare, xv

inwardness, 109, 110
IR, xi–xiii, xv, xix, xxi, xxiv, xxv, xix, xxxiv, 2, 3, 12–14, 22, 23, 124, 151; theory, xii, xxiv

Jemeinigkeit, 113. See also mineness

Lacoue-Labarthe, Philippe, 160, 162, 166–68, 172
Levinas, Emmanuel, xxxiii–xxxv, 27, 31, 50–55, 57, 58, 103–6, 109, 148, 179
Levinas's: critique, xxxiii, 54, 55, 57, 58, 105, 148, 179; ethics, 54
liberalism, xx–xxiii, xxvii, 155, 161
liberating solicitude, 122, 147, 148, 151, 154, 163, 171, 175, 183
Linklater, Andrew, xxii, xxiii, 3, 143
lived experience, 31, 38–42, 44, 49, 50, 57, 100
logic of composition, xiii, xxiii, xxv–xix, xxxii, xxxiii, xv, 1–4, 15, 23–25, 27, 29, 73, 80, 81, 93, 116, 117, 120, 147, 148, 150, 154, 155, 171–73, 178
Löwith, Karl, 107, 162

mastery of self, 18, 108
metaphysics, 4, 6, 11, 46, 53, 174; of the subject, xxviii, 9
method, phenomenological. See phenomenological: method
mimesis, 125, 162, 163, 166, 169–171. See also critical: mimesis; identification
mind, 4, 9, 16, 34, 45, 58, 65, 140, 179

mineness, 69, 70, 105, 106, 112, 113; Dasein's, 106. See also Jemeinigkeit
Mitdasein, 72, 73, 74, 137
Mitsein, 138, 157, 159–161. See also being-with; Mitdasein
modern: nonrelational subject, 71; subject, xii, xxi, xxiii–xxvii, xxix, xxxi, xxxiii, 2, 3, 11, 13, 15, 24–27, 29, 30, 50, 57, 58, 60, 115, 116, 149, 153, 154, 172, 173, 177–79, 184, 185
modernity, xiv, xxiv, xxv, 5, 7, 10, 12, 14, 77, 123, 157; autonomous subject of, 91, 180
modern subjectivity, xi, xiii, xxi, xxiv–xxvii, xxviii–xxxiv, 2, 6, 10, 13–15, 26, 27, 29–31, 48, 58, 59, 71, 81, 95, 102, 103, 108, 115, 184, 185; early, 2; features of, 2, 13, 15, 19, 25, 90, 180; ground of, xiii, xxvi, 1, 71, 102; unworking of, xxxiii, 80, 178
moods, 82–84, 91, 180; Dasein's, 83
moral subject, 129
morality, 101, 121, 122, 125, 128, 129, 132, 139, 145, 150, 182
mores, 127, 129

nationalist: Dasein's cohistorizing or historicity, 159, 163, 166–68, 170, 171; determination of Being-with, 162, 164, 184, 185; determination of community, 117, 156, 162, 172, 184; essence, 155, 171, 185; identification or mimesis, 167, 168, 170; reading of Being and Time, 163, 185

Natorp, Paul, 39, 40, 41, 43, 45
natural: attitude, 37; harmony of
    interests, 16; law or right, 18,
    19; sciences, 35, 37, 40
nature, 112, 131, 156, 157, 161,
    165; of the call of conscience,
    101; of Dasein, 112, 131, 156,
    165; of entities, 64; of the exis-
    tential analytic, 157; in Greek
    thought, 32, 33, 35; Hobbesian
    man's, 16, 24; human, 24; of
    the international system, 14,
    120; of the modern subject,
    14, 18, 21, 25, 43, 157; and
    phenomenology, 39; of public-
    ness, 56; state of, 2, 16–24; of
    world, 67, 68
Nazism, Heidegger's, 159, 161
neo-Kantianism, 35, 39, 42, 44,
    53, 60
neo-neo synthesis, 14
nonrelational subject. See subject:
    nonrelational
nonrelationality, xiii, xxiv, xxx,
    20, 23, 24, 26, 177
normalcy, 124, 125
normalization, 124, 125
norms: communal, everyday or
    public, 77, 121, 124, 127, 128,
    131, 139, 142, 182; construc-
    tion or codification of, 120,
    121, 146, 150, 181; ethical,
    130, 142, 144; and ethics, 124,
    125; habitual or customary,
    130, 138, 174, 182; humanitar-
    ian, 120; moral, 124, 130, 146;
    and otherness, 82, 88, 106,
    180; totality or web of, 59, 69,
    90, 138; unique appropriation
    of, 111, 112; universalized or
    universalizable, 120, 130, 146
nuclear conflict, xiv, xvii

objectification, 40–42, 47, 58, 66
objective world, ordinary, 37
one, the, 77, 78. See also "they,"
    the
ongoing coping, 60–62, 65, 66
ontological: assumptions, xxiv, 12;
    attributes, xxvii; basis of mod-
    ern subject, 2; categories, 34;
    centrality of modern subject,
    12, 13, 25; commitments of
    international relations, xxvii,
    xxix, 1, 12; Dasein's manifes-
    tation, 87; inquiry or exami-
    nation, xxv, xxxiii, 14, 15,
    26, 33, 44, 46, 50, 144, 179;
    relationship, 59, 66–68, 70, 81,
    88, 89, 95, 104,105, 110; tradi-
    tion of philosophy, 30, 32, 34,
    46, 163, 168, 172
ontology, xxiii, xxv, xxx, xxxiv,
    45–47, 49–54, 57, 71, 138, 144,
    179, 181; of anarchy, 22, 25; as
    critical activity,181; dangerous,
    13, 20, 21, 23, 25; destruction
    of, 31; and ethics, 51, 144; of
    friendship, 138; fundamental,
    31, 38, 45, 47, 50, 158, 159,
    161; genesis of, 32; of IR, xix,
    xxi; Levinas's critique of, 27,
    51–54, 57; method for, 36,
    45, 46; and phenomenology,
    xxxiv, 31, 45, 49, 50–54, 57,
    179; political determination of,
    158, 159, 161; and social and
    political theory,12; subjectivist,
    xxx, xxxiv, 6, 43, 71, 121, 141;
    traditional, 31, 45, 57
optics of coexistence, xxxiv, xxxv,
    27, 30, 31, 49, 50, 55, 60, 61,
    64, 66, 67, 70, 71, 79, 85, 90,
    103, 107, 112, 115, 120, 124,
    172, 181; elements of, 57–59,

76, 80–82, 89, 91, 92, 95, 96, 98, 104, 105, 108, 116, 119, 179
other-as-friend, 136, 137
otherness, xiii, xxii, xxix–xxxv, 8, 9, 21, 24–27, 49–52, 55, 57, 58, 80–82, 90, 106, 107, 120–24, 131–39, 141, 142, 173–75, 178–82; an ethics of, 148; role of, xiii, xxvi, 25, 29, 31, 54, 62, 92, 138
*ousia,* 4, 32, 33
ownmost: possibility, Dasein's, 99, 102, 104, 111; potentiality-for-Being-its-Self, 101

past possibilities, 164, 169, 171–73, 175, 184, 185
path, Heidegger's, 27
peacebuilding, xix, xx
peaceful coexistence, xv–xviii
peacekeeping, xix, xx
peacemaking, xix, xx
perceiving subject, 45, 58
perception, 36–38, 60, 87, 89, 125, 128
perceptual object, 36, 40, 45, 46
periphery, xvi, xviii
phenomenological: attitude, 37; description, 89, 156, 157; *epoche,* 37, 38; method, xxxiii, 30, 31, 36, 47, 50; reduction, 37, 38
phenomenology: Heidegger's, xxxiv, 31, 50, 59, 145, 158, 172, 185; hermeneutic, xxxiii, 43, 44, 47, 49, 57; Husserlian, 34, 35, 39, 40, 42, 43; and ontology, xxxiv, 31, 45, 49, 50–54, 57, 179; radical, 31, 39, 42, 50, 179; transcendental, 41, 44, 54

philosophy: Continental, 3, 27, 123; Heidegger's, 52, 54, 105; of the limit, 145; ontological tradition of, 30, 32, 34, 46, 163, 168, 172
political: coexistence, 1, 27, 153, 154, 159, 172; community, xxii, 116; decisionism, 103, 107, 108; order, 1, 10; philosophy, 2, 21, 25, 153; selfhood, 116, 155, 173; sociability, 156, 157; theory, 2, 11–13, 15, 22, 155; thought of coexistence 2, 26, 117, 154, 155, 158, 163, 171, 185
possibilities: ownmost, 99–102, 104, 105, 111, 113; past historical, 163, 164, 168, 169, 171–73, 175, 184, 185; repeatable, 140, 163, 168, 169, 173–75
post-1945 era or world, xiii, xv, xvii, xviii
postconflict reconstruction, xix
praxis: critical, 185; Dasein's everyday, 67, 69, 72, 81; international, xi, xii, xvii, xx, 177; and knowledge, 10
preconstituted subjects, 24, 25, 116
present-at-hand, 63, 66, 69, 72, 73, 102, 128, 165
primacy: of coexistence, 27, 49; of engaged immersion, 67; of otherness, 76, 91, 97, 107; of reflection, 64; of relations, 57, 59, 60, 92, 114, 154, 167, 171, 178
primary mode of Dasein, 67, 90, 180
priority, Dasein's paradoxical, 49
process of becoming-proper. *See* becoming-proper: process of

projection: future, 174; thrown, 85, 86, 89, 91, 110, 111, 180; upon possibilities, 100, 165, 166

propriety, 139–41, 143, 144, 146, 148, 174; Dasein's, 109, 112, 139, 141, 143, 174; and death, 111; and ethics, 140, 141; and heteronomy, 115, 141; and impropriety, 113, 131, 146; meaning or understanding of, 107, 146; process or movement toward, 114, 140, 141, 146 (*see also* becoming-proper: process of); and resoluteness, 109, 110; and silence, 137; struggle for, 131, 140, 144, 146, 148 (*see also* becoming-proper: struggle of). *See also* authenticity; becoming proper

public group: and Dasein's historicality, 163–66, 173–75; and ethics, éthos, or morality, 121, 122, 126, 127, 130, 132, 140, 183; and selfhood, 122, 138; and the "they," 128, 134

publicness, 78, 79, 82–84, 87, 92, 106, 125, 129, 132, 134

rationality, 13, 14, 20, 23; self-interested, 25, 26

rational subject, 14, 21

readiness: for anxiety, 110, 165; Dasein's, 111, 165; for death or finitude, 99, 107

readiness-to-hand, 62, 72

ready-to-hand, 62, 63, 65, 66, 71, 72, 87, 165

reality, 34–36, 39, 87

recognition, 113, 115, 130, 165; of contingency, 111; lack of, 128; of otherness, 111, 148, 160; of relationality, 111

reconceptualization of coexistence, 12, 95, 123, 146, 148, 178, 181

reduction, phenomenological. *See* phenomenological: reduction

references, 72, 106; other-created, 69, 128; totality of, 59, 63, 64, 66, 67, 68, 95, 114, 180 (*see also* referential totality); web of, 68–70, 81

referential totality, 35, 64–69, 79, 106

reflective subject, 60, 62, 66, 81, 157

relationality: articulated through human rights, 116; beyond knowledge, 53; controlled, 3, 24; Dasein's, 89, 97, 99, 111; ethical, 124; and éthos of survival, 21; human, 58, 90; nondeliberative, 60; primary, 75, 76, 99, 111, 167; radical, 153; reduction or concealment of, xxv, xxvii, 8, 117, 178

relations: Dasein's, 113–15, 133; disclosive, 66; international, xi–xiii, xviii, xx–xxiii, xv, xvii, xxxiii, xxxv, 1, 3, 22, 25, 29, 43, 71, 90, 95, 103, 120, 150, 154, 155, 177, 181–83; ontological, 104; primacy of, 57, 59, 92, 114, 154, 171, 178; social, xxi

repetition, 163, 164, 166–69

representation, xxviii, 8, 9, 60

*res extensa,* 7

resolute Dasein, 167

resoluteness, 97, 102, 107–9, 116, 159, 164–66

resource conflicts, xii

responsibility, 18, 21, 23, 99, 101, 107, 144

rights-bearing subject, xxi, 183

Scott, Charles E., 111, 125, 126, 139, 140, 142, 143
security, 16, 17, 23
self: coexistential, 57, 59, 90, 153, 154, 174, 180, 181, 183; ethical, 106, 117, 122, 124, 132, 140–48, 150, 153–55, 158, 163, 164, 169, 171–75, 182–85; habitual, 77; heter-onomous, 26, 29, 57, 79, 123, 138, 151, 153, 154, 174, 181, 183; masterful, 57; recovery of ethical, xxix, xxxv, 106, 117, 122–24, 140–44, 150, 152–55, 158, 163, 172, 173, 182, 183, 185
self-certainty, 5, 10
self-consciousness, 6, 115
self-determination, 6, 19, 166
self-dispersal, 77, 78, 89, 98, 100, 102, 109
selfhood, xxx, xxxii, xxxiv, xxxv, 15, 25, 30, 59, 90, 111, 115, 131, 138–40, 149, 151, 154, 179–81; constitutive role of otherness for, xiii, xxv, xxix; ethical, 117, 122–24, 150, 153, 163, 173, 182; heteronomous, xiii, 26, 57, 123, 151, 183
self-interested rationality, 25, 26
self-sufficiency, 13, 79, 89, 91, 92, 97, 109, 139, 153, 172, 177, 181
self-sufficient features of modern subjectivity. See modern subjectivity: features of
shared world. See world: shared
social contract, xxxiii, 2, 13, 20, 22, 24, 25, 29, 178
socialism, xv
socialization, Dasein's average, 124
social relations, xxi

social sciences, xxiv, xxv, xxx, 11–12, 15, 30, 71, 177, 179
solicitude: authentic or proper, 105, 106; average, 128, 131; and Being-with, 74, 75, 128, 149; Dasein's, 105, 128, 144, 147; forms of, 74, 75, 147; liberating, 122, 147, 148, 149, 151, 154, 163, 171, 175, 183
solipsistic self, 97
sovereign: nation-states, xxii, xxiv; subject 91, 97, 107, 115, 119, 156; subjectivity, 15, 79, 89, 96, 109, 131, 132, 178
sovereignty, xviii, 19, 22, 138
state: nation, xxii, xxiv; of nature, 2, 16–24
state borders, xii
state-centricity, xvii
subject: autonomous, 59, 91, 111, 131, 180; bare, 68, 75; Cartesian, 15, 48; of coexistence, the, xxi, xxxii, 154, 179, 181, 183; copresent, 71; dangerous, 29; Hobbesian, 17–19, 21, 23, 24, 29; human, 6, 7, 9, 30; indi-vidualist, 104; in IR theory, xii, xiii, xxi, xxiv, xxvi; isolated, 70, 103; juridical, xxiii; know-ing, 52, 62, 66, 70; master-ful, 30, 57, 81, 107, 108, 119; modern (see modern: subject); moral, 129; nonrelational, xiii, xxv, xxvii, 20, 23–25, 58, 71, 90, 92, 104, 178, 180; perceiving, 45, 58; philosophy of the, xxiii; rational, 14, 21; reflective, 60, 62, 66, 81, 157; rights-bearing, xxi, 183; self-interested, 2, 13, 178; self-suf-ficient, 30, 73, 77, 79, 95, 103, 115, 116, 153, 154, 178
subjection, 77, 128; passive, 111

subjectivism, 15; modern, 161
subjectivist: ontological premises,
90; ontology, 43, 121, 141;
presuppositions, 92, 108, 119;
self-sufficiency, 174
subjectivity, 3, 5, 8, 9, 11, 12,
20–25, 32, 53, 70, 75, 79, 113;
absolutization of, 13; belligerent, 24; Cartesian, 15, 90; conditions of, 35; configuration
of, 19, 20; Hobbesian, 17–19,
29; modern, xi, xiii, xxi,
xxiv–xxvii, xxviii–xxxiv, 1, 2,
6, 10, 13–15, 26, 27, 29–31,
48, 58, 59, 71, 81, 95, 102,
103, 108, 115, 184, 185; unworking of, 27, 80, 127
subject-object dichotomy, 38
submission, Dasein's, 114
substance, 4, 6, 7, 33, 34, 38, 44,
113
superpower conflict, xix
superpowers, xiv, xvi, xvii
surrounding work world, 71. See
also work-world
survival, xiv, xvi, xvii, xxix, xxx,
2, 16–22, 25; éthos of, 2, 16,
21, 25
synthesis, neo-neo. See neo-neo
synthesis

"they", the: and care, 91; and
Dasein's everydayness, 76, 96,
104, 156, 170; and death, 99;
and ethics, 124, 128, 129, 132,
139, 182; as manifestation of
being-with, 75–79, 156, 169,
170; and self-dispersal or lostness, 88, 97, 98, 109, 132–34;
and social conformism, 78, 80;
and subjectivity, 128, 131, 138,
157; and unique appropriation
of world, 111, 114, 115
thinking subject, 38
thrownness: and becoming-proper, 147; and care, 89; Dasein's,
83, 101, 111, 136, 171, 175;
of existence, 176; and fallenness, 86, 89, 91, 105, 181; and
heteronomy, 128; meaning
of, 102; and moods, 84; and
projection or projectiveness,
85, 86, 90, 91, 110, 165, 181;
state of, 83; transcendence of,
110, 111, 173
totality: and community, 163;
equipmental, 63, 65, 66, 69,
71, 72; Levinas's critique of,
51; of assignments, 64, 67,
68, 71, 83, 90, 95, 114, 138,
180; of meanings, 59, 64, 67,
70, 95, 142, 180; outlook
of, 98; of references, 59, 63,
64, 66, 67, 68, 95, 114, 180;
referential, 35, 64–69, 79, 106;
relational, 68, 70, 83, 90, 95,
114, 147
tradition: of community or public
group, 140, 162, 164; Hellenic
philosophical, 50; historical,
155, 159, 163–65, 167, 170,
173, 175, 184; of international
relations, 1, 2, 12, 13; ontological, 32, 34, 46, 163, 172
transcendence, 149; and becoming-proper, 108, 109, 111; of
danger, 19; finite, 110, 141; of
the state of nature, 18–20, 23;
toward the world, 110–12, 147
transcendental: ego, 38, 43, 45;
phenomenology, 41, 44, 54;
subjectivity, 37, 38, 60

universal: ethical construction,
120, 145, 146, 150, 182, 183;
ethics, 126, 145, 150, 151, 182;
humanity, 121, 149, 181
universalizable norms, 120, 130,
146
unworking of modern subjectivity,
27, 80, 178

violence, xii, xxxiii, xxxiv, 52–54;
ontology and phenomenology
as philosophies of, 50, 52, 57,
179
violent death, 19, 20
voice of conscience. *See* conscience: voice of

war: proxy, xvi, xviii; Second
World War, xiii, xviii, 51, 144
web of assignments, references,
and meanings, 59, 67–70, 81,
138

Wendt, Alexander, 3, 14, 15
West, the, xv, xvi, xix, 127
Western: culture or civilization,
127; metaphysics, 33, 129;
philosophical tradition, 50, 53,
57
withness: as an attribute of
Dasein, 75, 82, 90, 104, 106,
180; and the friend, 136; and
the "they," 76, 79, 84, 91, 95,
180
with-world, 73, 83
work-world, 61–65, 67, 71–73,
128
world: Dasein's, 70, 136; politics,
xi, xiii, xxi, xxvii, 120, 177,
181; shared, 69, 76–78, 112,
114, 147; society of individuals, 181
worldliness, 68, 88, 109, 115,
119
worldview, 14, 39

Louiza Odysseos is senior lecturer in international relations at the University of Sussex. She is coeditor (with Fabio Petito) of *The International Political Thought of Carl Schmitt: Terror, Liberal War, and the Crisis of Global Order* and (with Hakan Seckinelgin) of *Gendering the International*.